Until Our Last Breath

Until Our Last Breath

A Holocaust Story of Love and

Partisan Resistance

Michael Bart
and Laurel Corona

St. Martin's Press ♒ New York

www.stmartins.com

Library of Congress Cataloging-in-Publication Data

Bart, Michael.
    Until our last breath : a Holocaust story of love and partisan resistance / Michael Bart and Laurel Corona.—1st ed.
        p.   cm.
    ISBN-13: 978-0-312-37807-3
    ISBN-10: 0-312-37807-6
    1. Bart, Zenia Lewison. 2. Bart, Leizer. 3. Jews—Lithuania—Vilnius—History—20th century. 4. Holocaust, Jewish (1939–1945)—Lithuania—Vilnius—Biography. 5. Jews—Lithuania—Vilnius—Biography. 6. World War, 1939–1945—Jewish resistance—Lithuania—Vilnius. 7. Lithuania—Ethnic relations. I. Title.
    Includes bibliographical references.
DS135.L53 B3743   2008
940.53'1809224793B—dc22   2008006246

First Edition: May 2008

10   9   8   7   6   5   4   3   2   1

CONTENTS

Special Thanks   ix

Authors' Note   xiii

Map of Prewar Europe   xv

The Balcwinik and Bart Family Trees   xvi

Preface   xvii

One

Before and After   1

Two

The City That Went Forth a Thousand   18

Three

The Stones Burst into Tears   37

Four

Days with No Answer   51

Five

A Different Rhythm   74

Contents

Six
We Dreamers Must Turn Soldiers   90

Seven
Graves Are Growing Here   118

Eight
A Fire Inside   126

Nine
Love as Fierce as Death   146

Ten
Into the Free Forests   157

Eleven
Vanished Like Smoke   181

Twelve
Summon That Elusive Happiness   201

Thirteen
Under the Lofty, Silent Heavens   219

Fourteen
A World Was Here   240

Epilogue
Perhaps—Until Light   262

Members of the Family Who Died in the Holocaust   267
Notes   269
Bibliography   301
Acknowledgments   305

SPECIAL THANKS

With very special thanks to Michael Bart's wife, Bonnie, for her contributions. This book could not have been written without her encouragement and tireless efforts in editing, locating, and organizing documents, letters, family and archival photos; videotaping survivors' oral testimonies; and compiling the family endnotes.

Hitler aims to destroy *all* the Jews of Europe. It is the lot of the Jews of Lithuania to be the first in line.

Let us not go like sheep to the slaughter.

True, we are weak and without a protector, but the only answer to the murderers is—revolt!

Brothers! Better to fall as free fighters than to live at the mercy of the murderers.

Let us revolt! We shall fight until our last breath!

—Abba Kovner
First Proclamation of the United Partisan
Organization (FPO)
January 1, 1942
the Vilna ghetto

The disruption of enemy rail communications throughout occupied Europe, by the organized forces of the Resistance, played a very considerable part in our victory.

—General Dwight D. Eisenhower

AUTHORS' NOTE

Until Our Last Breath presents two interrelated narratives. One is historical, describing key events and other information pertaining to the Nazi occupation of Lithuania and the experiences of Jews during those years. All facts have been documented by the sources listed in the bibliography; to reduce distraction and preserve the flow of the narrative, we have provided endnotes only where the information might be questioned.

The story of Leizer and Zenia (Lewinson) Bart is woven together with this history. Many of the details they told directly to their son Michael, but some of it Michael has pieced together from other sources. Chief among these are letters Zenia wrote in the years immediately after the war. Several people helped Zenia write the letters in English, including a Red Cross worker known as Sister Bea. In these letters Zenia described some of the details of her life before, during, and immediately after the Nazi occupation. Other information came from survivors who knew Leizer and Zenia at the time. Central among these are

Maks Etingin, who lived with Zenia in the same ghetto room; Fania Bulkin, who introduced Leizer and Zenia in the ghetto; Fania Jocheles-Brancovski, who lived in the same bunker in the Avengers' camp; Joseph Harmatz, FPO member and partisan fighter; Motl Gurwitz, FPO member and partisan fighter; and several others. Additional details have come from relatives and friends in the United States who remembered things Zenia and Leizer told them. When using these sources, we have made the endnotes more frequent and substantive because we felt it was important to ensure the readers' confidence that this is a true story.

Prewar Europe
1939

Finland
Norway
North Sea
Estonia
Ireland
Sweden
Latvia
Denmark
Baltic Sea Lithuania
Great
Britain
East
Prussia
(Germany)
• Vilna
Atlantic Ocean
Netherlands
Soviet Union
Belgium
Germany
Poland
Luxembourg
France
Czechoslovakia
Switzerland
Austria
Hungary
Portugal
Romania
Spain
Italy
Yugoslavia
Adriatic Sea
Mediterranean Sea
Bulgaria
Black Sea

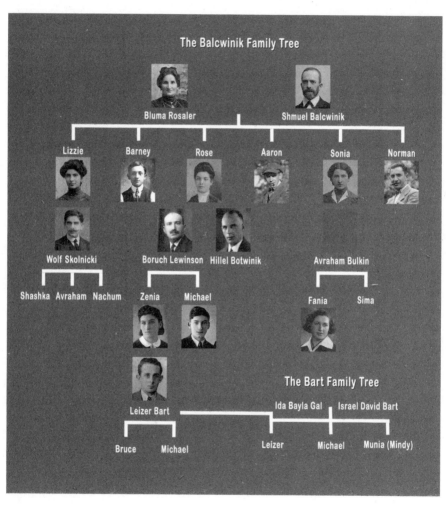

The Balcwinik Family Tree

Bluma Rosaler — Shmuel Balcwinik

Lizzie · Barney · Rose · Aaron · Sonia · Norman

Wolf Skolnicki · Boruch Lewinson · Hillel Botwinik · Avraham Bulkin

Shashka · Avraham · Nachum · Zenia · Michael · Fania · Sima

Leizer Bart

The Bart Family Tree

Ida Bayla Gal — Israel David Bart

Bruce · Michael · Leizer · Michael · Munia (Mindy)

BART FAMILY COLLECTION

PREFACE

The rabbi was coming to the end of the ancient Hebrew ritual for the burial of the dead. It was a bright fall day, shortly before Thanksgiving 1996, and the body lowered into the newly dug grave was my father's. Leizer Bart, or Leo, as he had been known in the United States, had just died at the age of eighty-one. I tossed a handful of soil onto my father's coffin and after a moment turned to look for my mother to take her home.

I hadn't noticed that a small, distinguished-looking man bending on a cane had come up behind me during the service, and when I turned around, he was so close I had to catch myself to keep from bumping into him. He looked up at me and, without introducing himself or even saying hello, he simply stated, "Michael, you are the son of Leizer and Zenia Bart," and then, lifting his cane to make his point, he added, "You need to inscribe 'Freedom Fighters of Nekamah' on your dad's headstone."

I didn't know what he was talking about. I asked him to

repeat what he had said, and he thrust his cane into the ground to emphasize each word as he repeated it. He was unaware that as he spoke, the cane had drifted and was now pounding the top of my foot. "Freedom Fighters of Nekamah. Say that!" Then he was gone, vanished into the small crowd of mourners.

I didn't have much time at that point to think about the man in the cemetery or the word "Nekamah," which I had heard for the first time that day, because I had noticed my mother was starting to become confused, a condition that would later be diagnosed as Alzheimer's. Over the next few months I began to spend more and more time at my mother's house to help with her care.

One day, while in my parents' living room, I remembered that my father had kept some old books and documents in the end table drawer. There, inside one of the books, I found an obituary for Abba Kovner, one of the most famous resistance leaders of World War II. In that article, I learned that the name of Kovner's fighting group was Nekamah. Remembering that my parents had always fondly referred to him as their commander, I knew that the stranger at the grave, my parents, Abba Kovner, and Nekamah were all inextricably linked. My parents' rabbi told me that the Hebrew word *nekamah* means "revenge," and to help in my quest for information, he recommended a book by Nora Levin, entitled *The Holocaust.* In it I found information about Abba Kovner and the Jewish partisans of Vilna. As I devoured that book, I realized it had given me a start into my own research on my parents.

I was certain there must be quite a tale to tell because my parents had clearly been involved with one of the most renowned Jewish underground resistance groups in World War

II. In fact, I remembered a conversation with my mother not too long before my father's death. She sat down on her sofa beside me and, using the affectionate Yiddish form of my name, said, "Michaeleh, Dad and I have an important story I believe needs to be told. So far we have only shared bits and pieces with you. It is very painful for me but even more so for your father. He is too weak now for us to add to his suffering. I think this story should be written down, but we will need to wait until after he is gone."

After my father died, I wanted to ask my mother what she had referred to, but it was becoming increasingly obvious that her memory was failing. She had lived with brain trauma from a Nazi beating, and this may have been a factor in why, late in her life, she became confused about where she was and who the people around her actually were. At times she would wake up in the morning fretting that she would be late to report to work for Anton Schmidt, the Nazi officer and righteous Gentile by whom she was employed while living in the ghetto. Other days, she would pack her bags and sit waiting for a ride back to Vilna. I knew that it was too late for her to tell me what she had wanted to say, and that it would be up to me to uncover it for myself.

My parents had been very generous with an outline of their lives, so I had a good base on which to build, but I wanted more details. I had heard from them the story of being forced by the Nazis into the Vilna ghetto, where they met and fell in love and were eventually married by one of the last surviving rabbis. They told me that they had been part of the resistance movement led by Abba Kovner, and that they had spent nearly a year living in a forest, blowing up trains, sabotaging telephone and other communication equipment, and otherwise thwarting the Nazi war effort. I knew that they had participated with the Soviet army in the liberation of Vilna, and that afterward they spent several years as displaced persons before coming to live with relatives in the United States.

I knew more about their partisan experience because they, especially my father, were very proud of it. For two years they had lived in the ghetto, where they were treated like animals. When they escaped to the forest and joined the partisans, they were able to regain their dignity. They were very proud of the fact that my dad had gone out on many partisan missions, including blowing up trains. They spent less time describing their ghetto experiences to me, and I realize now it was probably because they, like all Jews, had been so humiliated by the Nazis. It was understandable that they preferred to focus on how they had been able to escape the Nazis and fight back. As a child I had been satisfied hearing stories I could easily imagine, or even see and touch, such as why my father had a scar from a bullet wound in his side, and why my mother had a permanent bump on her head.

While they were alive I could see how the pain of the Holocaust was always there for them, and I rarely asked about their experiences unless they brought the subject up first. After my mother was gone, I had many unanswered questions. I knew that connecting the dots was going to require not only more knowledge of my parents but also general research into the world in which they had lived. I began a multipronged approach to my research, the first part of which was locating all my parents' records and important documents. These included letters my mother had written to the United States from Vilna after the liberation, and later from Rome where she and my father lived as displaced persons. Her first correspondence was a postcard sent from behind Russian lines to an uncle whom she had never met; she only knew that he lived in "America Springfeld." Remarkably, the postcard eventually arrived eight months later at the right address in Springfield, Massachusetts, and it became my parents' lifeline to a new world.

I also found a document issued by the Chief Rabbi in Rome certifying my parents' marriage in the Vilna ghetto. Their wedding in the ghetto had taken place quickly, and they were afraid that Jewish law had not been followed precisely enough for the marriage to be valid. Just to be certain, they had two of the surviving witnesses, who were also living in Rome, go with them to the rabbi to attest to the marriage and help them get a certificate validating the original ceremony.

At the same time, I was pursuing the second prong of my research, which involved contacting Holocaust survivors who had known my parents, using their old address books and other means. I reasoned that their California friends might not have known them during the war, but that Jews from the East Coast and Israel might possibly have shared wartime experiences with them. I began calling numbers I found to tell people that my father had died and to ask if they had any information about him and my mother. My elation at hearing that there was someone on the other end who remembered them often turned to disappointment because most were not willing to discuss the past. "Talking about those times is like walking in a graveyard," one of their friends told me. "It is no wonder we take no pleasure in it."

But each person I talked to told me something, and I discovered that by going in constant circles between my handful of good contacts, I could get confirmation from one of what another had told me, and as I learned more and more I found each contact was willing to tell me more and more. This circle of contacts included my mother's cousin, who had introduced my parents in the ghetto and became a partisan herself; a close friend of my mother's family, who shared a room in the ghetto along with as many as thirty-five other prisoners; several resistance fighters who escaped the ghetto, some through the sewers; and another cousin with whom they were very close right after immigrating to the United States and to whom they had told the story of their lives during the Holocaust.

The third part of my research involved accumulating a library of books about Vilna, the ghetto, the resistance movement, and the partisans. I learned that Vilna had been known as the Jerusalem of Lithuania and that my parents had thus been witnesses to the deliberate destruction of one of the most important and vibrant centers of Jewish culture and scholarship in the world. I learned that Lithuania was the place Hitler designated for the first trial of the Final Solution, and that my parents and other Jews could have had no way of knowing that the Nazis' plans involved the systematic extermination of every last one of them. I learned that on the eve of the German invasion there had been approximately seventy thousand Jews in Vilna, whereas on the day the Soviet army and the partisans liberated Vilna there were roughly five hundred, a number that rose only to approximately three thousand as survivors began to trickle back into the city from hiding places, work camps, and unoccupied parts of Europe. I learned that of all the ghetto resistance movements in Europe, the Fareynegte Partizaner Organizatsye (United Partisan Organization), known as the FPO, was one of the largest, best organized, and best connected with other underground groups. I learned that even within the broader partisan movement, anti-Semitism was so rampant that Jews had to watch their backs around campfires and while marching through the woods on the way to and from their missions.

Another aspect of my research involved contacting various Jewish and Holocaust organizations, including the United States Holocaust Memorial Museum, the Simon Wiesenthal Center Museum of Tolerance, YIVO Institute for Jewish Research, and the American Jewish Joint Distribution Committee in the United States; Yad Vashem and the Ghetto Fighters' House in Israel; and the Vilna Gaon Jewish State Museum in Vilnius, Lithuania. At the Simon Wiesenthal Center Museum of Tolerance Library and Archives in Los Angeles, my wife, Bonnie, and I went through file after file, envelope after envelope, photo after photo of material pertaining to Vilna in the Holocaust. We found nothing that added to our knowledge of my parents, but one archivist said she thought there might be one more box somewhere if we were willing to wait while she looked for it.

I was ready to give up. It was lunchtime, and it seemed unlikely this one box would be different from the others. My wife persuaded me to stay just long enough to look at this one last box. We were nearly to the bottom, and disheartened to have found it also contained nothing to help us, when we pulled out a photograph we had never seen. I immediately recognized

Abba Kovner, with a group of partisans. To my astonishment, there, to his left, were my parents, both brandishing rifles.

I had told no one except my wife that I was thinking about writing a book, and the two of us had trouble picturing how we would do this, but after we found that photograph we both started believing that a book was meant to be. This feeling was reinforced in 2002, when I had already been researching for about six years. I received word that Sol Margoles, my mother's cousin in "America Springfeld" with whom they had shared many of their wartime experiences, was in failing health at the age of ninety-eight. I wanted to go see him before he died because he had been such an important part of my family's history. When Bonnie and I walked into his room, he greeted me with a huge smile. "Michael, is that you?" he asked. "Are you going to write a book about your parents?" I was astonished, as there was no way he could have known that was on my mind. As the nurse helped him into his wheelchair, he immediately began telling her about my parents. For the next four hours he entertained us with intimate stories about my father and mother, some of which I had never heard.

He died two weeks later. Looking back, I think I realized once and for all in that last visit with him that it was time to turn my research into a book. The next hurdle was to find the right writer. Jews often use the term *bashert* when things come together as if they were always meant to be. That was what it felt like when Laurel Corona gave a guest lecture in a class Bonnie and I were taking. Convinced of the power of the story, within a few months she began to write, amid piles of books and photographs I had amassed during my years of research, and with the partisan photo of my parents over her desk.[1] One last step remained, and in the summer of 2004 the three of us made an emotional and revealing journey to what is now called Vilnius, Lithuania. We saw the properties where my family lived and owned businesses, and walked what little remains of the ghetto after postwar reconstruction. Along with Fania Jocheles-Brancovski, who was also a member of the Avengers, we went to the Rudnicki forest, where the Avengers' camp, including the bunker where my parents and Fania slept, is still standing. We also visited Ponary, the scene of the mass executions of somewhere between fifty and sixty thousand Jewish men, women, and children from Vilna.[2]

In August 2005, Bonnie and I made a second trip to Vilnius. On our first day we were walking through the remnants of the old ghetto, and to my surprise I heard a familiar voice in front of the old *Judenrat* building on Rudnicka Street. Standing in front of me was former partisan fighter Joseph Harmatz, surrounded by a large group. He was visiting Vilnius with his family and was telling them about life in the ghetto. I approached Harmatz and asked, "Do you know who I am? I call you in Israel all the time." Ten heads immediately turned around and stared at me. When I told him my name, his response was, "You look like your father, except taller." He then introduced me to his family, and took me by my arm in front of the *Judenrat* so his family could take pictures of the two of us together.

Joseph Harmatz has been one of my best sources, and I have grown to have the utmost admiration and respect for him. Our chance meeting was an emotional experience for both of us. Harmatz had been one of the chief weapons smugglers for the

FPO in the Vilna ghetto, and had gone on numerous sabotage missions with my father while they were partisans in the forest.

The next day my wife and I had the great pleasure of meeting former partisan fighter Motl Gurwitz. He had also gone on many train sabotage missions with my father—too numerous to count. Motl spent the next two days with us sharing stories and walking the old ghetto, and he joined us and Fania on our road trip to the former partisan base in the Rudnicki forest. After this very emotional and informative trip, we knew that we had enough information to finish the book.

I had long since realized that the single thing that had the most impact on my life happened before I was even born. The Holocaust had taken from me all my grandparents, aunts and uncles, and first cousins who were living in Nazi-occupied Europe. More than anything else, it shaped the lives of my parents, who in turn shaped mine. They tried to be careful not to overburden my brother and me with the nightmares of their past, in large part because they did not want us to grow up hating people and having a pessimistic view of the world. Nevertheless, their pain was an important part of the backdrop of our home life.

Perhaps because I saw how their pain was never far below the surface, I had been reluctant to bring more of it onto myself by spending a lot of time delving into the experiences of the Jews in World War II. That changed in 1996, when my desire to know more about my parents overcame my hesitations. I found, once I was deeply involved in my research, that I was energized by what I was learning about my own heritage, and with a great sense of pride I became more and more active in the local and national community of survivors and their children. As the book evolved, it became very important to me not only to pay tribute to my parents but to honor all the victims of the Holocaust by focusing as much as possible on the dignity and heroism with which they dealt with such incomprehensible evil.

Through my mother's cousins in Israel, the United States, and Lithuania, other Holocaust survivors, archives, libraries, scholars, and specialists, as well as other relatives and friends, I had gradually come to know my parents in a new way, as the main characters in a remarkable story of love and heroism. The Holocaust swept them up along with millions of others, and though they did not choose what world to inhabit, they did make two choices that make their story extraordinary: They chose to fight the Nazis, and they chose each other. When I told one of the local Holocaust survivors I was working on a book about my parents, she said simply, "Your parents are a love story." That story is the foundation upon which *Until Our Last Breath* is built.

My goal for this book is that it be as factually accurate as possible. My parents were both very straightforward people, and my dad in particular was very precise on details. I have tried to maintain the same values as my parents in the writing of this book.

As I stand in synagogue on their *yahrzeits,* the anniversaries of their deaths, I repeat the moving words of the prayer known to Jews as the *amidah.* I stop at one of its phrases, which praises God for keeping faith with those who sleep in dust. I believe this book has done that. It has kept faith with my parents and relatives, and with all who are now gone, whether shot in Nazi-occupied Vilna or in the forests by Nazi sympathizers, or whether dead now of old age in Lithuania, Israel, the United States, or elsewhere.

In fleshing out the facts I know with the overall reality of the lives of the Jewish resistance fighters, first in the Vilna ghetto and then in the forests of Lithuania, this book tells a larger story than my parents' own. It tells a story that is not in the end about victimization but about empowerment under unimaginable circumstances. Set against a backdrop of incomprehensible cruelty and misery, it nevertheless shines with all that is best about being human, including the ability to find the strength to stand up together and be counted when it most matters.

I can picture my mother and father at this moment, saying they just did what they felt they needed to do under the circumstances and conducted their lives in the only way they knew how. But they did far more than that. They pledged to fight, and they pledged to love each other until their last breath. They are my heroes, and this is their story.

Until Our Last Breath

One

BEFORE AND AFTER

He stands, cradling his wife in his arms. Her left shoulder is pressed upward toward her chin as she leans back, letting him hold her upright for the photograph. She wants to be strong and tough in this moment, but her head is tilted to one side, as if the thoughts crowding in behind her eyes are too heavy to bear. Her face looks taut with pain. In her right hand she holds a rifle.

Towering behind her, his body and face are all angles. His jaw is clenched. The shadows under his narrowed eyes make smoky triangles in the bright sunlight. His shoulders, shrunken from years of hunger but still strong, are swallowed up in the folds of an oversized army jacket. He stands as if every nerve in his body is crackling with rage.

They are Leizer and Zenia Bart. Two weeks have passed since they left their base in the Rudnicki forest of Lithuania to participate in the liberation of Vilna from the Nazis. The once-pale cheeks of their fellow partisans now glisten and redden in the sun as they stand together squinting into the camera lens

The Avengers
USHMM, COURTESY OF YIVO INSTITUTE

of a Soviet army photographer. A few women grin and embrace. The men strike either fierce or nonchalant poses with their weapons. One man cups his hands to light a cigarette, while next to him Abba Kovner, the renowned poet-hero of the Jewish resistance, stares off to the side.

Zenia does not look at the camera. For her there is no victory on this day. As of the beginning of the battle for Vilna, her mother and brother were still alive in the work camp where they had been interned. As quiet settled over the city, she and Leizer had gone to look for them. There, among the scattered corpses in a courtyard, they found the crumpled body of her mother. A few feet away her younger brother lay sprawled, shot in the back.

It is the sheer spite of it—of the Nazis, even as they drove away from the camp, not allowing the last Jews to live—that pummels Zenia with a grief more ferocious than any Nazi artillery fire. Too late. Too late. Now, only a day after finding their bodies, she stands for a photograph meant to commemorate a victory, but for her there is nothing to do but bury the dead. That, and learn how to go on.

The future lies beyond the camera's lens. Only the story of how Leizer and Zenia came to be in each other's arms at the end of the war, posing with one of the most illustrious resistance groups of World War II, can be told as the shutter clicks and the moment is recorded forever.

Ten o'clock Sunday morning, June 22, 1941. Summer mornings come early to the northernmost cities of Europe, and by the time Zenia Lewinson stepped out of the entrance of her home at 29 Zawalna Street the sun had been burning for hours in the cloudless cobalt sky over Vilna. The leaves glowed an almost iridescent green, as yet unsullied by summer's heat and dust. The colors of the flowers seemed to explode out of balcony pots all along the street. Unencumbered by thick winter coats and heavy shoes, the people on the street no longer hurried to their destinations with their heads down, but nodded at passersby and stopped to chat with neighbors in the street.

The municipal government had announced there would be another air-raid drill that day, and it had almost derailed Zenia's plans for the morning. Her mother, Rose Lewinson, and her stepfather, Hillel Botwinik, had been unwilling to let her leave the house, out of concern about where she would be when the sirens went off. Even the most ordinary things could be risky for Vilna's Jews, and Zenia's pretty face and smile might not be enough to keep her from harm if she went too far or stayed away too long from home.

Hillel Botwinik, who had married Rose after the premature death of Zenia's father, was a prominent lumber merchant.[1] On occasion he helped Rose with her office supply store on the ground floor of another large building owned by Zenia's family a few blocks away on Sadowa Street.[2] Both Hillel and Rose had prospered, serving Jews and Christians alike. Zenia's family had a loving and devoted Christian housekeeper, Kajya, who had also served as a nanny for Zenia and her brother, Michael, known as Misha, when they were younger. Michael was only a year younger than Zenia, but still a boy, a very nice one, far away from adulthood.[3] All of Zenia and Michael's friends were Jewish, but this was typical, and Zenia felt no doubt that in the world of Vilna they would both find a comfortable place to build their lives.

Zenia's liberation for a few hours was probably, at least in part, due to the influence of her maternal grandmother, Bluma Balcwinik. Bluma was a successful hay and grain merchant, whose business was on the ground floor of a family-owned three-story building.[4] Bluma lived above the store in spacious private quarters, as did two of her daughters, Rose and Lizzie, who lived in separate apartments with their families. Lizzie, her oldest daughter, was married to Wolf Skolnicki, with whom she had three sons: Shashka, Avraham, and Nachum. Bluma's daughter Sonia also lived in the city with her husband, Avraham Bulkin, and their two daughters, Fania and Sima.[5] Zenia's was a strong and loving family, and a successful one.[6] Bluma's business had flourished since the time of the Russian czars,[7] when brightly uniformed soldiers of the cavalry had brought

Left: *Rose, Michael, and Zenia*   Center: *Hillel Botwinik*
Right: *Kajya the nanny, pictured when Zenia was young*

horse-drawn wagons through the building's covered entry to buy feed. Even then being Jewish made life precarious, but business was business, and horses needed to be fed.

Bluma's own strong spirit provided the argument that daughters blossom and thrive when their parents do not constrict their lives quite as much as Rose and Hillel wanted to do with Zenia. She was a vivacious young girl on the verge of high school graduation, who had been cooped up for months by a Baltic winter, and, after all, life went on and there were still errands to run. Rose and Hillel had relented, and Zenia was free. The necessary task of returning a borrowed item to her stepfather's niece Sonia Etingin, whose house was only six or seven blocks away, had resulted in the good fortune to be out amid the bustle and clanging streetcars and horse-drawn carriages of Zawalna Street.

For Jewish parents in Vilna even a perfect summer day gave only a fleeting sense of well-being, barely enough to let a Jewish

Left: *Sonia Bulkin*   Center: *Grandma Bluma Balcwinik*
Right: *Wolf and Lizzie Skolnicki*   BART FAMILY COLLECTION

child venture out alone. Nerves had been jangled and raw for months. Crimes against Jewish property, and physical assaults including occasional murders, had characterized life in Vilna for as long as anyone could remember, and some gruesome tales of persecution were centuries old. But many seemed to think the situation was going to get steadily worse, and they were not just the people who were always shaking their heads and prophesying doom. The diatribes of Adolf Hitler in Germany had encouraged all the old ethnic hatreds, and if a person could get away with hurting a Jew, well, what was going to stop him? The latest problems were whispered about at night and downplayed in front of the children the next day. The only thing Jews knew they could count on was that almost everyone—Pole, Lithuanian, and Russian, atheist and Christian alike—would think it was perfectly all right if the Jews simply ceased to be.

Cease to be? Impossible. Certainly their allies were few, but far more people were indifferent to their presence than hostile to it. This fact had kept life in Vilna more than tolerable—in fact quite pleasant—for Jews like Zenia Lewinson. They could all find a way to make a living, go where they wanted, and do more or less what they wished.[8] Her family kept the holidays and went to the synagogue unmolested.[9] They followed Jewish dietary laws and other customs as a matter of tradition, belonged to Jewish clubs, and contributed to Jewish charities. There was a fit for Jews in Christian-dominated Vilna, despite the many cultural differences between the two groups, and despite a hate-driven fringe that could not leave the Jews alone.

Zenia knew a little about the hatred against Jews fomented by Hitler in Germany, but she had other things on her mind that June. She was working a few hours a week for Grandmother Bluma, and she heard the low chatter of mothers murmuring how pretty she was and how good a match she would make for their son or nephew. She was graduating from the Epstein-Szpeizer Gymnasium, a private Jewish school for the privileged class of Vilna,[10] and life seemed on the verge of getting far more interesting. She might even consider continuing her education at a local university, but nothing specific appealed to her. Though she would remain living at home, graduation would give her a bit more freedom to be herself before she settled down with a good Jewish husband, had babies, grew stout, and turned into her mother.

To most of Vilna's Jews, Hitler was a madman soon to be set right by an outraged world. Until that happened, Vilna seemed safer than many places, as measured by the steady stream of Jewish refugees from Poland arriving there each week. Zenia had met a few at meetings of Betar, a right-wing

Pictured on the left is 29 Zawalna Street. A horse-drawn carriage is turning into Bluma's hay and grain business.
COURTESY OF LEYZER RAN'S *JERUSALEM OF LITHUANIA*

group of young Zionists preparing to go to Palestine to resist the British, whose policies were perceived as hostile and overly restrictive to Jews who wished to settle there. They had told her of terrible murderous rampages against Jews by occupying Nazi troops, rumors of mass graves outside Polish cities, and plans to imprison all the Jews of Poland in ghettos.

When Zenia arrived at Sonia's house on Zeligowsky Street,[11] the family was out, and there was nothing to do but turn back toward home. As she made her way back along Zawalna Street, her ears picked up the distant drone of engines in the southern skies. Within seconds, the air-raid sirens howled, their shrill urgency freezing everyone in the street. Was this the real thing, or only the scheduled drill? If it were possible to simply stand there and endure the screaming sirens for a few minutes, perhaps they could all just go about their day afterward.

It was no drill. Within seconds, planes flew high overhead, then dropped to skim low above the city streets. A loud thud in the distance near the Porobanek Airport was followed by the shadow of a plane streaking down Zawalna Street. The rolling roar of a blast from the direction of Sonia's house unfroze her feet, and she ran for home.

Safe inside, she watched as Bluma turned the radio dial. Signals swam in and out of hearing until one came in clearly. They recognized the rasping, pulsing voice immediately, and though they did not speak German, Yiddish was similar enough for the meaning to be clear. Adolf Hitler was announcing that Operation Barbarossa, the invasion of the Soviet Union, was under way. In two weeks, he vowed, he would be addressing the world from Moscow's Red Square.

Michael and Hillel had been out but had returned home quickly with the news that Sonia's building had been hit by a bomb. Zenia had averted certain death by only minutes. She had no way of knowing how many times in the next few years she would again be just outside the reach of death, but that morning of the invasion had marked the first time. Sonia's family had been in the park when the bombs fell, and they were safe. The couple sharing the same staircase in their apartment building was not so lucky. They, along with their young child, lay dead in the rubble.[12]

There is a before, and then there is nothing but after. A voice on the radio told the grim news: The Germans had invaded and had crossed the Nieman River. Impossible as it

A droshky, or horse-drawn carriage
COURTESY OF LEYZER RAN'S *JERUSALEM OF LITHUANIA*

seemed for an army to move that quickly, they were already only sixty miles away.

It had been commonly agreed among Vilna's Jews that it was a good thing that, as a result of the August 1939 Nonaggression Pact between the Germans and the Russians, Vilna had once again become part of Lithuania, as it had been before World War I. Otherwise, the Nazi occupation of Poland in September of that year would have already put them in Hitler's grasp, instead of under the protection of the Soviet Union. But being part of Lithuania had its own nightmarish qualities, and it was hard to know how much worse the situation would get under the Germans. Because Vilna had been a part of Poland for two decades, Lithuanians who lived there were actually a minority group, smaller than either Poles or Jews.[13] For many Lithuanians in the Vilna area, the easiest means to strongly, quickly, and cohesively assert their new status as part of Lithuania had been to reject whatever or whoever was un-Lithuanian among them. Thinking of themselves as patriots, gangs had spent the previous few years terrorizing and assaulting Poles as well as Jews,[14] primarily in rural and outlying districts of Vilna, not only as a means of stamping the area as Lithuanian, but also as a form of resistance to the suppression of national and ethnic identity occurring everywhere in the Soviet Union.

The Poles disliked the Lithuanians, and had the numbers and the political power in Vilna to keep the ugliness from escalating. But the Poles were equally anti-Semitic,[15] and most of the violence against Jews was not ideological or even political. It was centuries-old, inbred hatred, pure and simple.

Nevertheless, tensions between Jews and non-Jews had shown signs of abating somewhat in the last year, though not so much so that Jews had relaxed, or even much noticed. Since the Soviet Union had cut short Lithuanian independence by annexing the country in 1940 as a means of strengthening its position against Nazi territorial aggression, the Soviets had retaken control of the government and the police. Anyone, Jew or non-Jew, who was considered hostile or otherwise a threat to the Soviet regime was dealt with harshly,[16] and street violence by ordinary citizens against Jews was harder to get away with, because the Soviets simply would not tolerate disorder, regardless of who the perpetrators or victims might be. The random anti-Semitic cruelty displayed by Lithuanians who beat up Jews in the street or who ransacked the shelves of Jewish merchants epitomized a debased humanity the Soviets hoped to destroy altogether in favor of a new world order without the divisive forces of nationality and religion.

The ideological distaste that Communists felt for Lithuanian thuggery against Jews was tempered, however, by inbred anti-Semitism that ran as deeply in Russian history as it did in Poland or Lithuania. Exploiting the general illiteracy and ignorance of the peasantry, the medieval church had sought for centuries to protect its image as God's agent and messenger by accusing those who had not embraced Christianity of causing natural disasters and all human afflictions. The Jews were the particular target of such preaching because it had been the Jews among whom Jesus had lived and preached. This fact evolved into the erroneous but universally held belief among medieval Christians that the Jews had been responsible for the crucifixion.

Branded as "Christ killers," the Jewish population had been the target of violence and subjected for centuries all over Europe to constriction of rights and privileges. Since the reign of Russia's Catherine the Great, the Jewish population had been concentrated in Lithuania, Poland, Ukraine, and elsewhere in Eastern Europe. In 1791, she established what was known as the Pale of Settlement along her empire's western border, and by 1794, all Jews were uprooted from other parts of the Russian Empire and forced to resettle in the Pale.[17] There, life was "isolated, stifling, and oppressive,"[18] but despite hardships and restrictions on their activities, a lively Jewish culture evolved over the next century and a half.

Vilna was a jewel of that culture, proudly called the Jerusalem of Lithuania. Jews came there in such large numbers at the time of the Russian decree that at one point the sixty-four thousand Jews in the city constituted almost 40 percent of the total population. It was natural for Jews to gravitate to Vilna, for it had been a center of Jewish spiritual life for several centuries. Earlier, in the second half of the seventeenth century, of the twenty-five hundred Jews in Vilna, forty were rabbis, and hundreds of others devoted their lives to Talmudic study. In the eighteenth century, the great scholar and spiritual leader the Gaon of Vilna brought the city even greater fame among the Jews of Europe. If a Jew wanted to do business, the saying went, he should go to Lodz, but if he wanted wisdom he should go to Vilna. The prestige of Vilna as a spiritual center gave special status to all Jews living there and, whatever their occupation, to be Jews from Vilna gave families like Zenia Lewinson's a source of great pride.

Any sense of special status the Jews of Vilna may have felt in the generations leading up to World War II did not extend beyond the Jews themselves. Like all other Jews, they were banished to the outskirts of the Russian Empire, and subject to the whims of the czars, who from time to time unleashed rampages of pillage, rape, and murder known as pogroms. These official purges by the Russian cavalry were frequently mimicked by ordinary citizens holding ancient and irrational grudges against the Jews. By the time Zenia was born, the same joke had been told a million times, about how non-Jews always seemed to be able to spot them from a mile away. It wasn't the basic and stereotyped physiognomy at all, not the shape of the nose, or the build, or the hair. It was the look of eternal persecution on their faces.[19]

Only a week before the air raid, Zenia's mother, Rose, might have served as an example of the type. The local police had arrested a number of prominent members of Vilna's Jewish community, including some of its most socially active businessmen and scholars. Most were deported to Siberia,[20] a remote and frozen wasteland, where they were put to forced labor in conditions so harsh few of them survived. It was part of a general purge of those considered anti-Soviet, and all told, seven thousand of Vilna's Jews were among the thirty-five thousand deportees from all over Lithuania.[21] There had been no provocation, no crime, but their families were so certain they would never return that they took the unusual step of *kriah,* the ritual tearing of clothing that began the Jewish mourning process for the dead, even in advance of knowing for certain their loved ones had died. Rose lived in fear that Hillel would be next.

Everybody knew there was no easy way to be a Jew in Vilna, in Lithuania, or anywhere else in Europe, for that matter. There never had been. It might be a little better, a little worse, but nothing was really new. But as the Nazi bombers fueled up, and as Zenia walked out on that summer Sunday, the world of the Jews was about to become worse beyond anyone's ability to imagine.

On the outskirts of Vilna in a large brick building known as the Cheap Houses, Leizer Bart had slept in that Sunday morning. The apartments at 37 Subocz Street had traditionally been the place that the newest arrivals in Vilna went to live, and the left-wing Zionist group Ha-Shomer ha-Tzair, the Young Guard, to which Leizer belonged, was no exception. Zionist groups had been outlawed by the Soviets, and thus they lived in small groups scattered within the Cheap Houses and conducted their business with as much secrecy as possible. Some of the members, including Leizer, had come from a *hakhsharah,* or Zionist training camp, located in Czestochowa, Poland,[22] where they

Leizer Bart (top row, left) with fellow Ha-Shomer ha-Tzair members, 1937
BART FAMILY COLLECTION

had learned survival skills, agricultural methods, and physical fitness, in anticipation of immigrating to Palestine. In the evenings they continued their studies of agriculture, basic engineering, and other subjects they would need to build a Jewish homeland.[23]

Rumors had been flying since the night before about the invasion, and everywhere in the Cheap Houses people hovered over their radios listening for news. At 11:00 A.M., the Soviet foreign minister finally took to the airwaves to say that the unthinkable—the invasion of the Soviet Union—was under way.

Leizer and his friends had escaped from Poland just ahead of the occupying Nazi army, but apparently they had not run far enough. And now it seemed everyone was on the move.

Young Zionists lived in the Cheap Houses at 37 Subocz Street.
COURTESY OF LEYZER RAN'S *JERUSALEM OF LITHUANIA*

Cars, laden with suitcases and furniture, were already creeping up Subocz Street. Other people were walking, pushing their belongings in small carts or carrying them by hand. It seemed almost impossible, at the rate cars and people were moving, to make it even to the next town. And what would be the point of that if the Nazis could move with the lightning speed they had already demonstrated?

Leizer had nowhere to go. All he and his Ha-Shomer ha-Tzair group had to fall back on was each other. For the time being, they would remain in the Cheap Houses, watching and waiting to see what happened next.

He heard the drone of engines overhead shortly after noon. The sound grew louder, merging with the crackling sound of antiaircraft rounds. Flames from an incendiary bomb lit up the sky in another part of the city. Inside the rooms of Ha-Shomer ha-Tzair members, the attitude quickly changed from shocked silence to frantic activity. People were coming in and out with information about the German advance. Some were talking about leaving Vilna to be with their families, while others had already decided to join the Red Army to fight against the Nazis.

Leizer worried about his parents and his younger brother and sister at home in Hrubieshov, a Polish town near the Bug River. Though the town was under Nazi occupation, the river marked the boundary between Soviet and German territory, and his family felt a small measure of safety in the possibility of escape across the river if things grew worse. Now it was obvious that the Nazis did not intend to respect any borders, and if the German army, the *Wehrmacht,* pushed across the Bug as easily as it had just crossed the Nieman, the entire Bart family would be completely trapped.[24]

Leizer had left home almost two years before, unable to get the others to come with him while they still could. His dream of going to Vilna to find a way to get exit visas for his family to go to Palestine had come to nothing. He had managed to get a transit visa for himself from the office of Chiune Sugihara, the Japanese consul in Kovno who had defied his government by issuing hundreds of transit visas to local Jews. These visas could be used to cross the Soviet Union by train, en route to Shanghai.[25] The visa had done him no good because he had already decided he would not use it if it meant leaving his family behind in Poland.

And now, what would happen? The Germans were coming, laden with centuries of hatred, spurred on by a madman, and all he could do was watch and listen in disbelief.

Two

————

THE CITY THAT WENT FORTH
A THOUSAND

The city that went forth a thousand shall have a hundred left,
and that which went forth one hundred shall have
ten left to the house of Israel.

—AMOS 5:3

The aerial assault on Vilna died down overnight but resumed the following morning. Soviet officials claimed the Red Army was repelling the German advance, but few in Vilna believed them. All Sunday afternoon, the sidewalks on the streets where Soviet officials lived were clogged with possessions being loaded into cars. Crying children were pushed into backseats of cars with their mothers, while grim-faced fathers waved good-bye and promised to follow after completing the final orders of their superiors.

The Red Army had been in full retreat along the highways leading east of Vilna since Sunday evening. Grodno and the capital, Kovno, had been abandoned as well. Trains packed with Vilna residents sped southeast toward the Lithuanian border with Byelorussia, then on to Minsk and elsewhere.

Prewar Vilna BART FAMILY COLLECTION

Among those seeking to escape by train, or even on foot, were several thousand Jews. Few would survive the trip. Those who were not picked off on the roads by *Luftwaffe* strafing runs, or blown up in aerial attacks on trains, were stopped at the border and told that only those who could prove they were returning to homes in other parts of the Soviet Union could cross. Many Jews who had made it to the border had no recourse but to go back to Vilna. Many did not survive the return trip, dying at the hands of Lithuanian ambushers or German sharpshooters while on the road.

In Vilna, by Monday morning, June 23, almost all signs of the Soviet government and army had vanished. The Soviets had left without any directives to the residents or local authorities, leaving behind only the Lithuanian police force to keep order. Many of its officers did not even try. The city was in a state of chaos approaching total anarchy. A perfect time, some thought, to settle scores with the Jews.

The majority of Vilna's seventy thousand Jews[1] barricaded themselves in their homes for fear of falling prey to Lithuanian thugs. It was widely felt among Vilna's Jews that the Lithuanians were looking forward to the Germans' arrival. The Jews were certain that the Lithuanians hated them more than they hated the idea of another foreign occupation. The Jews, therefore, had to worry not only about the danger of collapsing buildings and ordinary people so crazed by fear they might do desperate things, but also about people with a more cruelly calculated agenda about the Jews. Anti-Semitic posters had appeared on walls overnight, and young men sporting swastikas had already begun swaggering down Vilna's streets.

Among the most fearful inhabitants of Vilna were Soviet soldiers. Most had managed to get on one of the convoys leaving town, but for those left behind there was little refuge anywhere. To the Germans roaring toward Vilna, the Soviets were the enemy, to be shot on sight. To the people of Lithuania, Soviet soldiers were the most visible representatives of an unwanted occupying force that had been suddenly and unexpectedly sent packing. Anyone in a Soviet uniform out on a Vilna street was taking his life in his hands.

But Soviet soldiers, desperate to hide their identity with civilian clothing, presented their own threat to the people of Vilna. Soldiers were killing people in the streets for their boots, or their hats, or their jackets, or even for a loaf of bread, because clothing other than a Soviet uniform and provisions would improve their chances of making it safely back to the Soviet border.

It was a deeply frightening turn of events for all of Vilna, but particularly for its Jews, who knew from centuries of experience that when respect for human life weakened, respect for their lives tended to disappear altogether.

Zenia's family pondered their options. Hillel had a property called the Boulders less than an hour outside Vilna where they went each summer to get out of the city and harvest vegetables and fruits they put up for the winter.[2] One possibility, quickly rejected, was to go there. Given the anti-Semitism they had observed in the nearby village, it was possible the house had already been vandalized or occupied, and even if it hadn't, they would be too vulnerable there.

It was too late to act on Rose's three brothers' long-standing invitation to come to the United States. Rose and her sister Lizzie had sailed to visit them once as teenagers, and when Lizzie expressed interest in staying, Rose had convinced her to return to Vilna rather than put down roots in America. Vilna provided a much easier life, Rose had insisted, and besides, it was where their other sister, Sonia, and their parents were.[3]

Most Jews in Vilna saw that it was really too late to go anywhere. Even other cities in Europe offered little chance of refuge. Many communities with sizable Jewish populations were in German hands, and the previous October, Warsaw's Jews had been forced into a ghetto. Ghetto residents who were still alive were hungry and sick, and losing hope that the war would be short enough for them to be saved. Even those not in ghettos were prey to all kinds of unspeakable violence all over Nazi-occupied Europe.

No, Rose and Hillel concluded, it was best to stay in their home in a city that was at least familiar. Jews who left everything behind and took their chances elsewhere now would be like rabbits scurrying in a field under the eye of circling eagles.

The decision of most of Vilna's Jews on June 22 and 23 might have been different if they had known the war was not going to be as short as many people were predicting. Surely the great armies of Europe could unite to overrun this menace Hitler, they thought, and there was always the hope that the United States would put a quick end to the situation by entering the war. Surely Roosevelt would have to listen to the many delegations of Jews already telling him how precarious their chances for survival were in Europe. At the beginning of the invasion, it seemed that the best chance to stay alive and protect their property was to stay put, lie low, and hope that the occupation would not be too bad, or too long.

Their decision might have been different if they had known the enormity of the evil the Nazis would unleash. Isolated atrocities and a general murderous rampage across Europe had already left thousands of Jews dead, but large-scale, systematic exterminations of Jewish population centers were not yet part of the landscape of war in June 1941.[4] The Jews of Vilna had no way of knowing that Lithuania had been designated as the place to try out Hitler's blueprint for mass murder. As it happened, close to half of those who made the choice to stay in Vilna were dead in less than two months. Leaving no Jew alive would become to Hitler more important than transporting and supplying his own troops. In the end it would have an even higher priority than winning the war.

The first German tanks, part of the Seventh Armored Division, entered Vilna at dawn Tuesday morning, June 24, 1941. When the first Germans arrived on motorcycles, Lithuanian girls rushed into the street to throw flowers. Tanks were next, emblazoned with swastikas, followed by artillery units. Truckloads of soldiers followed. Young men on the sidelines practiced uncoiling their arms into taut Nazi salutes. Thousands waved Lithuanian flags. Some carried anti-Semitic signs and chanted slogans denigrating the Jews.

Spirits were high. The occupation meant that the German bombing was over, the Soviets were gone, and Lithuanians were allied with what they were sure was the winning side. Good times were ahead. Communists, Poles, Jews—it would be good to be rid of them all.

Within a few days the Jews of Vilna were already experiencing the downward spiral that would lead them to the ghetto seventy-four days after the arrival of the first German troops.[5] However, at the outset of Nazi occupation, under hastily formed local provisional governments, things were worse for Jews in other parts of Lithuania. Pent-up resentments against Jews in the capital, Kovno, triggered a massacre on June 25, just as the *Wehrmacht* was arriving. Sixty homes were destroyed and twelve hundred Jews, including women and children, were killed. In the next few days, the numbers of the dead nearly tripled, to thirty-five hundred, and by the middle of July, five thousand of the thirty-six thousand Jews of Kovno were already dead.[6] Similar loss of life occurred in Shavli, the third-largest city in Lithuania, as well as half a dozen smaller towns.

In Vilna, however, there was no such immediate wholesale violence. The Third Reich could take care of the Jews. Asserting themselves as Lithuanians was what mattered most to the relatively small group of people of that ethnicity in the city. The important thing was to make a first impression on the Nazis that Vilna was indeed a Lithuanian city, and that the Nazis should deal with the Lithuanians, not the Poles, in the government.[7]

Consequently, in the first days there were no pogroms against Vilna's Jews. Instead, sixty Jews and twenty Poles were taken hostage by the provisional Lithuanian government on June 24 and 25. The hostages were claimed to be necessary to ensure compliance by Poles and Jews with the orders of the interim authorities serving until the German authorities arrived. The Poles were released quickly, but the Jews were held in prison for a month, at which time six were released and the remaining fifty-four were killed.

Their deaths were a prophecy that went unheard by Vilna's Jews. In the ensuing occupation, the Nazis would persuade the increasingly skeptical Jews time and time again that their behavior and cooperation could ensure their survival. These first hostages had committed no offense, and the populace had been compliant. The hostages died because the prison was the easiest place to start in on what was the true plan for every last one of the Jews of Vilna.

The Provisional Lithuanian Government, formed while *Wehrmacht* tanks still raced down the highways toward Vilna, functioned for a short while, but it was clear that the Nazis had no interest in Lithuania's ethnic quarrels. To the disappointment of many Lithuanians, the Germans did not recognize Lithuania's independence or the validity of the interim government. Hitler's intention was to create a large protectorate made up of all the Baltic states, without regard for any national borders. But because the Reich was busy with the war effort, it left the provisional government in place until early August.

The disdain of the Germans for Lithuania's view of itself as an occupied sovereign nation rather than simply part of an enlarged Third Reich disappointed many Lithuanians, who saw themselves as kindred Jew- and Communist-hating souls, working at a single purpose with the Nazis.[8] Many believed this should have given them special, elevated status among the occupied nations, but they did not yet understand that in the Nazi hierarchy, non-German populations were only one step above Jews. There would be no respect forthcoming for Lithuania or Lithuanians.

A brief period of cooperative command with the German military lasted until the beginning of August, when the military

Lithuanian policeman assists German soldier on motorcycle.
COURTESY OF GHETTO FIGHTERS' HOUSE, ISRAEL

authorities moved further east to take charge of more recently conquered territory. Arriving in their place, the German security police, the *Schutzstaffel* (SS), made it clear that the Lithuanian government was now superfluous. Surprised and disappointed at being so summarily ignored and dismissed, Lithuanian authorities and hundreds of private citizens sublimated their disappointment by taking on with relish the dirty work so clearly modeled by Nazis elsewhere in Europe. German collaborators in Vilna were at the outset mostly paramilitary groups of local Lithuanian residents, supplemented later by Ukrainians, Estonians, and Lativans brought to Vilna by the Nazis to carry out the mission to destroy the Jews.[9]

The Nazis encouraged local efforts intended to humiliate, weaken, and decimate the Jews, such as the activities of the Lithuanian paramilitary groups. To the Nazis, it was a way of showing the world that the Germans were not the instigators of anti-Semitic violence, but were simply supporting a long-standing European desire to be rid of Jews. To this end, special German agents infiltrated neighborhoods and villages to whip up anti-Jewish frenzy and ensure that the body count was already high before the victims could be laid at the feet of the Reich.[10]

These special agents were followed by mobile units known as *Einsatzgruppen,* formed by the Reich specifically for the purpose of killing Jews. There were four *Einsatzgruppen* in Soviet-occupied territories, each with approximately a thousand men. As the *Wehrmacht* swept east out of Lithuania on its way deeper into Soviet territory, a subgroup of *Einsatzgruppen,* known as the *Einsatzkommando,* followed in its wake, working with Lithuanians to round up Jews, take them to places where their bodies could be easily disposed of, and shoot them. Approximately 72 percent of the Jews of Lithuania, and almost every last one of those living in villages in the provinces, were already dead by the end of August 1941, at the hands of the *Einsatzkommando* and their Lithuanian collaborators. Though figures vary widely, in part due to the uncertainty regarding the numbers of those, such as Leizer Bart, who had recently arrived in Vilna, as well as those who managed to leave the city in the days and months before the German arrival, records indicate that only a little more than half of the approximately seventy thousand Jews living in Vilna survived the summer.[11]

What was to come over the next two months was only hinted at in the first few days of the occupation. Immediately after the arrival of the German army, a curfew for Jews was announced. Though most Jews, and in fact much of the general population as well, would not have ventured far from home after dark in any case, Jews now knew that being caught outside could mean an immediate bullet in the back. Anyone who saw Jews on the street could do anything at all to them without fear of penalty other than that provided by his or her own conscience.

Soon after the Nazis' arrival, Rose had pulled out her sewing basket, looking for white cloth with which she could fashion the armbands that all Jews had been ordered to wear. She and Zenia patched blue Stars of David on five thick strips of cloth, which the family began wearing around their arms when they went outside. Though many of Vilna's established Jewish families would have been recognizable without the symbol, the point was at least in part to force them to announce on their own bodies that they were government-sanctioned targets.

Over the next few weeks Vilna's Jews sewed new patches as the Nazis changed their minds about the exact colors, size, and location of the symbols before deciding on a yellow Star of David on the left side of the chest and on the back of coats and jackets.

Many of the initial problems of the occupation affected Zenia's mother more than any other member of the family. Kajya rarely came anymore, because her family was fearful she might be victimized on the street if people knew she was still working for a Jewish family. For Rose, the job of maintaining her business and household became more onerous as new edicts decreed that Jews could buy food only during specified hours late in the day. Rose would go out with Michael or Zenia, and they often came back after several hours with only a few bedraggled carrots and greens, or a small piece of meat, because the vendors had already run out of everything else.[12]

Each new day meant dealing with new humiliations and hardships. Zenia, Michael, and their friends could no longer go to the movie theaters, because Jews were forbidden to go inside all public places, including movie houses, concert halls, libraries, barbershops, and even their own schools. Michael's bicycle, like those of all other Jews, had been confiscated, along with other items such as phones and radios. When they went outside they had to walk in wet, leaf-strewn gutters, because the sidewalks were reserved for everyone else. Some, like the Lewinson family, took to cutting holes in walls to create makeshift safes for their valuables because marauders simply broke into their homes and demanded them.

Rose was growing more tired and discouraged by the day. They all were, but it seemed to show the most on Rose. Hillel

Choral Synagogue
BART FAMILY
COLLECTION

knew it was only a matter of time until he was forced completely out of the lumber business by Nazi decrees, and he was spending most of his time trying to liquidate his inventory to build a hedge against what he knew were difficult times ahead for his family. Still, he struggled to be upbeat when he came home, greeting Zenia and Michael with a nod and an approving look. Bluma seemed like a rock, which rain could pelt, sun could scorch, and wind could pummel without changing at all.

To go between the house and Rose's store required a circuitous and difficult route after Zawalna Street and a number of other major thoroughfares were decreed off-limits to Jews altogether.[13] This edict was particularly bitter for Vilna's Jews because the Choral Synagogue was on Zawalna Street, just a few blocks from Zenia's home. Jews would no longer be able to stop to admire the beautiful white tablets of the law on its roof. Families like the Lewinsons who had worshiped there for

Zawalna Street, c. 1925   BART FAMILY COLLECTION

generations had seen its Torah paraded through the congregation for the last time. So much had been ripped away by Nazi decrees, and now it seemed as if they were marching into Jews' heads to destroy their memories as well.

The day of Zenia's high school graduation passed without note, because her school had been forced to close.[14] The family had planned to mark the day nonetheless with a dinner just for themselves. Kajya had not arrived to help because a new edict forbade Christians and Jews to have any contact with each other. The Nazis would probably have let Kajya go with a warning, but they could have punished Rose's family in any way they wished. Later, as the bloodlust and murders escalated, even Kajya might not have gotten a second chance.[15]

Neither Zenia nor Michael could remember a time when Kajya had not been in their lives, and this edict weighed particularly heavily on them. It was followed by another that seemed especially cruel for someone as outgoing as Zenia Lewinson. From that point forward Jews were not even to look at anyone in the street who was not Jewish. They were to keep their eyes trained on the ground and their mouths shut. Even if she saw a customer she knew, Zenia was to avert her eyes and say nothing, not even hello.

Decrees limiting Jews' behavior and rights were only one aspect of life in the immediate aftermath of the German invasion. Jews were required to register for work and to report to an address on Strashun Street, from which long lines of men were marched each morning to work sites permitted by the government to use Jewish labor. The Nazis were getting more organized as each week passed, and opportunists were not missing the chance to use the Jews' misfortune to enhance their profits.

It was difficult for young men like Leizer Bart and his fellow members of Ha-Shomer ha-Tzair to avoid being marched off on work details. After all, with their efforts to prepare themselves for the hard labor of building a Jewish homeland in Palestine, few if any Jews in Vilna were more suited for hard labor than they were. The group dispersed, focusing on staying out of Nazi clutches while they waited to see what happened next and what they might be able to do about it.

Leizer and his friends had heard rumors of the possible creation of a ghetto in Vilna similar to that in Warsaw. If the Nazis created a ghetto, the alternative to going there would be to stand one's ground and be killed on the spot. That or go into hiding, for it was clear there was no safe haven anywhere in Europe. Leizer was not about to bow his head to the Nazis, but neither did he want to lose his life in some small, ineffectual act of defiance. He might live in a society that saw his life as valueless, but he certainly did not agree. But how to reconcile his chances to survive with his need to hold his head high? In a world where death and indignity were facts of everyday life, the answer was not at all clear.

Within Ha-Shomer ha-Tzair, a response to the dilemma that plagued them all was brewing in the mind of one of their leaders, the wild-haired poet Abba Kovner. Still, at the moment nothing could be done except remain alert, avoid unnecessary risks, and wait to see what the Nazis would do next. Though they had to lie low and minimize contact with each other, especially in vulnerable places like the Cheap Houses, they all knew they needed to remain bonded in spirit, ready on a moment's notice to come together. Ha-Shomer ha-Tzair intended to counteract the menace that had entered their lives. They just didn't know how, or when.

Conditions deteriorated so swiftly for Vilna's Jews that it was soon hard to remember ever having felt safe or happy. With the arrival of the Germans a group of somewhere between 100 and 150 Lithuanian and some Polish men,[16] known formally as the Ypatingas Burys, or Special Squad, and informally as Hapunes, or Snatchers, began to kidnap Jewish men from the streets and turn them over to Nazi authorities. Though some might have done it for nothing but the sadistic pleasure of hurting a Jew,[17] most were enticed by the small bounty they received for each victim. The abducted Jews were supposedly offered as day laborers to the Nazis, but it quickly became clear that few of the Snatchers' victims ever came back.

Hillel, having liquidated his lumber business and closed Rose's office supply store, pocketed his work permit every morn-

Michael, Rose, and Zenia Lewinson with Hillel Botwinik, c. 1940
BART FAMILY COLLECTION

ing as he marched several miles outside the city with a labor detail. This piece of paper conveyed that the holder was doing approved work for the Germans or their contractors, and thus was
off-limits to the Snatchers. Such permits were necessary because
the Snatchers had become brazen enough to kidnap whole work
crews, creating a circular situation whereby they brought them
back to the authorities to collect the finder's fee for pulling Jews
off the street for labor.[18] The employers' concern was that productivity was suffering because no one could count on his forced
laborers showing up if they ran into Snatchers on the way to
work. The fact that a sizable number were never seen again was
of concern to few other than the Jews.

Michael was only a few months too young to be con-
scripted for labor, and Hillel ordered him to stay at home so

Jewish men being led to Ponary (photo found in the possession of a German soldier on the Eastern Front) USHMM, COURTESY OF YIVO INSTITUTE

as not to be kidnapped by Snatchers. Michael busied himself around the house while Zenia and Rose went out to find food. Without Kajya, every housekeeping task had to be done by the family, and because they were home so much more, the house seemed more dismal with each passing week.

By the first week of July, Rose and her older sister Lizzie, who lived next to Zenia's family in another apartment in Bluma's building on Zawalna Street, had received an order to report for work in a unit that repaired military uniforms. Each day they marched off, and each day they arrived home exhausted. Like many other Jews they believed that the key to their continued existence was to be diligent, productive workers. The Germans needed labor, and since Jews received little more than a few pennies for their work, it was in the best interests of the Nazis to ensure at least some minimal standard of living and level of safety for working Jews. Or at least so it seemed.

Indeed, the war effort required a wide range of labor, from sewing buttons on uniforms to loading supplies onto trains to manufacturing equipment to cleaning officers' quarters. Though the work was debilitating, as long as it was clear they would be back at home at night, the Jews of Vilna simply said that it could be worse.

Most of the men who marched off in the morning came back at night. People assumed that those who did not return had been taken too far to come back the same day. Stories of faraway labor camps calmed the nerves of Vilna's Jews, and from time to time postcards would arrive in Vilna from men who had not been seen in some time, saying where they had been taken and that they were safe.

On July 13, Hillel Botwinik, the man Zenia called father, did not return home.

About a week after Hillel's disappearance, Zenia's family got the news that he had been seen as part of a group marching toward the Ponary forest outside Vilna. People were saying there was a secret labor camp there, because so many work crews had headed that way. Nazi labor camps were fearsome places, where prisoners often died of hunger, exhaustion, or exposure, or were simply shot when they were no longer strong enough to work. Still, painful as it was to picture Hillel slaving with Nazi guns at his back, it was at least an image of him alive.

But the rumors about Ponary were growing more ominous by the day. Stories of gunshots heard after groups of Jews had

Jewish men being led to Ponary (photo found in the possession of a German soldier on the Eastern Front) USHMM, COURTESY OF YIVO INSTITUTE

disappeared into the forest had begun to circulate among Vilna's Jews. People whispered that there was no labor camp in Ponary, and that the Nazis shot all the people they took there. The inference was clear. Hillel might have been dead even before they knew he was missing.[19]

Three

THE STONES BURST INTO TEARS

It seemed to me that stones,
Seeing us, burst into tears. . . .
Old people and children walked
Like cattle to the altar. . . .
Rare are those who still have everyone.
—FROM "IT WAS A SUMMER DAY," A SONG OF
THE VILNA PARTISANS

Before World War II, the name "Ponary" conjured up images of lighthearted Sunday strolls, bicycle rides, family picnics, and bonfires each spring on the Jewish holiday of Lag Ba'omer. For Zenia and her family, this beautiful wooded area a few miles outside the city limits of Vilna was so inconceivable as a place of death that they continued to prop up each other's hopes that if Hillel had gone there he must just be working.

It took all their energy—all the energy of all the Jews of Vilna—simply to maintain their lives in the summer of 1941. They did not have the time, and most of them did not have the morbid imagination, to form any clear picture of what Nazi intentions really were.

And in the beginning the Nazis covered their tracks very

Execution pit at Ponary   COURTESY OF DEATHCAMPS.ORG

well. The *Einsatzkommando,* German military units following
behind the fighting troops to maintain order in newly occupied
areas, had begun working immediately with the Snatchers to
use Ponary to disguise the murders of small groups of Soviet
prisoners and Jews. When the Soviets had controlled the area,
they excavated parts of the Ponary forest to store fuel tanks,
but they had not gotten farther than digging large pits. It was a
fairly uncomplicated matter to bring victims to Ponary, watch
them from the top of embankments as they marched single file
to the ditches lining the pit, and then shoot them. Hillel
Botwinik never returned home and was, presumably, one of
the first to be caught up in this newly streamlined operation.
By late July 1941, the process had become so efficient that an
average of five hundred Jews died there each day.[1]

It took Rose several weeks after Hillel's disappearance to understand that she would have to take on his role as the backbone of her family. Soon she, Bluma, and Lizzie had put together a plan to wall off a corner of a storage area in the granary that could be accessed through a trapdoor in the floor immediately above. In this way, when people with hostile intent were detected in the immediate area, everyone living in the house on Zawalna Street was able to go into an enclosed space that was not likely to be discovered from the outside.

Jews all over Vilna were creating hiding places of this sort. They were called by the Hebrew name *maline,* harkening back to the biblical reference to building a lodge within a cucumber garden.[2] German soldiers, Lithuanian police, and Snatchers would move in quickly and unexpectedly, using cars or other vehicles to surround a neighborhood, and conduct door-to-door searches for Jewish men. Even those with work permits were dragged away while their families were herded into courtyards or streets. They watched the Germans and Lithuanians parade out of their building with their possessions, and when they tried to return home later, they found the doors sealed, rendering them homeless.

The existence of a killing field at Ponary was still only a rumor at the time Hillel disappeared, and those who so much as suggested it might be true were roundly criticized for promoting unnecessary fear and low morale among Vilna's Jews. Nevertheless, the murderous inclinations of the occupiers were clear to everyone. Jews were already being killed in various places, by various means, and using various pretexts. Shootings and fatal beatings took place openly, always with some claimed provocation or violation of Nazi orders. As the situation worsened over the summer of 1941, some Jews even began to think the German civilian authority, due to arrive shortly, might actually be an improvement over the military one, which had governed Vilna since the beginning of July. At least then the lawlessness of life in Vilna, where everyone except their fellow Jews seemed to be armed and on the lookout for them, might possibly be brought under control.

Reports filtering in from the Warsaw ghetto indicated that the German soldiers stayed outside the ghetto walls, and that the Jews didn't have Snatchers taking away their men. As long as German labor needs were met, the occupants of the ghetto were by and large left alone. Once behind the ghetto walls, the prisoners were not allowed out, but hostile townspeople and bullying soldiers and police were not allowed to just walk in either. To many Jews in Vilna, the idea of having their own space sounded like an improvement over their current situation.

In Warsaw, an institution known as the *Judenrat,* or Jewish council, served as a mechanism by which the German occupiers could maintain an administrative liaison with the Jewish community even before they had been walled into a ghetto. This was taken as a sign to many of the Jews of Warsaw and elsewhere that some degree of cooperation between Jews and Nazis might be achieved, and that this might help keep them alive. Others were more skeptical. Though Jewish community councils were a long-standing part of life in European Jewish communities, serving on a Nazi-ordained *Judenrat* simply felt too much like collaboration, however good the participants' intentions.

On July 4, 1941, the German military command gave the Jews of Vilna twenty-four hours to put together their own *Judenrat*.[3] No one wanted to serve. There was no bargaining with the Germans, however. A respected doctor stood up at an emergency meeting of fifty-seven Jewish leaders that same day and told them to put their fear and disgust aside and participate in the *Judenrat*. "Although we are aware of the peril confronting us, it is our obligation to do so. All who are elected must not refuse; they must make themselves available for service," he said, before bursting into tears as he sat down.

The first group serving on the *Judenrat* maintained the respect of the Jewish community, despite having to cooperate with the Nazis. They worked tirelessly to solve problems such as homelessness and kidnappings. To put an end to the snatching, sealing of houses, and sudden roundups of men, the *Judenrat* offered to supply a steady and reliable daily pool of Jewish labor to the Nazis. Kidnapping and pillage greatly decreased by the end of July 1941, but the trade-off was a deeply troubling one. The *Judenrat* had to choose which individuals would go out on risky, long-term, or questionable work details, from which it was quite possible they would not return. The Jewish community began to realize that the *Judenrat* was allowing, and perhaps even calculating, the deaths of some Jews in order to save others.

The *Judenrat* was responsible for other means of appeasing the Germans as well. Nazi leadership changed near the end of July, when the civilian command under the leadership of Hans Hingst moved in to take charge of Vilna. Hingst and his assistant in charge of liaison with the Jews, Franz Murer, quickly made clear their intent to profit personally from the situation.

Nazi District Commissar Hans Hingst; behind him, on the right, Franz Murer
COURTESY OF
LEYZER RAN'S
*JERUSALEM OF
LITHUANIA*

Murer took three members of the new *Judenrat* hostage, and told the others to spread the word that he planned to shoot all three if the Jews did not meet his demand for five million rubles by nine the following morning. Murer claimed at that meeting that his demand would not only save the three hostages but buy the safety of all the Jews of Vilna.[4]

The other *Judenrat* members were, in fact, in an impossible situation because a curfew prohibited them from going house to house that evening, but nevertheless they began a frenetic appeal for as many donations as each family could possibly afford. Nearly two hundred watches, a million and a half rubles, thirty-three pounds of gold, and many bags full of miscellaneous items like candlesticks were delivered to Murer.[5] The violence abated. For a little while it looked as if the Jews of Vilna had gotten something for their money.

The 461 Jews killed during the entire month of August equaled only what had typically been killed in one day in July. Mass roundups, snatchings, and pillaging of homes and property ceased almost completely. Perhaps, many Jews thought, the tribute money had been enough after all. Perhaps the Nazis had satisfied their anti-Semitic lust to a sufficient degree, and had decided to keep the rest of the Jews alive as a labor force.

The Jews of Vilna spent August concentrating on settling down for what was likely to be a long-term Nazi occupation. They focused on finding jobs that would give them the work permits they believed would keep them and their families safe. The *Judenrat* worked with the Germans to match Jews with potential places of employment. Jews developed secret connections to get adequate food, built more *malines,* and figured out ways, in the absence of all but a few radios and with no phones, to hear news of the war and to stay in contact with Jews of other communities.

Though gossip and rumors kept the Jews of Vilna in a frenzy of anxiety, August was a relatively calm month. Unknown to the Jews, the calm came about as a result of another set of concerns among the Nazi occupiers. Commissar Hans Hingst had orders to begin the complete elimination of Vilna's Jews as soon as possible, and his officials were using August to familiarize themselves with the city, make contacts among Lithuanians who might be helpful, and develop the procedures by which this mission could be accomplished in an orderly fashion.

In fact, some of the deaths of Jews in August were meant as training in murder for soldiers newly assigned to Vilna. Unlike the *Einsatzkommando,* whose primary assignment was killing, most of these new soldiers had not yet been initiated into the bloody ways of the Third Reich. It was a common practice, therefore, to create situations that would ensure they each personally had blood on their hands.[6] Groups of Jews would be arrested and taken to the location selected for their execution. New soldiers and the civilian security police known as the SS were told to kill the Jews individually with rifle shots and to help with removal of the bodies. Officers participated directly in these firing squads, to increase the psychological pressure not to resist becoming a murderer. The Jewish victims in these "practice runs" were almost always males, so as to avoid complicating the soldiers' emotional response by including mothers and children. "It is difficult to expect that people who are themselves family men can do this with any enthusiasm," commanding officer Alfred Filbert remarked.[7]

As a result, the Jewish population other than adult males had as yet been largely untouched, and Filbert told his squads of executioners that in the future they would "have to murder Jewish women and children, as the number of those liquidated so far has been too small."[8] But it was unnecessary to kill Jews, male or female, old or young, in August. There was always September.

On Sunday afternoon, August 31, 1941, in a square at the corner of Wielka and Szklanna streets, a small group of German soldiers sat in a café near a movie house. Unnoticed, two Lithuanians entered a house overlooking the square. From the upstairs window, one of them stuck out a rifle and fired in the direction of the soldiers. None of them were hit. The Lithuanians ran out a minute later saying that Jews living in the building had fired the shots. Immediately, the Germans picked up their weapons and ran inside. A handful of SS officers soon came out of the house, prodding several Jews along with their rifle butts. They took the Jews to the middle of the square and began beating them savagely. They shot one as he lay motionless

Wielka Street, looking in the direction of Szklanna Street
BART FAMILY COLLECTION

on the ground, but dragged the rest to their feet and shot them where they stood.

The Jews gave the event the acidly ironic name of the "Great Provocation." It was obvious to the shocked Jews that the entire event had been staged. The clearest evidence of this was that a full five hours before the event even took place, government radio had already announced that German soldiers had been shot on Szklanna Street, and that Jews had been executed in reprisal. In addition to the clairvoyant news broadcast, Nazi retaliation was far too well coordinated not to have been preplanned. In the wake of the Great Provocation, the SS moved within hours to begin to clear every Jew from the area known for centuries as the Jewish Quarter.

The Jewish Quarter was where the most vulnerable of

Vilna's Jews lived—those who were poor, or elderly, or alone. They surrendered their keys and took one last look at their possessions, often within view of hovering non-Jews eager to grab up everything the minute they were marched away. They were taken to Lukiszki Prison, where they were held without food, water, or sanitary provisions. From September 1 through 3, a total of 3,700 Jewish men, women, and children were taken in groups to Ponary, where they were all shot.

On September 2, the first *Judenrat* was disbanded. Its members were lined up and marched to the prison. Most died the next day at Ponary. The clearing of the Jewish Quarter and the slaughter of the *Judenrat* marked the inception of the systematic campaign to eliminate Vilna's Jews. No one was kept from the pits at Ponary because of a work permit or role in the community, and in fact the identity of most victims was not ascertained at all before they were marched off. A Jew was a Jew, and that was a death sentence in and of itself.

The Jewish Quarter had been cleared for a reason other than simply to kill that segment of the population. Since mid-August plans had been drawn up to use the quarter as a ghetto in which to imprison Vilna's Jews. The Germans wanted several blocks of vacant houses for this purpose, so they would have a coordinated and efficient base from which to take a steady flow of victims to their deaths. The Jewish Quarter was, to the Nazi officials' way of thinking, the ideal place.

This would cause greater immediate suffering for many of Vilna's Jews than for those in other Lithuanian cities where ghettos were established, such as Kovno. In Kovno, ghetto walls were built around a place where the majority of the Jews already lived. Those who lived elsewhere were assigned to houses vacated inside the walls by non-Jews. Thus, many of Kovno's Jews were able to keep whatever meager possessions had not yet been confiscated or stolen, whereas almost all of Vilna's Jews would find themselves forced to leave almost everything behind when the order came to move to the ghetto.[9]

To the Jews of Vilna, that order seemed to be more imminent every day. Zenia watched from the window as the doors opening onto Zawalna Street directly across from her house were boarded up and cross streets were closed off with wooden fences.

On Friday, September 5, a notice was published that all owners of carts and horses were to appear at a market on the corner of Zawalna and Nowogrodzka streets at five o'clock the following morning. This may have been a ruse to ensure that nobody could help Jewish friends or neighbors take their possessions to the ghetto, or perhaps to minimize the number of people who would see the roundup occur, but whatever its purpose, many Jews interpreted this to mean the order to go to the ghetto would come while the cart owners were occupied at the market. Christians were drawing the same conclusion, and in a macabre twist on the biblical story of the escape of the Hebrews from Egypt, many Christians placed crosses on their doors to keep the twentieth-century versions of the angel of death at bay.[10]

Zenia knew many relatives and friends who had already sewn small valuables into the linings and hems of their clothing, to carry secretly if they were forced to leave in a hurry. On the night of September 5, 1941, she too was busy with needle and thread. Family photos, documents, and memorabilia lay on the dining room table, alongside other heirlooms and Rose's wedding silverware with her initials *R* and *L* on every piece. Her mother had taken the painting from in front of the ragged opening Hillel had hacked in the wall. Most of what was on the table would stay in the hole behind, in the hope that the family would be coming home soon.

Over the course of the night in Zenia's home, as everywhere in the city, practicality eventually overcame sentiment. Family photos and treasures of little monetary value were placed in their hiding places with the solemnity and tears of a funeral. One suitcase or parcel for each hand was prepared and left by the door, and the Jews of Vilna went to bed to lie sleepless until morning.

Zenia and her family stayed in Bluma's apartment that night, fearful of being separated in the morning. Lithuanian soldiers pounded rifle butts against Bluma's front door a little after 5:00 A.M. on September 6, 1941, before kicking it in and pulling them all from their beds. "Get outside," one of them said. "You have five minutes."[11]

They all were fat and stiff already with the layers of clothing they had worn to bed, but each of them put on another layer or two as they prepared to leave. Each of them bent awkwardly to pick up a suitcase and a bundle made from a sheet whose four corners had been knotted. They waited inside, until the soldiers came back.

"Get out," one of them said, waving the barrel of his rifle toward the door. They struggled to carry their burdens down the stairs and were herded into the street, which had already begun to fill with people who looked much as they did, with heavy loads and grim faces.

The entrance to the ghetto was only a little over six blocks away, but a brisk ten-minute walk on an ordinary day was transformed for Zenia and her family that morning into a slow, seemingly endless ordeal. For Jews living farther away, the experience was worse. One minute it was raining, and a few minutes later it was unseasonably hot. Padded with so many layers of clothing drenched with sweat and rain, people struggled not to faint and staggered under their loads. Those who fell or stopped to rest were kicked and beaten with rifle butts. Those who could not go on were shot.

It was early enough so that only small groups of Lithuanians, roused by the noise, had come down to the streets to watch. "Are you going to Palestine?" some yelled out over and over again. Others were shouting, "Good riddance, Jews." A few seemed genuinely disturbed by what they were witnessing, but no one moved to help the Jews.

Zenia turned onto Rudnicka Street and saw the pink and white belfries of All Saints Church up ahead. The crowd was too thick for her to see the ghetto gate, but she knew it was near. Her eyes stung from perspiration and her elbows and shoulders were screaming with the strain of carrying her baggage. Bluma had fallen back in the crowd, and Rose had lagged behind in the hope of being able to find her. Zenia and Michael had not seen them for close to an hour.

Jews finally turning the corner toward the ghetto gate may have felt some relief in knowing they were almost there. But where? It wasn't like arriving at the entrance to their homes, laden down with bags and anticipating a cool living room where they could fling themselves into a comfortable chair and rest their feet. Whatever it meant, it certainly wasn't the same

Corner of Rudnicka and Zawalna, and the belfries of All Saints Church
COURTESY OF LEYZER RAN'S *JERUSALEM OF LITHUANIA*

as almost home. Their living rooms, their unmade beds, the kitchen with the last glasses and cups quickly rinsed and laid aside—were there already people inside making off with their things? Whatever happened, no one would be coming back to the lives that had existed inside those homes, if they came back at all.

Four

DAYS WITH NO ANSWER

So many days
with no answer,
with no certainty.

—FROM "LAST STORM"
BY ABBA KOVNER

It sounded like a river at flood stage, so powerful a force that the shutters of the top-floor apartment on Bosaczkowa Street rattled.[1] Zenia stood at the window with the other occupants of the apartment, staring at the sight in the small park below them. Thousands of Jews were converging from side streets, moving slowly toward the narrow lane leading to the ghetto gate. Crowds spilled over into the park, the solid wedge of their bodies obliterating all signs of the trampled grass beneath as they struggled to carry heavy burdens over their shoulders, or bent with strained arms under the weight of their suitcases. The sounds of fabric rubbing against thighs and arms padded with extra layers of clothing created an eerie rustle, mingled with murmured words of lamentation in the streets below. The clamor rose in waves so palpable it almost seemed as if they could have reached out and grabbed handfuls of sound.

A courtyard off Bosaczkowa Street accessed from Rudnicka Street, where the Etingin and Lewinson families lived
COURTESY OF GHETTO FIGHTERS' HOUSE, ISRAEL

Hillel's niece Sonia Etingin and her family were friends of the apartment owners, and they had been living there since their own home was bombed on the first day of the Nazi invasion. It was Sonia to whom Zenia had been sent on her errand the day the bomb fell. Now, by an odd twist of fate, the Etingin family's misfortune that day had begun to seem like a stroke of good fortune compared to what the rest of Vilna's Jews were experiencing. By luck, their friends' apartment was on the edge of the newly formed ghetto, with its entry on Bosaczkowa Street, outside the ghetto. When the old Jewish Quarter had been cleared, their apartment had been overlooked. As a result, the Etingins' friends were one of the few families whose home actually ended up inside the perimeter of the Vilna ghetto, and the Etingins were one of only a few families who were not scrambling that day for a place to stay.[2]

When the Jewish Quarter was originally cleared by the

Germans and the walls began to go up, arrangements had been made for Rose and her family to move in when the time came. While most Jews would have to find a space to settle in when they arrived, Zenia's family had already known where to go.

Zenia and Michael stared down from the apartment window at the crowds beneath them, crowds Zenia and her brother had been a part of only an hour earlier. For months before that day, people had wondered aloud what the world was coming to. That day, no one needed to ask. What the world was coming to could be observed outside the window. Soldiers were beating many of the Jews heading toward the ghetto, but the screams of horror and groans of pain and anguish were muted by the roar of so many bodies moving like a giant wave toward the gate that lay just out of sight around the corner.[3]

Behind them, the streets and houses now empty of their presence teemed with other activity. The nightmare for the Jews of Vilna was a dream come true for many of the non-Jews of Vilna, who had wasted no time ransacking the Jews' homes for their valuables, carting off furniture, paintings, antiques, china and silver, clothing, bedding, and anything else left behind. Many who had trusted their Christian neighbors to watch over their property would find themselves quickly betrayed,[4] while others would discover they had put their trust in people who were as good as their word.

The ghetto, consisting of only a few square blocks, would be unimaginably congested. Zenia's family was grateful to have an apartment with people they knew, and the owners were equally glad to have their first new tenants be almost like family. But the sight of the numbers pouring through the gate, coupled with their intimate knowledge of the few

Zenia with Maks Etingin
(postwar photo, September 1948)
BART FAMILY COLLECTION

oddly shaped and narrow
streets of the medieval Jewish Quarter, led them to realize quite quickly that many
strangers would be sharing
the apartment with them by
the end of the day.

Even the idea of sharing a single bedroom as a family
turned out to be unachievable. The ghetto was truly going to
test the age-old tradition that "Jews must help Jews. Who else
will?" Bluma, Rose, Zenia, and Michael were quickly con-
strained to sharing a bedroom with Sonia, her husband, Abram,
and their boys, Maks and Chaim. By the end of the day, reality
was even worse than that, as four more families brought the
capacity of the single bedroom to twenty or more. Beds would
be shared by as many as could fit. Everyone else would sleep
on the floor.[5]

Within a few hours, fights were breaking out over space
everywhere in the ghetto. In the interior courtyard of Zenia's
new lodging, many more people were sitting on their suitcases, and others were stopping in the covered entryway and
putting their bags down as if they intended to walk no farther.
By midafternoon the flood of Jews pouring across the park
had not abated, and every apartment in the building already
had dozens of occupants.[6]

By nightfall, another dozen people were in the other bedroom of Zenia's new apartment and over a dozen more in the

parlor and living room. They were the lucky ones. No formal mechanism had been created to allocate housing, and the Germans had not even bothered to figure out the ratio of existing housing units to the number of Jews they had driven through the ghetto gates. Planning for the ghetto had not extended beyond setting its boundaries and herding the Jews into living spaces that turned out to allow less than one square yard per person and one bed per twenty residents.[7] Late-arriving Jews found themselves living indefinitely in alleyways and open courtyards, shivering and often drenched by early autumn rain.[8]

Leizer was one of the unlucky ones who slept in a crowded stairwell that first night. He knew he was in big trouble. He had been in town less than two years and had no family in Vilna, and no friends other than the members of Ha-Shomer ha-Tzair. Most of them, having come from elsewhere, were in the same predicament. Jews might help other Jews, but family and old friends would come first. And clearly in this situation there would not be enough of anything but misery to go around.

The chill of the stone landing seeped through his clothes. Autumn was closing in, bringing night frost and then the inevitable first snowfall. Where would all these people be sleeping then? Though some Jews on that first night might have already been worrying about that, for most, including Leizer, the immediate future commanded all their attention. Tomorrow, Leizer told himself, he was going to find a place to live, and a bed to sleep in.

The opportunity Leizer was looking for arose by midmorning the next day, when he heard about job openings with the newly formed ghetto police. Many of the senior ghetto administrators and ghetto police officers would be able to live in the

Housing for ghetto officials and police on Konska Street
COURTESY OF GHETTO FIGHTERS' HOUSE, ISRAEL

building on Konska Street designated for the *Judenrat* housing.[9]
Leizer rushed to get in line to apply. By the end of the day he
was sitting on a bed in an apartment, pleased with his good fortune. How bad could it be keeping order in the ghetto? He had
been told that the Gestapo planned to stay out and let the Jews
handle their own affairs. Being in the ghetto was bad enough,
but at least they would be safely out of reach of trigger-happy
Germans while they waited out the war. Jews keeping the peace
for Jews. He liked that idea.

A few days after their arrival, the small bedroom into which
Zenia's family and two dozen other people were crammed had
been organized to provide a modicum of privacy. Sheets were
hung to form curtains, cordoning off tiny sections of the bedroom into claustrophobically small spaces for each family.[10]

Zenia's family was luckier than some, in that one of the beds was inside their space.

Though their changed circumstances had shocked some of Vilna's Jews into psychological paralysis, the most optimistic had already begun to point out that the Jews had lived in ghettos before and had managed to survive. They would just wait for things to change, and then they would go about their lives again. They knew what it felt like to be hated, and it was something they had always been able to withstand.

Everyone was hoping the Americans would enter the war and it wouldn't be long before they could go home. There were so many Jews in America, and almost everyone had some connection there through family or friends. They were certain President Roosevelt was aware of the deteriorating and now deadly conditions facing the Jews of Europe. Surely Roosevelt would help them. But he needed to move quickly. They had never seen anyone as full of hate as Hitler. He had so much political and military power, and it seemed he had everybody wanting the Jews dead. Now here they were, still alive, but feeling more helpless than ever.

Monday came, and the Jews were told to report to the same place they had worked at before the ghetto, marching out in columns under German or Lithuanian guard. Rose went back to the uniform repair shop, and Zenia, Michael, and Bluma registered for work with the *Judenrat,* along with Lizzie, her husband, Wolf Skolnicki, and their three sons and their families, who were living elsewhere within the ghetto walls.[11] Zenia was told to report to the kitchen of a hostel for German soldiers displaced from their units, called the Lost Gathering Point.[12]

The Judenrat *building on Rudnicka Street*
COURTESY OF LEYZER RAN'S *JERUSALEM OF LITHUANIA*

The next morning she marched out through the ghetto gate to her new workplace across from the train station. Michael was assigned to work nearby, helping to lay bricks.[13] Bluma was not so lucky. At her age she was unable to get a work permit for anything at all.

The plan was for Bluma to stand in the food line each day while everyone else went to work. It was an unnerving task. In the courtyard of the *Judenrat,* the Jews had already heard the buzz in the air that only those who worked would be protected from being deported. And then there was this rather disturbing business of the other ghetto. The Nazis had established two ghettos in Vilna, a large ghetto, known as Ghetto 1, with a population of thirty thousand; and a smaller ghetto, known as Ghetto 2, with a population a little under ten thousand. They were deliberately separated from each other by a major thoroughfare, with no means of communication between them.

The Jews had been forced into whichever ghetto was closer to their home, but within a week a sorting process had begun, with orphaned children, the sick, and the elderly told to go to Ghetto 2 and healthy adults moved to Ghetto 1. Without a work permit Bluma feared she might be forced to leave her family behind and go to Ghetto 2. Separation from the family was the least of her fears, for doomsayers were already saying that the Germans intended to use Ghetto 2 as a halfway point for those they planned to exterminate next.

In fact, the German plan for Ghetto 2 was even more sinister and devious than Bluma or anyone else realized. Because the two ghettos could not communicate, no one could know whether those transferred actually arrived at the other ghetto. The Ger-

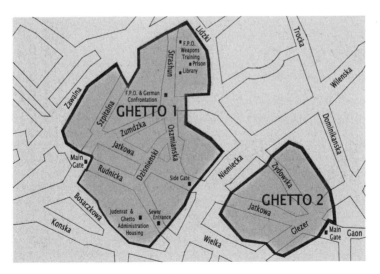

Map of Ghettos 1 and 2   BART FAMILY COLLECTION

mans lured Jews out of one ghetto by claiming they were taking them to the other. This was true some of the time, but it took a while to figure out that many who marched out of one ghetto never arrived at the other. To confuse matters further, the Germans claimed to be operating a third ghetto in Vilna, and that all the missing people were there. Ghetto 2 would be almost empty by mid-October, before the people of Ghetto 1 had any clear understanding of what the Nazis were doing.[14]

The dreaded order that all those without work permits were to go to Ghetto 2 came less than a week later, throwing Zenia's family into a panic. What should they do? If Bluma went, would they ever see her again? But what would happen to her if she stayed and was discovered? In the end the family decided Bluma would not go. To be on the safe side, she would hide in the apartment, and they would all hope for the best.

Bluma, it turned out, had made a good decision. Of the three thousand people who marched out of the gates of Ghetto 1 that day, only six hundred reached Ghetto 2.[15] In Ghetto 1, soldiers and police made only a cursory search of the buildings, and Bluma was safe, for the time being. Still, the unnerving games of the Nazis were taking a psychological toll on Bluma and her family, as well as on the rest of the ghetto. It was impossible to know on any given day whether it was best to do what the Germans said, gambling that today they were telling the truth, or to hide from them, on the assumption that today they were telling yet another lie.

It still seemed a better choice to hide, and it was obvious Bluma needed a real *maline.* Soon she had one. The owner of the apartment took Zenia and Bluma to the attic one afternoon the following week, to show them something. The attic was not quite tall enough to stand up in, and only a few stored items were visible in the dim light. He knelt down and pried open a false wall. The attic was very hot, made worse because the roof was made of metal sheeting.[16] Anyone who used this *maline* would pray that the Germans didn't come on a hot day.

As Zenia watched Bluma's gray head descend from the attic, she remembered how her grandmother had stood her ground with customers over the prices in her store, attacked rats in her storage shed with a straw broom, and scolded Michael when he had tarried too long after being told to set the table. And she remembered Bluma's full-skirted lap that she had loved to bury herself in when she was small, and the kisses, and the wonderful *cholent* Bluma cooked for the family's Shabbos dinner.[17] Bluma was a force. There was no one in Zenia's world she had gravitated more to, or spun in such happy circles around. The Germans wouldn't dare try to take her.

The attention of most Jews the first week in the ghetto was focused on such basic concerns as finding a place to stay, registering for work, getting food, and, for those who were particularly vulnerable, finding a *maline*. However, almost from the first minute in the ghetto, many Jews began working to set up the administrative and social services the ghetto would require. A new *Judenrat* was immediately assembled, headed by Anatol Fried, a local businessman, who quickly pulled in several surviving members of the former *Judenrat* to work with him. The choice of Fried was not a popular one.[18] Before the war Fried was one of those who seemed to have forgotten they were Jewish, or at least wished everyone else would. Jacob Gens was a more popular choice as chief of police. He had a strong military background and a great deal of administrative experience, and was respected in the Jewish community.[19]

Both of them and their appointees worked at a frenetic pace, beginning only hours after they reached the ghetto. Gens organized three police precincts and a gate guard with fifteen to twenty officers each, as well as a unit to guard the ghetto jail and one whose job was to force reluctant Jews to leave the relative safety of the ghetto and go to work. Fried set up departments to handle health, labor, housing, and food. Within days an orderly process was already in place to handle housing problems, issue work permits, and maintain public health. With the minuscule budget provided by the Germans, the new food department of the *Judenrat* purchased food, created ration cards, and set up soup kitchens for the most needy.

Leizer was a bit disappointed when he was assigned to duty guarding the gate. It seemed rather dull to simply stand in one place all day, but he wasn't about to complain. Young men without families were the first to be sent out on the most questionable and dangerous work details, and the least likely to ever come back. He had gone from being one of the most vulnerable people in the ghetto to one of the safest.

Zenia too was one of the more securely situated people in the ghetto, although life in her apartment was close to intolerable. The one hundred occupants had to share a small kitchen, and quarrels often erupted in the kitchen over who could use the stove first. It was only the simple fact that most people had nothing to cook on a given day that kept the situation under control. The single bathroom in the apartment was the worst point of stress. Not only were people constantly pounding on the door, but the pipes were not intended for

Portraits of Jewish policemen who served as guards at the entrances to the Vilna Ghetto 1, 1942. The portraits at the upper right are of Jacob Gens, Ghetto Chief of Police (left), and Police Commissar Salek Dessler. Leizer Bart, sergeant in charge of the ghetto gate, is in the second row beneath Gens, third from the right. COURTESY OF GHETTO FIGHTERS' HOUSE, ISRAEL

such heavy use, and though water remained consistently available, toilets all over the ghetto easily became clogged.[20] Likewise, electrical circuits meant for use by a few thousand people had broken down under the strain of lighting every last room in the ghetto, regularly plunging whole buildings into darkness.[21]

Still, Zenia lived in an apartment. For weeks after the ghetto opened, people still crowded together in open courtyards, lacking even a few square feet of space in any of the buildings. Women used suitcases for pillows, their children resting on their bellies. Men stood in clusters talking about winter closing in, and wondering how desperate things could get.

By the end of September, most people had found some place to stay. People got up to join their work parties and marched under guard through the city streets to their workplaces, while children went to school and day care.[22] Those without work permits spent the day trying to get food. The rations allowed by the German administration amounted to only about four hundred calories a day per person, and only those with work permits could have ration cards. The ration cards in Zenia's family had to stretch to cover Bluma as well, making it even more important that Bluma spend her time selling off any remaining valuables in order to buy more bread on the black market, and occasionally a few potatoes, for the family.

People quickly found ways to move in and out of the ghetto to get food, and within a few weeks the black market was thriving. Still, food supplies were woefully inadequate, and Bluma would despair that her daughter and grandchildren would come back exhausted, and all she could offer was bread and a potato, or more often than not, just bread.

Living with constant pressure simply to survive took its toll on everyone in the ghetto. Some people seemed more able than others to resist being overwhelmed by depression, and Zenia was one of these. Affectionate and cheerful by nature, she managed to keep her characteristic personality in the ghetto. She was fed a bowl of soup every day at her workplace, and when there was only a little food at home, she gave her share to her family, to make sure they had enough.[23]

Leizer was eating a little better than most, as the *Judenrat* and the police had special allotments, but it was still not enough to keep the weight on his already slim frame. He had made one or two friends among the police, although most of the force was Betar.[24] Betar members were a natural fit for service as ghetto police, since the group had been focused on training and learning the skills necessary for resisting the British in Palestine. Leizer and the other members of Ha-Shomer ha-Tzair, on the other hand, had plans to work the land and establish the agricultural communities that would be the foundation of a Jewish homeland. Though both groups dreamed of immigrating to Palestine, beyond that they agreed on very little and had not usually gotten along well together.

Leizer's general aloofness toward members of Betar had a few exceptions. One of the highest-ranking policemen, Joseph Glazman, was a Betar leader, and he stood out in contrast to some of the other police, who seemed to want the job for the power it would give them in such an otherwise powerless place. Glazman seemed to picture it more as Leizer did, as a peace force and not just an arm of the Nazis in the ghetto.

For the most part, Leizer simply reconnected with his old friends from Ha-Shomer ha-Tzair in the ghetto, rather than making too many new ones in the police residence. From the moment they regrouped in the ghetto, the members of the organization had agreed to do whatever they could to help each other. Housing, jobs, food—whatever one of them needed, the rest would do what they could to provide. Though a few in Ha-Shomer ha-Tzair could not disguise their opinion that working on the ghetto police force was too much like working for the Nazis themselves, most felt it couldn't hurt in the long run to have a friend working at the ghetto gate—especially someone like Leizer Bart, who by all accounts was dependable, considerate, and levelheaded.

Leizer, for his own part, hoped his impulsive decision to join the police wouldn't come to cost him his few friends in the ghetto. Still, overall, things were going about as well as they possibly could for him on the job. Only one thing troubled him: Jacob Gens. Gens had told the gate guard during their training that it was clear people would need to smuggle food in through the gate if they were to stay alive. As chief of police, he couldn't exactly contravene orders, but he had made it clear that he trusted the gate guard to become adept at looking the other way.

It wasn't, however, quite that simple. Gens also told them that if the Germans thought they weren't doing a thorough enough job, they would put nothing but Lithuanian and German soldiers at the gate. The inference was obvious: If that happened, it would mean more people caught, more beatings, more hunger. An effective Jewish gate police, Gens said, was the single best way to show the Germans that the Jewish administration could manage the ghetto without German interference.

Leizer could hardly argue with that, but what it meant had only slowly dawned on him. Most of the time they might be able to get away with pulling aside a few Jews and giving them a cursory patdown. However, when high-ranking Germans like Murer or Hingst were at the gate, the searches would have to be convincing. From early on, Leizer had seen

A meeting of the gate guards, including Meir Levas, head of the
gatekeepers (standing next to the wall, top left corner), and Leizer Bart
(also next to the wall on the left, behind a man with a mustache)
COURTESY OF LEYZER RAN'S *JERUSALEM OF LITHUANIA*

people staggering through the gate after an encounter with a
fellow Jew needing to make a good impression on the enemy
at the gate.[25]

Police stationed elsewhere in the ghetto were getting a horrible reputation as well. Some of them were labeled Snatchers,
the invective coming from their willingness to grab any Jews
they saw if work details were short. They also sniffed around
looking for *malines* they could uncover, all in the hope of improving their own position and thus their chances of surviving. Another group was known as the *shlegers,* or strongmen,
whose job it was to beat up Jews who were uncooperative with

the police or who broke ghetto rules.[26] Jews roughing up Jews? The job on the police force was not turning out as Leizer had envisioned.

When the ghetto was first established, employers had been concerned that their Jewish workers, prisoners working long hours for almost no pay, would not be permitted to leave the ghetto to come to work. These employers were permitted to give their workers a piece of paper that would function as an identification document that would get them through the gate. These employer-issued documents all looked different and their legitimacy was often difficult to ascertain. As a result, by mid-October 1941, when the chaos of opening the ghetto had died down, the German administration centralized the power to grant work passes in one office, the *Arbeitsamt.* Employers had to apply to the *Arbeitsamt* for workers, and the *Arbeitsamt* would decide how many workers were needed. It would then issue to the chosen workers a uniform pass, printed on yellow paper.

This became known to the Jews as a yellow *Schein.* Spouses and two children under the age of sixteen were covered by a *Schein,* and these dependents were given blue cards to carry with them to show they were protected. Since from the beginning the Nazis had made clear their intention to use Jews as a workforce and preserve only that portion of the Jewish population that was useful for this purpose, the Jews did not need to be told that from that point forward only those in possession of a *Schein* or a blue card were secure in the ghetto.

Only three thousand yellow *Scheins* were issued, which meant that at the most twelve thousand of the approximately

A yellow Schein   COURTESY OF LEYZER RAN'S *JERUSALEM OF LITHUANIA*

twenty-seven thousand Jews in the ghetto were protected by them. Clearly, the Germans intended by this move to leave well over half of the ghetto population vulnerable to immediate extermination. The Germans had actually calculated that the number of protected Jews was substantially lower, because many *Schein* holders had no families.

Rose, Zenia, and Michael, in fact, were all able to get *Scheins* because they were employed on work details considered important to the war effort, and their employers were influential Nazis. A number of people in their apartment were not so lucky. Older people like Bluma were the most vulnerable of all, because they had no hope of being assigned to a work detail.[27] It was apparent that the Germans were getting better organized, and the ghetto waited for the *Aktion* they were sure would come to rid the ghetto of all those without legitimate papers.[28]

The Gestapo inspecting returning workers at the main ghetto gate at Rudnicka Street COURTESY OF LEYZER RAN'S *JERUSALEM OF LITHUANIA*

It did not take more than a day after the issuance of the last yellow *Scheins* for the Germans to order all those carrying them to come to the ghetto gate with their covered family members. They were marched with their families to their workplaces and stayed there the whole day. The inference of what became known as the First Yellow Schein Aktion was clear: Anyone found in the ghetto that day was Nazi prey.

All day, Zenia could think of nothing else except Bluma, whom they had had to leave behind. Her anxiety increased when she was delayed at her work and barely made it back before the curfew for outside workers. When she arrived at the apartment she saw that the living room had been ransacked. Frantic, she pulled back the now graying sheet of their cubicle. There, sitting on the bed, was her mother, hugging Bluma.

Michael sat white-faced next to his mother. Zenia kneeled between them silently and put her arms around them all.

Most days when Leizer guarded the gate, things went smoothly. The Lithuanian guards in particular wanted bribes more than they wanted to find Jews with contraband, and soon Leizer could size up when he came on duty whether the day would be an easy one. When only Lithuanians were on duty, they would cast glances at the Jewish police from time to time, and at the Jews coming home from work. Once in a while, a few would be pulled out of the line and searched. If

Main gate at Rudnicka Street, where Leizer Bart worked
COURTESY OF DEATHCAMPS.ORG

they were carrying bread, or sugar, or any other contraband, German soldiers would beat them, but usually they would then be sent through the gate to nurse their wounds at home.[29]

It was different when high-ranking German officers, particularly Franz Murer, were there. Everyone, Lithuanian and German guards, and the Jewish police as well, needed to look tough then. Even a few Jews embraced the sadism of their German captors. Meir Levas, appointed head of the Jewish gate guard in February 1942, was Murer's brutal equal.[30] Levas would watch the performance of each of his officers and coldly dress anyone down who had not been violent enough to impress the Germans. Sometimes he would savage a randomly selected Jew passing through the gate. His hapless victim sometimes simply hadn't heard of a change in the rules and had made the mistake of bringing something through the gate that had been permitted the day before. Levas had a reputation throughout the ghetto for beating Jews so savagely he had once fainted from the effort.[31] Even some of the more brutal ghetto police grew silent and stone-faced when the subject of Levas's treatment of Jews came up.

Leizer's involvement with Ha-Shomer ha-Tzair was the only positive thing in his life. Ha-Shomer ha-Tzair had to that point been largely a mutual aid organization in the ghetto, a source of the tenuous sense of security that being among friends in a dire situation can provide. A single leader of Ha-Shomer ha-Tzair had clearly emerged since the German invasion, but he was not even in the ghetto at that point. Abba Kovner had been hidden away by the Mother Superior of a convent a few miles outside Vilna.[32] Leizer had heard that a Ha-Shomer ha-Tzair meeting would take place at the convent in a few days, and though he would not be able to make the trip without missing his next shift, it would buoy his spirits if Kovner had something positive to say about the importance of having some of their people on the police force.

It would be no problem at all to hold such a meeting, despite the Jews' incarceration in the ghetto. By that time, many ways to get in and out of the ghetto were already in place. Some people went out on phony work details, escorted by cooperative ghetto police. Others went individually over rooftops and fences, through unboarded windows, or through holes in walls created either by bombs at the time of the occupation or later by determined ghetto smugglers. Once outside, some would take off their jackets with the Stars of David and stroll through the streets, faking nonchalance, while others with less bravado would scurry from alleyway to alleyway to get to where they were going. Such exploits by Jews who were often barely in their teens soon became honored in song and verse, a vicarious pleasure for those who had neither the means nor the inclination to try to outwit their persecutors.

Leizer saw someone approaching the gate give him a signal that meant he was trying to smuggle something through. Leizer allowed him to walk almost abreast of him before pulling the man next to him out of the line. The man with the contraband passed safely through the gate.

Leizer made a good show of patting down the man he had grabbed. When he felt something in the man's jacket, Leizer kept his hands moving and his face expressionless.

"Go on," he said, sending the puzzled man off through the gate, still possessing whatever it was that might easily have cost him his life.[33]

Five

A DIFFERENT RHYTHM

But brother, a different rhythm will soon reach your ear. . . .
One's step has a sound, an entirely different song
When you walk, knowing why.

—FROM "BY ONES, TWOS, THREES,"
SUNG IN THE GHETTO THEATER IN SUMMER 1943
BY ACTOR JACOB BEREGALSKI

Sundays most of the Jews did not work because their Christian employers outside the ghetto closed their shops. As usual, Zenia had plans to go out to meet her cousin Fania Bulkin. The streets of the ghetto were always crowded, especially on Sundays, because people like Zenia and Fania all wanted to use the day off to meet with friends or just to get out of their cramped living quarters for a while. Zenia couldn't wait to leave the suffocating and stale air of the apartment. The smells and the arguments were a constant assault on her nerves. On Sundays, some in the apartment would try to get extra sleep to recuperate from their harsh six-day workweeks, but even asleep, so many people in one place made everyone claustrophobic and on edge.

It had been almost a week since she had seen Fania because they worked in different places and lived on opposite ends of the ghetto.[1] Though the ghetto was only a few square blocks, curfews and sheer exhaustion meant that most people, despite the crowding and the noise and the smells, went straight home at the end of the day. Getting outside on Sunday, however, could hardly be called recreational or restorative. The incessant press of the crowd, bumping and jostling from all sides, was as tiring in its own way as the long, orderly marches to work the rest of the week.

Within an hour, Fania had had enough. When she suggested going back to her apartment to meet some of her friends, Zenia agreed, even though she didn't expect to enjoy the visit that much. Fania's friends were Ha-Shomer ha-Tzair members, and people in Zenia's family joined the conservative group Betar if they joined any Zionist youth movement at all. Zenia didn't care for politics much either way. She wasn't at all interested in having to endure a boring discussion with a polite, frozen smile on her face when she would so much rather be outside enjoying the daylight and the blue sky.

Fania's apartment seemed less crowded than Zenia's, and half the living room was still being used for its intended purpose. A dozen young men and women sat on the chairs and on the floor, in the middle of a heated discussion that went silent when Zenia and Fania entered. One young man stood up to greet them. Fania introduced Zenia, going around the room saying each person's name so rapidly there was no way Zenia could remember any of them.

"And this," she said, motioning to the young man who was still standing, "is Leizer Bart."[2]

He had very blue eyes, and he didn't look anything like most of the boys Zenia knew. Blonder. Handsome too, she thought.

And he wasn't from Vilna—she knew that right away by his Polish accent. Awfully thin, but who in the ghetto wasn't?

Zenia had been brought up so strictly that she had never even kissed a boy, but that didn't mean she didn't love to flirt.[3] All of a sudden she was very glad she had let Fania drag her upstairs. She cocked her head and smiled at Leizer before it occurred to her that she recognized him from somewhere. And then she remembered where. "I've seen you before," she said. "At the gate."

Leizer couldn't just shrug his shoulders and pretend it was nothing. There was no denying the stigma that had become attached to his job. Zenia's voice was cold and flat as she acknowledged the introduction. She ignored him for the rest of the time they were in the apartment, and left without saying good-bye.

"Leizer was interested in you," Fania said when they were once again on the street. "I know him. Believe me, he's one of the good ones."[4]

Left: *Fania Bulkin*   Center: *Leizer Bart*   Right: *Zenia Lewinson*

To Zenia this was a contradiction in terms. A decent gate guard? But Fania insisted. Did Zenia think that Ha-Shomer ha-Tzair would let him darken their door if they thought he was just like the others? It was rare for Fania to be so annoyed with her, and Zenia wished that she hadn't been so rude. A nice-looking man, and now, look at what she had done.

Leizer had seen Zenia come through the gate several times since the day in the Ha-Shomer ha-Tzair apartment a week or so before, but he had not been able to talk to her again. He didn't acknowledge her at the gate, for fear of calling the attention of the other police to her, but instead each day he had passed by her entryway on Rudnicka Street as slowly as he could, hoping for a chance encounter. Finally, in despair, he turned to Fania. On the night she had arranged for them to meet, Leizer showed up at the appointed hour in the courtyard of Zenia's building. He took her by the elbow for a second to direct her through the courtyard and out the passageway. Too shy to hang on to it, he put his hands in his pockets as they started down Rudnicka Street.

Leizer was too nervous to say much of anything. Zenia was so full of life she could make a stone happy. She was feminine to the core, and even in the gloom of the dirty ghetto streets she smiled and pranced as if she were promenading down a tree-lined boulevard on a summer afternoon. She was the most beautiful and vivacious girl he had ever laid eyes on, and he didn't know what to do.

Grandmother Bluma's experience hiding in the *maline* had shaken her badly, but it had been much worse for others in the ghetto. Many people in their building had been taken to

Lukiszki Prison when their hiding places were discovered. One *maline* hiding one hundred people was cleared out elsewhere in the ghetto. In all, close to four thousand Jews were taken first to Lukiszki Prison, then later to the Ponary forest.[5] None had returned. There was no question that Bluma was in grave danger. The next time the Germans would look harder for *malines,* and the next time harder yet. However, unknown to Bluma and her family, she was about to get a reprieve.

Leizer and Zenia had begun to see each other regularly, and Leizer was well aware of how worried Zenia was about Bluma. He said nothing to Zenia as he formulated a plan. The next time he was in the *Judenrat* headquarters, he went to one of his contacts and told him he needed a *Schein.* Though the number of Jews protected by work permits was supposed to be strictly limited, among the ghetto police and authorities, friends asked no questions.[6] Leizer left a few minutes later with the precious yellow document in his pocket. Now, Zenia's beloved grandmother would not only be protected from Nazi purges, but she would also be eligible for a ration card, and the entire family would eat a little better.

When the Jews passed safely through the gate after a day of work, they knew they had survived another day, and their relief was so palpable Leizer could feel it. But that evening, as Leizer stood with the *Schein* in his pocket, Zenia was having no such feelings. The kitchen and laundry room at the Lost Gathering Point, where she worked, was always buzzing with news and gossip about the war. German soldiers returning from or going to the front in the fall of 1941 spent much of their time talking among themselves, and because Yiddish was similar enough to German, the Jews were able to eavesdrop on them. Groups of soldiers had begun talking about something so casually it seemed it must be a fact—that all of the Jews taken from the ghetto were being killed. This wasn't happening just in Vilna, but was part of a bigger plan that hadn't yet gotten fully under way, a plan to kill every Jew in Europe.

Zenia still could not believe what she and the others were hearing at work. The Germans obviously didn't care if they killed Jews, even hundreds of them, right and left, at random. She had accepted by now that that was probably Hillel's fate. Though people didn't discuss it, the assumption was that many of the old people and young orphaned children taken from the ghetto were dead. Everyone knew it was the policy of Jacob Gens—the true leader of the ghetto rather than Anatol Fried and the *Judenrat*—to offer up the most helpless and, in Nazi eyes, most useless ones when the Germans demanded that five hundred or a thousand Jews assemble at the gate. She couldn't imagine that the Germans would have the heart to be simply taking care of old people and orphans elsewhere. But could it possibly be true that everyone else who had disappeared was dead?

As many as seventy thousand Jews were living in Vilna when the Nazis arrived, especially if the new arrivals like Leizer were factored in. There were still a little over twenty thousand in Ghetto 1 where she lived, and who knew how many more in Ghetto 2. Where had the others gone? Was killing that many people even possible? And who would have such a crazy idea in the first place? Even Hitler couldn't think he could do such a thing. And how many thousands of people would he need to help carry it out? Blaming the Jews for everything that went wrong in the world was stupid, but murdering them all? What problem would that solve?

Thousands and sometimes even millions of people died in wars, but it was mostly on the battlefield or when their cities were destroyed. Had there ever been any human beings who deliberately set out, in cold blood, to kill thousands and thousands of people—their neighbors, no less—for no reason? It just wasn't possible. People might be misled, but they weren't evil. They wouldn't let it happen.

Unknown to Zenia, there were such human beings, spread all over conquered Europe. Using common sense, and drawing on past experience of how to survive persecution, Jews had assumed that as long as they remained a productive part of the German war effort, the Nazis would put aside their race hatred and let at least most of them live. Like Gens, most of them understood that the Nazis would demand victims, and there would be no way to avoid surrendering a certain number, but doing so seemed to be postponing the loss of the rest.[7] *Scheins, malines,* food smuggling, and work might be enough to save at least the strongest among them. The Germans surely could have no interest in killing such a huge slave labor force when their own people were off fighting a war.

Though the ethics of turning over some rather than others to the Nazis was one of the most hotly contested issues in the ghetto, and Jacob Gens the polarizing figure in this debate, the Jews knew they were in an individual as well as a collective fight for survival. The cornerstone of Gens's strategy was that only productivity would keep the Jews alive, and most Jews accepted this, battling to get *Scheins* to protect their own family members even if it meant the sacrifice of others who were helpless and alone.[8] What happened to them? Most people in the ghetto simply tried not to think about that too much.

The ghetto was a constant, roiling sea of rumors and conflicting interpretations of what appeared to be facts. People desperately wanted to believe that a few postcards, purportedly sent from distant labor camps, meant that stories of mass executions in the Ponary forest were the work of just the kind of defeatists the ghetto could do without. But the whispers from Ponary were getting louder and louder. The first stories had filtered back as early as July, and the first survivors to pull themselves from the pits had made their way back to the ghetto soon thereafter. Their accounts had been hushed up in order not to create panic in the ghetto, but the rumors could not be contained.

Though Zenia and Leizer tried not to talk about such things, the spectre of Ponary hung over them as it did everyone in the ghetto. For Leizer and his friends, however, Ponary had been seen for quite a while as only one part of a larger picture. Many Ha-Shomer ha-Tzair members had read a book that had been circulating in the ghetto about the Armenian genocide, and the most pessimistic were convinced that what they had read about was also already happening to them.

As far as Leizer knew, only Ha-Shomer ha-Tzair was actively engaged in discussing what to do about the threat posed to every last one of Vilna's Jews by the Nazis.[9] The typical ghetto resident still seemed to see the situation as an endurance contest with the Nazis, but Leizer had come to think that even the Jews' immense capacity for perseverance was not going to be enough to save them this time.

Several Ha-Shomer ha-Tzair members had reassured Leizer that it was good he was a gate guard. Whatever lay ahead, they were going to need people they could trust at the gate. Though such comments were far from numerous, Leizer had begun to sleep better and had found his shifts at the gate less of a torment. When the time came, he would be part of a greater effort, an agent for a movement that did not yet exist. *But it will,* he told himself. *It will.*

Gloomy as things seemed that particular evening, there was one bright note. Shortly after he was alone with Zenia in the courtyard of her building, Leizer pulled Bluma's yellow *Schein* out of his pocket and held it out in front of her.[10] It took a moment for her to understand; then, without speaking, she began to cry. He moved closer and put his arm around her for the first time. As he turned toward her in the dim light of the courtyard, their lips met. They pulled away, startled at what had just happened.

Something seemed to be settled between them. He took her hand, and this time he held on to it. Neither of them could speak for a while as they sat on the low stone wall of the courtyard. When the silence reached a point where it was more uncomfortable than whatever words they might have to say, someone spoke. The subject moved from one thing or another that was, however gruesome or depressing, somehow easier to talk about than what had just happened between them—something like ration cards, or news from the front, or Jacob Gens.

Leizer rarely shared any views about the person who was his ultimate boss, but a few minutes of conversation were enough to agree that Gens was at the very least an extremely confusing man with a frightening amount of power. There were times he had gotten the Nazis to take a few dozen people rather than the few hundred they had demanded. If the war ended soon, it was undoubtedly a way to save the greatest possible number of

Jews, but it was deeply troubling how he seemed capable of choosing one person to die instead of another.

What kind of a Jew does that to a Jew? Their question went into the night air unanswered.

It was time for Zenia to go inside. She put the yellow *Schein* in her pocket. It was not an easy thing for her family to give a ghetto policeman a chance, but perhaps this gift for Bluma would alleviate the tension Zenia had felt since she had begun her relationship with Leizer. Bluma safe, and her first kiss, all in one day. Even if she had to return to an apartment reeking of stale urine and sweat, where people were complaining about nearly everything, for her it was the first completely good day in the ghetto.

Leizer had gotten Bluma a *Schein* not a moment too soon. In less than a week Jews with the coveted yellow passes were told they would be moved with their registered family members to Ghetto 2 for three days. The significance of the longer removal was obvious. Few Jews had *malines* suitable for so long a stay. And since everyone who was legally in the ghetto was temporarily gone, Jews caught out in the open would be killed or marched away, no questions asked. Three days would give soldiers the chance to be very thorough in looking for the thousands who were likely to be hiding, returning again and again to search for any signs of life under floorboards, in the backs of closets, or behind hidden openings in walls.

When the residents of Ghetto 1 arrived in Ghetto 2, it was immediately clear that the Nazis had been using the second ghetto as a phony pretext for some time. Its original inhabitants were gone, and those who had been marched there

Inside Ghetto 2
COURTESY OF VILNA GAON
JEWISH STATE MUSEUM

later were gone as well, if they had actually ever arrived. Doors hung limp on their hinges, and broken glass littered the ground. Not a single Jew was in the streets or staring from the windows. Bluma's *maline* had undoubtedly saved her life, but perhaps as many as ten thousand others had not been so lucky.

The first order of business was to find a place to stay for the few days of the *Aktion*. Many places were uninhabitable because of the strong smell of decay. Contributing to the stench were the rotting corpses of Jews, some of whom were dead of asphyxiation in their *malines*. A few dozen surviving residents of Ghetto 2 gradually emerged from their hiding places when they heard people speaking Yiddish outside. Somehow they had managed to evade the final liquidation, but their bodies were debilitated by sickness and hunger, as well as from the forced immobility of life in their tiny *malines*. The *Aktion*, unknown to the Germans, had given these Jews a new chance for life. When the three days were over, they blended in with the returning residents of Ghetto 1 going back to a world of ration cards and chances to walk openly on the streets.[11] Even in the ghetto, there were from time to time such victories.

It took a confirmed story from Ponary to bring Abba Kovner out of hiding. In late December, a messenger came to tell him that a teenage girl was in the Vilna hospital, recovering from wounds suffered when she survived a firing squad at Ponary.[12] Jacob Gens had insisted the girl was hallucinating when she told him her story. Later, after being convinced what she was saying was true, he told her that if she revealed her story to anyone he would see that her father, at that point her only surviving family member, would be in the next group offered up to the Nazis.[13] Such a story, Gens knew, was likely to create panic and possibly serve as an excuse for Nazis to enter the ghetto on a murder spree. Despite the threat, the girl secretly spoke to a few people summoned to her bedside in the hospital, including Kovner, who had clandestinely entered into the ghetto on Christmas Eve 1941 to meet with her.

After hearing the story firsthand, Kovner called a meeting of Ha-Shomer ha-Tzair. In the candlelit cellar, he wasted no time getting to the point: They were fooling themselves if they continued to believe that any of those who had been marched from the ghetto were alive. The longer the people in the ghetto believed false stories, the longer they would do nothing. And as long as they did nothing, the Nazis would continue to operate as they pleased.

Kovner was now convinced that the Nazis intended to kill all the Jews in every corner of Europe. Lithuania was just the beginning. Someone stood up and said that if what he said was

A Lithuanian soldier stands guard as the Jews of Vilna are being murdered at Ponary.   USHMM, COURTESY OF YIVO INSTITUTE

true, they should escape by whatever means they could. A few voices murmured assent, but Kovner shook his head. There was no escape. They might escape from Vilna to some place that seemed temporarily safer, but Bialystok and Minsk and other cities would be part of the extermination plan as well, sooner or later. "Listen to me," Kovner said. "Flight is not an answer to our predicament. Revolt and armed self-defense is the only way for the Jews."[14]

The room exploded as people argued among themselves over the implications of Kovner's words. At the end, Kovner said that he knew it wasn't easy to take in what he was saying, and that everyone had to make up his own mind as to whether he spoke the truth. "But hear me well," he said. "No matter what course we take, we are doomed. The cowardly will die

Execution of Vilna Jews at Ponary   USHMM, COURTESY OF YIVO INSTITUTE

along with the courageous. The only thing left to decide is if you want to die the way the others have."

"If you knew for certain we were all going to die, it would be different," one voice called out, "but how do you know the war won't end by spring? How do you know we can't last the Germans out?"

"I don't know," Kovner said. "Only one person will know for sure. When they take the last Jew in Europe to Ponary—he will know for sure."[15]

Snow was falling, and drunken German soldiers were staggering through snowdrifts on Vilna's streets on New Year's Eve 1941. Shortly before the welcoming toasts to 1942 were offered up in the German officers' quarters, by ones and twos people stole across the rooftops and through the shadows of the ghetto streets toward a public soup kitchen at 2 Strashun Street. For several days, word had spread about a meeting to discuss resistance against the Germans, and by midnight 150 people, mostly in their late teens or early twenties, had gathered.

Leizer slipped in at the last minute and tried to remain unnoticed in the shadows, because he was sure the police would not be welcome.

Kovner suddenly walked into the room, and a hush fell. "Jewish youth," he began, "do not trust your deceivers. Of eighty thousand Jews in Vilna, only twenty thousand are left."

Over a low murmur in the audience, Kovner continued talking about the many times Jews had been taken away before their eyes. People nodded and murmured among themselves.

"Destroy your illusions!" Kovner said, looking up from his papers at the crowd. "Hitler aims to destroy all the Jews of Eu-

"LET'S NOT GO LIKE SHEEP TO THE SLAUGHTER!"

"Jewish youth, don't trust those who mislead you: out of the 80 thousand Jews of the Jerusalem of Lithuania there remain only 20 thousand.

. . .Rip off the illusion of those in despair: your children, wives and husbands are no more. Ponary is not a camp – those taken there were all shot. Hitler devised a method to exterminate all Jews of Europe. We are destined to be the first.

Let's not go like sheep to the slaughter – the only worthy response to the enemy is RESISTANCE!

Brethren! It's better to die as free fighters than live at the mercy of the murderer! Let's resist to our last breath."

Kovner's proclamation COURTESY OF LEYZER RAN'S *JERUSALEM OF LITHUANIA*

rope. It is the lot of the Jews of Lithuania to be the first in line. Let us not go like sheep to the slaughter. True, we are weak, and without a protector, but the only answer to the murderers is revolt!"

The room was stirring. Kovner's voice rose. "Brothers! Better to fall as free fighters than to live at the mercy of the murderers." As the crowd rose to its feet, Kovner cried out, "Let us revolt! We shall fight until our last breath!"[16]

Leizer looked at the people around him. Some were crying, some were cheering so loudly their faces were a ghastly purple in the dim light, and some were raising fists. He slipped back out and felt the welcome cold of snowflakes on his cheeks after the stuffy air inside. A feeling of exhilaration welled up in him, and he shut his eyes. The words of the *Shehekiyanu,* the Hebrew blessing for special, long-awaited occasions, came into his mind, and he repeated it softly. "Blessed art thou, O Lord God, King of the Universe, who has given us life, sustained us, and enabled us to reach this day." As he walked away, the voices in the room behind him faded. The only sounds were German soldiers singing from beyond the ghetto walls, and the crunch of his boots in the snow.

Six

WE DREAMERS MUST
TURN SOLDIERS

Our fingers stretched through bars
To capture the shining air of freedom.
We dreamers must now turn soldiers. . . .
—FROM ABRAHAM SUTSKEVER,
"THE LEAD PLATES OF ROMM'S PRINTING HOUSE"

Leizer stood at the gate, scanning the returning Jews. In the distance he saw a man suddenly begin to limp. As the man drew closer, Leizer looked toward the guardhouse on the other side of the gate. A few Lithuanians were visible inside, but none were out on the frozen streets. Leizer sauntered over to another Jewish gate guard, positioning himself to block the other officer's view of the limping man. Blowing into his gloves, he started an idle conversation with the other guard, until out of the corner of his eye he saw the man go through the gate. Leizer went back to stand at his post, another piece of contraband safely inside the ghetto.[1]

It was early February 1942, a little over a month since Kovner had read his proclamation in the soup kitchen. Within a few weeks, sympathetic members of Ha-Shomer ha-Tzair, Betar, and

Main gate at Rudnicka Street, winter 1942
COURTESY OF LEYZER RAN'S *JERUSALEM OF LITHUANIA*

the Young Communists had formed a united underground resistance movement, known in Yiddish as the Fareynegte Partizaner Organizatsye, or FPO. Its primary goal was to prepare for an armed defense of the ghetto if the Germans should move to liquidate it. The commander in chief, known by the code name Leon, was Isaac Wittenberg, a forty-year-old Communist and union leader. Abba Kovner, who took the code name Uri, was one of two deputy commanders under Leon.

Due to his cautious nature, Leizer wanted to keep the knowledge of his membership limited, so as not to jeopardize his job with the ghetto police.[2] Kovner had reassured him that the FPO would be organized in such a way that even its own members would have little idea who else was involved. The other commander under Leon was dubbed Abraham. Secrecy was so well

Ghetto library on Strashun Street
COURTESY OF LEYZER RAN'S *JERUSALEM OF LITHUANIA*

kept that it was not for some time that Leizer found out that Abraham was actually his own boss, the assistant chief of police and leader of Betar, Joseph Glazman.

Secrecy was also maintained about the headquarters of the FPO. The ghetto library at 6 Strashun Street had a large unfinished cellar with several rooms, and the FPO had broken through the floorboards, installed a trapdoor and ladder, and run electrical lines from the library to illuminate the damp, cavelike space that would serve as the FPO training center and weapons cache. By that point, the FPO had mapped routes through corridors, down alleys, and over roofs, so that their members could go anywhere at any time during the nightly curfew. Once inside the secret basement room, members learned to construct and use grenades made from old lightbulbs and practiced with unloaded guns. To rise up against the Nazis when the time came, they would need to be well disciplined and trained, with a large stock of conventional and improvised weapons and ammunition. To create this kind

*Entrance to the weapons
training center*
USHMM, COURTESY OF
WILLIAM BEGELL

of fighting force using
one small, secret room
and without firing a
single bullet took inge-
nuity and determina-
tion, and despite the
meager circumstances,
that little basement
room became a source
of immense pride to
the FPO.

Though having no
outlet for their wea-
pons training was frustrating, members of the resistance had
already been able to find other ways to attack the Germans. In
army vehicle workshops, saboteurs began to botch repairs so
that tanks and transports would break down on the way to the
front and have to be abandoned. Other, more skilled saboteurs
rigged fuses that would cause the vehicles' gas tanks to blow up
far from the shop, so sabotage would not be suspected.
Firearms were sent out rigged in such a way as to explode in
the hands of their operators.[3]

In addition to sabotage, workers began stealing things for
use by the FPO. Anything that could be stolen would be, either for direct use or to sell to get money for arms and ammunition. In one daring undertaking, an unused printing press

was dismantled and brought piece by piece into the ghetto, where it was reassembled to print FPO manifestos and other flyers, as well as false documents and ration cards.[4] In another, two FPO members pretending to be city sewer workers making a repair thrust pipes into a manhole. These pipes were filled with rifles, which were then retrieved inside the ghetto.[5]

Leizer's job was to do whatever was needed to get weapons and contraband through the gate. By then it was clear which of the Jewish police could not be trusted, so he stood in their line of vision or created distractions to pull their attention away from the people coming back home through the gate.[6] He faked searches so well that the German or Lithuanian guards would stay in their covered sentry posts and simply watch. Such a level of vigilance left Leizer exhausted after a long day. He would meet Zenia most evenings after his shift, too tired to say much more than hello and look for a place to sit quietly with her.

Zenia could be counted upon to supply the energy. Even in the worst of times, she managed to be upbeat, as if there were nothing in the world to be troubled about. Fortunately, because she always had at least one amusing story or thought to share, Leizer was usually able to say very little. He was by nature very quiet, and Zenia had already learned he had a hard time sharing his feelings. More than that, however, the most significant part of his life, his underground work at the gate, he could not share with her anyway. "You never get in trouble if you keep your mouth shut," he was known for saying.[7] He hid his secret identity so well that he was quickly promoted to the rank of sergeant and became a supervisor of the Jewish police at the gate. Even years later, some survivors would be amazed to learn this quiet and polite ghetto guard, one of the "good ones," had been part of the resistance all along.

Life in Zenia's apartment, and in the ghetto as a whole, lurched along through the winter and spring of 1942. The killing sprees seemed to have ended, and though the dark cloud of Ponary hung over every conversation, most in the ghetto felt secure as long as they were working, and many still continued to refuse to believe the stories about mass exterminations. Few had any inkling there was a growing underground resistance movement preparing for armed combat.[8]

Food, as always, was the main thing on people's minds. Bluma, who spent her days combing the ghetto for things to help the family, would come home with whatever food she could obtain. She knew every ghetto merchant, whether they sold their wares from their pockets or from a table on a street corner. Because three family members were working, and they had four *Scheins* at that time, they had a little more to eat. Also, at this point even the Germans had been forced to acknowledge that if their own rules were strictly followed, their workforce would starve. To address this problem, the Germans announced that Jews who had valuables outside the ghetto could apply to get these returned to them in the ghetto to use on the black market to supplement their income. In this way, Zenia's family, through Bluma's efforts, was able to manage a little better. This sudden magnanimity came with a price, for the Jews had to agree to let the Germans keep half of whatever valuables were retrieved.[9]

Some weeks, seemingly at whim, the German authorities relaxed their rules and allowed returning workers to bring in a certain amount of bread or potatoes; then, just as quickly, permission would be withdrawn. A number of ghetto residents, particularly children, had long since become adept at avoiding the gate altogether, sneaking in and out over rooftops or through loose boards in the ghetto walls to bring in food to sell.

The *Judenrat* was the biggest customer for ghetto smuggling when German crackdowns meant it could no longer bring cartloads of food directly through the gate. It used its supplies to make thousands of lunches and dinners that were free for the most destitute Jews and available for pennies to others who were unable to support themselves even at the meager level of the other ghetto residents. It sold the excess contraband at a profit to Vilna residents and used the proceeds for ghetto services such as garbage removal and operation of the hospital and bathhouses, as well as for the incessant bribes to the Germans and Lithuanians that were necessary to keep the ghetto alive. To supplement its budget, the *Judenrat* levied a 20 percent income tax for those working outside the ghetto, as well as charging fees for such things as medical and burial services.[10] It became a principle among the Jews that if they had had a close escape from death on a particular day, they would donate that day's wages to the *Judenrat*.

Despite these reductions in their income, the Jews of the ghetto saw clearly what they were getting for their money and did not spend too much time complaining. With an initial bread ration of 1.3 pounds a week per person, supplemented by small amounts of flour, sugar, and meat,[11] a person who had no other source of food would consume somewhere between two and four hundred calories a day and be dead of starvation in a few months. Even when the ration was later doubled, it was still far from sufficient to sustain life. Posters appeared on the ghetto walls, stating a bold mission: "No Hungry People in the Ghetto."[12] Indeed, unlike some other ghettos in Europe, in the two years of the ghetto's existence not one of Vilna's Jews died as a direct result of starvation.[13]

Equally remarkable, diseases such as typhus, which raged outside the ghetto, were stopped in the ghetto after the first few cases through prompt quarantine and medical attention from Jewish doctors. Quarantines had to be kept secret, for the Nazis simply murdered possibly contagious Jews and non-Jews alike to keep diseases from spreading. Suspecting an outbreak of typhus in Kovno, a Nazi arsonist had already burned a hospital to the ground with its patients, visitors, and staff inside. Ghetto quarantines involved keeping two sets of books: one for ghetto officials and the Germans, and a more accurate one for hospital staff. Similar tactics were used by the Jews to hide pregnancies and births in the ghetto, for pregnant women and newborns would be prime targets for extermination.[14]

The hospital and outpatient clinics operated by the Jews were only part of the herculean effort to keep the ghetto's weak and hungry inmates free of diseases that could easily have killed or further debilitated them. The Sanitary-Epidemiological Committee in the ghetto, which functioned under the auspices of the *Judenrat,* ensured that every crowded apartment was kept scrupulously clean, and that everyone in the ghetto made use of the public bathhouses on a regular basis. To enforce this, they would not allow anyone to receive a ration card who could not produce proof of having recently bathed.[15] They oversaw garbage removal and laundry services and ensured that residents could get boiled water for drinking and washing up. Children in school were regularly treated for lice, bringing the percentage of children with lice down from 80 percent to a stabilized 1.5 percent for the duration of the ghetto.[16] Largely because of such efforts, no epidemic ever swept through the Vilna ghetto, nor did any resident die as a result of exposure to the extreme cold of a Baltic winter. In fact, statistics culled later showed that, despite the fact that all but a few thousand of Vilna's Jews died violently at the hands of the Nazis, only 3 percent of the Jews died of natural causes in the ghetto, up only 2 percent from the prewar annual rate.[17]

If anyone had asked Zenia after six months in the ghetto to characterize life there, she would have said it boiled down to an oppressive and dreary scramble not to starve or be shot. As the winter of 1942 dragged on, however, residents of the ghetto began to look beyond the constant hunger and menace in their lives, fighting back against the mind-numbing weariness and gloom by forming associations to promote activities they had enjoyed before the war. When the weather warmed, the residents set up a basketball court to help occupy the ghetto's large population of children and teenagers.[18] Competitions with prizes were the talk of the ghetto for days on end, but the prizes were not the usual ribbons or medals. Instead, the winners each proudly brought home more practical rewards, such as a half kilo of butter or sugar.[19]

As time passed, theater productions, cabarets, musical revues, recitals, and other cultural events gave people something to do every week. As far back as January 1942 the first public concert had been held, a mix of poetry, song, and piano music. Such concerts were not without their detractors. As people began approaching the school building where the concert was to be held, a small group of angry ghetto residents were chanting, "No performance in a graveyard!"[20]

Though some remained critical, even some of those who had called for a boycott changed their minds when they saw the faces of the Jews streaming out of the hall. It took no more than the din of an orchestra tuning up, the lone note of the oboe piercing the clamor, and the applause as the conductor, Volf Durmashkin, came on stage to have the audience in tears before the music even came to life. It was a chance to feel normal again,[21] to forget their shabby clothes and the aches and pains of hard work and hard floors to sleep on, to think about something other than cold, and hunger, and fear.

Other concerts followed. Soon several ghetto theater companies, performing serious drama as well as lighthearted comedies and satirical revues, struggled to put on enough performances to meet the huge demand. Professors whose university careers in science, history, and literature had been cut short by anti-Semitism even before the ghetto was established gave lectures and courses. Two choruses were formed, one singing in Yiddish and one in Hebrew.[22]

Thirty-three professional musicians, under the direction of Durmashkin, founded a symphony orchestra and began rehearsing in February 1942. In March, as the orchestra tuned up on stage for their inaugural performance, several German and Lithuanian officers walked in and took seats up front. One of them, obviously drunk, stumbled over the legs of his chair and

Hebrew choir with the conductor, Volf Durmashkin, December 2, 1942
COURTESY OF LEYZER RAN'S *JERUSALEM OF LITHUANIA*

had to be grabbed by the arm to keep from falling. To the Jews such behavior was disgusting and disheartening. They were doing all they could to create small and temporary refuges against their imprisoners and executioners, and yet at the news of some Jewish entertainment, Nazi officials saw nothing wrong with barging their way into the ghetto and insisting on the best seats in the house.

It was particularly galling because the same musicians and performers who were loudly and often drunkenly applauded one night were simply anonymous Jews the next day, to be shot on sight or taken to Ponary if they were too slow laying bricks or shoveling snow. But such thoughts were temporarily put aside when Durmashkin took the stage for the first performance of the symphony orchestra and signaled the first lush notes of Ippolitov-Ivanov's "Caucasian Sketches." As if tied to earth only by an invisible weaving of violins and clarinets, cellos and flutes, the spirits of the transfixed audience seemed to rise

Anton Schmidt   COURTESY OF LEYZER
RAN'S *JERUSALEM OF LITHUANIA*

somehow over the ghetto, as
close as they could be to free.

The reality of life in the ghetto
did not take long to come
crashing back in, when word
came that spring that Anton
Schmidt, the Nazi officer who
was director of the German
hostel where Zenia worked, had been shot by the Nazis. Zenia
had known him only as one of the few "decent Germans,"
who shielded his workers from the Gestapo and made sure
they were treated well and fed adequately while at work.[23]
Zenia's work in the kitchen sometimes kept her there after the
rest of the hostel staff had marched back to the ghetto, but to
ensure her safety—because Jews could be shot if they were
seen walking alone outside the ghetto—the cook had been directed to walk her back personally if he kept her late.[24] Leizer
had been on duty on several occasions when this had happened, and he would watch from a distance as Zenia appeared,
walking in the gutter, her jacket emblazoned with a yellow
star, while the cook towered above her as he sauntered down
the sidewalk.

Sergeant Schmidt had been a familiar figure to Leizer and
others in the FPO. Schmidt despised Hitler and called himself an officer in the "accursed German Army."[25] On several
occasions while he was stationed in Vilna, he helped a num-

*After work, Zenia would have walked in the gutter down Szpitalna Street
(left), then turned onto Rudnicka Street to the main gate of the ghetto
(right).* COURTESY OF VILNA GAON JEWISH STATE MUSEUM

ber of Jews escape by the extraordinary tactic of having them
transported over the Byelorussian border in German military
vehicles.[26] When an FPO delegation wanted to go to Warsaw
to check on the situation there and share information about
the fate of Vilna's Jews, Schmidt helped them get safely across
the front.[27] During the Yellow Pass *Aktionen* he hid many
Jewish workers in his headquarters.[28] When his activities
were uncovered, the Nazis made an obvious and public example of him, sending his wife the bloody shirt, with twenty-
seven bullet holes, in which he had been executed.

Despite the severity of Baltic winters, many Jews dreaded
the end of the winter of 1942. Warm weather, they feared,
would unleash a new program of *Aktionen*. Instead, bread ra-

tions went up to 2.6 pounds a week, and new work permits served only as a means to take a census rather than to set up a new slaughter, lending credence to Jacob Gens's motto of "Work to Survive." Demand for labor also went up, giving the Jews the idea that perhaps the Germans intended to keep them alive indefinitely.[29]

The Jews had no way of knowing that this comparatively bloodless period, which lasted through the end of 1942, was simply a hiatus caused by dissent between the German army officers responsible for winning the war and the SS officers responsible for killing the Jews. The same blitzkrieg tactics that had enabled Hitler to occupy much of Europe without too great an expenditure of resources had failed on the Russian front, and what was to be a two-week invasion passed its first anniversary in June 1942. Keeping the Jews alive and fit to work at jobs serving the war effort was a critical need of Hitler's Third Reich, but the SS leaders had their orders too.[30]

By early 1942, unknown to the Jews of Vilna, the Final Solution had taken a diabolical turn at Auschwitz and elsewhere in neighboring Poland, with the opening of the first death camps. There would be no simultaneous extermination effort in Vilna, however, because the conflict within the Reich was resolved that spring by a decision to keep Vilna's Jews alive, for the time being at least, as long as their labor was essential to winning the war.

Work remained linked to hope, although the Jews were working too hard, with too little nourishment, for such a situation to continue indefinitely. Eventually, when their strength failed, death from illness or a bullet at Ponary awaited them all. In July, with the Germans still bogged down on the Russian front, Jacob Gens consolidated his power by dissolving the *Judenrat* and having himself appointed the sole "Ghetto Representative" by the Nazi commissar, Hans Hingst. The *Judenrat,* Gens claimed, had not been efficient enough in meeting German demands for labor, and this, he argued, put the ghetto in constant jeopardy. The sorting out of the productive from the nonproductive Jews was at an end, and the ghetto, Gens argued, had become in essence a factory town—a captive one, to be sure, but one where high output justified the continued German investment in their lives. It required a decisive leader, Gens claimed, not the endless discussions and votes of a committee such as the *Judenrat.*

Vilna's railway station, where Zenia worked for Schmidt in the German soldiers' hostel COURTESY OF GHETTO FIGHTERS' HOUSE, ISRAEL

Gens took credit for the reprieve in the killings, but the Jews did not share his confidence that he could keep the Germans at bay. Every tic in the behavior by the Germans, every development—whether major, as in the case of the dissolution of the *Judenrat,* or minor, such as a visit to the ghetto by a high-ranking Nazi official—was dissected for what it might mean for the future of the Jews. Did the building of a more permanent wall mean the Germans intended to keep them alive? Did a visit of Nazi commissar Hans Hingst to Gens suggest a new *Aktion*? Though Jews were no longer being taken by the thousands to Ponary, violence and death were still never far from the minds of the living.

One name in particular conjured up the most frightful images of humiliation and brutality among the Jews: Franz Murer, the aide-de-camp in charge of "Jewish Affairs" for Hans Hingst. When Murer appeared at the ghetto gate or toured ghetto workshops, it seemed to be linked to a personal blood-lust that required frequent satiation. He would randomly order a group of Jews to strip, men and women together, and if he found someone holding even the smallest amount of money or food, he would order the person beaten with a nightstick or leather strap. Sometimes he entertained himself by taking over the beating himself. Women who tried to cover their nakedness were forced to stand shamefaced before him, while he scrutinized their bodies. Sometimes, pronouncing them "too fat," he would immediately slap new restrictions on food brought into the ghetto.[31]

The Jews had come to expect such behavior of the Germans, but what caused the greatest demoralization and rage

Jacob Gens
COURTESY OF LEYZER RAN'S
JERUSALEM OF LITHUANIA

was the complicity of some of the top-ranking ghetto police. Gens himself was not above whipping a Jew he thought had done something to antagonize the Germans, and Meir Levas was known by all as a true sadist. Salek Dessler, appointed as Gens's replacement as chief of police when Gens became the undisputed single head of the ghetto, had an equally sordid reputation. The ghetto population included Jews with criminal backgrounds and underworld ties, whom Dessler enlisted to serve him directly as spies and enforcers.[32] Over time even Gens became afraid of Dessler, who was seen by all in the ghetto as a man who would do anything to ingratiate himself to the Nazis and thus increase the chances of his own survival. On one occasion when the Germans demanded a certain number of workers, Dessler used his own police force to round people up, and then sent the unsuspecting officers with the group to fill the quota when their efforts fell short.

In early fall of 1942, Joseph Glazman was no longer one of Leizer's superiors on the police force. After Gens appointed Salek Dessler to replace him as chief of police, Glazman resigned from the police rather than be forced to report to Dessler. He had then been appointed head of the ghetto housing department. Glazman, whom Leizer had by now learned

was indeed Abraham, the other deputy commander of the FPO, had by that point emerged as something of a ghetto hero. He was one of the few who had stood up to Gens, and who had kept his integrity, even while surrounded by Jews like Levas and Dessler, and by Germans like Murer and Hingst.

Glazman, the highest-placed member of the underground in the ghetto administration, was in a good position to report what he could glean about the intentions of the Nazi regime. The ghetto seemed to be safe for the time being because the Germans were at that point more focused on the growing partisan movement outside. In some of the work camps in the surrounding countryside, Jews were escaping to link up with them. Young people trapped in the remaining village ghettos were also fleeing to partisan camps near the front. Even in Vilna, a buzz was growing, particularly among young people, that escaping the ghetto to fight the Nazis was a better idea than trying to defend it. The word was that, once the winter had passed, the Soviets were likely to have a significant partisan network in the Vilna area. Then, many thought, an exodus from the ghetto and surrounding work camps would begin in earnest.

Ilya Scheinbaum, leader of the Yechiel Struggle Group COURTESY OF LEYZER RAN'S *JERUSALEM OF LITHUANIA*

This idea excited many of the young, but it was a source of dread to the leadership of the FPO, in particular Abba Kovner, who had been the instigator and architect of the plan to defend the ghetto. The FPO had, by fall of 1942, close to two hundred members, all of whom were engaged in weapons and tactical training for armed revolt. Hundreds of potential members among the ghetto youth were not part of the FPO because of its need to be highly selective so as to avoid infiltration, and because many of the young people were perceived as too hotheaded or individualistic to accept its strict paramilitary structure.

Other groups existed outside the FPO, and these groups, as well as many unaffiliated individuals, were also smuggling in arms. The FPO command worried that renegade young people might trigger a liquidation of the ghetto by acting on individual—and inevitably suicidal—urges to open fire on German soldiers. But competing organizations were an even greater threat to the FPO's plans than such individuals. One such group, Yechiel, called after the Hebrew name of its founder, Ilya Scheinbaum, had been in existence since shortly after the time the FPO was formed. Largely because of personality conflicts with Kovner and the others, Scheinbaum had not been asked to join the FPO command. Since then Yechiel had functioned on its own, attracting dozens of unaffiliated youth by its looser organizational structure and its emphasis on escaping to join the partisans at the first opportunity.[33]

Yechiel was a small group not posing much of a threat to the FPO until the spring of 1942. At that point, several FPO members who had lost their enthusiasm for the idea of armed revolt within the ghetto quit to form a new faction known as the Struggle Group. They soon merged with Yechiel to become the Yechiel Struggle Group. Among the members of the newly merged group were Shlomo Brand, one of Leizer's friends from his hometown, and several ghetto policemen, including Borka Friedman and Nathan Ring.[34]

Leizer shared many views with the Yechiel Struggle Group and was willing to help them, but he did not formally join, in part because of his personal loyalty to Abba Kovner. It was true that Kovner was a dreamer, Leizer knew. His greatest appeal was that his plan did not abandon thousands of Jews to the mercy of the Germans, but offered a chance to fight back. In the end, all Kovner really had to offer, however, was a dignified, heroic death in an uprising that could not help but be wiped out by the might of the Nazi regime. And then there was the risk such a revolt would entail. Even though the idea was not to rise up until the liquidation began and the deaths of the remaining ghetto residents were imminent, it was possible that some who might have otherwise avoided what looked like certain death would die as a result of the Nazis' fury over the revolt—including a certain girl and her family, who were never far from Leizer's mind.

Leizer began attending some of the Yechiel Struggle Group

meetings with Shlomo Brand. The underground organization a person favored often depended upon his or her personal circumstances. Those who had few ties to Vilna and simply wanted to damage the Germans were eager to escape. Those with family ties in the ghetto wanted to defend what they most cared about. As a result, this latter group found it difficult to consider escape to the forests even if the alternative meant certain death.

Leizer found himself juggling two destinies. He was young, he was willing to fight, and, more than that, he wanted to survive the hell he was in and go to help build a Jewish homeland in Palestine. He didn't want to abandon the ghetto, but he didn't want to die accomplishing nothing in the end. And besides, his family might still be alive, and he wanted to live to see them. But if he left Zenia and her family to die, what would that say about him as a man? Leizer went back and forth between the FPO and the Yechiel Struggle Group, maintaining good relations with both but formally joining neither for the time being.

As fall progressed, and the Jews took out coats in preparation for a winter few believed they could survive, tensions between the Yechiel Struggle Group and the FPO continued. Arsenals were still small, and the chance for survival in the woods even smaller, so outright clashes were kept at bay. Membership continued to grow in both groups as more and more people came to understand that despite the lull in the killings in Vilna, the Germans had no intention of allowing any Jews to survive the war.[35]

Stories about the death camps at Auschwitz, Majdanek, and

Treblinka had been trickling back steadily since late summer 1942, and the death rate from starvation and disease in the Warsaw ghetto was a horrifying reminder of what might await them even if the Germans never sent another Jew to Ponary. Those who felt they needed to do something—anything—about the situation were drawn toward young, charismatic leaders such as Scheinbaum and Kovner, and other figures of shining integrity such as Joseph Glazman and Isaac Wittenberg, the leader of the Young Communists within the ghetto.

Jacob Gens viewed Kovner and Scheinbaum with begrudging respect because of their followings, but it was Wittenberg and Glazman he kept the closest eye on. Glazman was the most difficult for Gens to bear. When Glazman defied and embarrassed Gens by stepping down as assistant police chief, people in the ghetto held up the two men for comparison, and Gens had come out the clear, abysmal loser. "Do something about Glazman," Gens's supporters often told him, but for the time being Glazman was keeping a low profile, running the housing department, and giving Gens no pretext for removing this thorn in his side.

Gens was, most agreed, not a bad person, unlike Levas and Dessler.[36] Many ghetto residents were sympathetic toward a decent man who had gotten himself in a terrible mess. Gens had been naïve in his views of the Germans and wrong about the length of the war, and by the end of 1942 he was so far down the path of appeasement that there was no other choice but to try to muscle his policies through an increasingly embittered and skeptical ghetto populace.

Gens was a pragmatist not just about the Germans but about the underground as well. Hedging his bets about the

Isaac Wittenberg, first commander of the FPO COURTESY OF VILNA GAON JEWISH STATE MUSEUM

outcome of the war, he courted Wittenberg's approval because he suspected that after liberation the city would be controlled by the Soviets and he wanted to keep his name off the Communists' list of those on whom to take revenge. He also secretly passed funds to the FPO and the Yechiel Struggle Group and on more than one occasion intervened to keep their leaders, including Kovner, from deportation, or their smuggling operations from discovery. When the end came, Gens often told underground leaders, he would come to the barricades and fight with them. Many people believed there was more than just pragmatism in such statements. Gens, in his own way, also saw himself as a fighter against the Nazis.

Gens had the continuing, indomitable optimism of the Jews working in his favor as the anniversary of their imprisonment in the ghetto came and went in September 1942. When twenty of the ghetto police were given uniforms in October 1942, many Jews thought this was a sign that the Germans had long-term plans to keep the ghetto functioning. Until that point, Leizer and the others had simply worn a special armband and hat, but the twenty put in uniform now had a sturdy leather coat, blue pants, and special peaked caps with a Star of David on the crown.

FPO headquarters
COURTESY OF VILNA GAON
JEWISH STATE MUSEUM

Only a few of the ghetto's Jews commented at the time how odd it was that on the very day they were first put in uniform, the same twenty officers were quickly escorted by truck away from the ghetto, accompanied by Dessler and Levas. By that point the spy network of the underground was substantial, and the destination of the police was soon known. They were headed for Oszmiana, a small town between Vilna and the Byelorussian border. This area was of particular concern to the Germans because of partisan activity there, and Reich authorities had decided to create a buffer zone that was *Judenrein,* or Jew-free, in the region as a means of ensuring that young Jews did not escape to fight against the Germans.

An FPO courier, a young woman named Liza Magun, was immediately dispatched to Oszmiana to warn the residents that they should suspect a ruse. The actual intention of the Germans was not clear, but the FPO believed the presence of the Jewish police might simply be a ploy to calm the town's leaders into thinking Oszmiana was only undergoing some kind of

Liza Magun COURTESY OF LEYZER RAN'S *JERUSALEM OF LITHUANIA*

harmless registration and reorganization for work. If Jews were in charge and German soldiers were nowhere to be seen, the residents were unlikely to become suspicious, and if indeed an *Aktion* were in the making, they would not move to save themselves until it was too late. Liza Magun's message was rejected by the people of Oszmiana precisely for the reason the FPO had feared. Magun left briefly; then, when she returned to try a second time to warn its residents, she was captured by the Germans and killed.

The ghetto police, at least the majority of them, had no idea they were being used for an *Aktion* against the Jews of Oszmiana. Once there, they carried out a registration of the population, dividing it into those who could work and those who could not. Small groups of Jews were summoned to the square, and the strong and healthy were told to wait in the synagogue. Once the approximately five hundred ill and elderly in a population of a little over two thousand were the only ones left in the town square, the Germans moved in to take them out of town and execute them in the presence of seven Jewish police officers. They then let the other Jews out of the synagogue.

It was the first time the Jewish police had been used in an *Aktion,* and the news rocked the Vilna ghetto. Though it was clear the majority of the police had had no idea what their true role in Oszmiana was to be, Dessler and Levas, the supervisors of the operation, had been briefed by Gens, who had approved what was going to happen to the town. The purpose of the *Aktion,* Gens told a meeting of ghetto leaders after the return of the police, was to weed out only the unproductive residents of Oszmiana. His willingness to make the tough decision to use the police to facilitate a peaceful sacrifice of the few for the many, he claimed, had resulted in saving the rest of the population from total liquidation.[37]

It was an argument Vilna's Jews were finding harder and harder to accept. The gate guards had groused a little when they first heard they would not be getting the warm leather coats that were part of the police uniform, but the complaints quickly stopped when the coats and hats served to identify clearly those police who, wittingly or unwittingly, had betrayed an entire Jewish town. What happened in Oszmiana was a turning point for many in the ghetto, too great a blurring of the distinction between the Jews and their captors, and the police who had been left behind were relieved to have had no part in it.

The ghetto was upset by the police role in Oszmiana, and Rose and Bluma made some cutting remarks about Leizer and his job with the police that hurt Zenia deeply. Leizer believed she had strong and sincere feelings for him, and he didn't want to lose her, but he knew it would be much easier for Zenia to live with her mother and grandmother if she gave him up. And of course he couldn't beg her not to. It wouldn't be fair. And if she did leave him, in some respects it would make things simpler. He could leave for the forests as soon as spring came.

But it wasn't going to be that easy, his heart told him. Perhaps it was time to tell her the truth about his involvement with the underground. She was right that he was different from most of the police, but that was only the smallest part of who he was. How would she react? Would she hate him for keeping secrets? Admire him for having the courage to work undercover at the gate? Be frightened off at the risk to him, or be angered by what she might see as the possible danger to her or her family? He had no idea. Still, he was sure things would be clearer if he got it off his chest.

One night in late fall, Leizer took a breath and told her about his secret life.[38] Though sweethearts weren't supposed to keep such important things from each other, he was reassured by the fact that she had no idea an underground even existed. If she didn't know, others weren't likely to know either, and that was good.

"What if they catch you?" she asked.

"You mean at the gate? Probably kill me." He tried to sound offhand, but he knew what he was saying was the truth. New regulations that spring clarified that any ghetto policeman suspected of helping smugglers at the gate would be shot without warning or trial.[39] If they discovered Leizer was part of the underground, they would take him off and torture him for information first, before killing him.

For a brief moment, Zenia wondered what he had gotten himself into, but she knew Leizer was a strong man, with a great sense of personal dignity, one who would do what he could to keep his integrity and pride intact. He was, she realized, exactly the kind of man she had hoped she would find, even though she had found him in circumstances she could never have imagined. In the end, she decided, she believed in him and trusted he would do what was right.

Seven

GRAVES ARE GROWING HERE

Hush, hush, let's be quiet
Graves are growing here. . . .
There are roads that lead to Ponary
There are no roads back.
Hush, my child, don't cry, my darling.
Wailing doesn't help.
—FROM "HUSH, HUSH," SUNG BY THE VILNA PARTISANS
AND GHETTO RESIDENTS

The year 1943 opened on a clear and blisteringly cold Vilna night. The ghetto police had invited residents to a New Year's Eve party. The hall was not large enough to hold everyone, and those with tickets were the envy of others who had not moved quickly enough to get them. The hall was meltingly, deliciously warm and filled with golden light, though it had the heady and cloying smell of wet wool and body odors trapped in clothes badly in need of cleaning. Ghetto musicians played a toe-tapping mix of klezmer and traditional Yiddish songs. Refreshments were meager by prewar standards, but to the hungry and disheartened Jews, it was the most festive event of their time in the ghetto.

Precisely at midnight Gens strode to the front of the room. The orchestra instantly stopped playing. Something in Gens's stiff and serious manner made the whole crowd freeze up in anticipation of yet another piece of horrible news. Then he smiled. His eyes made a slow sweep of the room, the smile seeming only to grow broader as he picked out and acknowledged a few faces in the crowd. A rustle of soft exhalations and relaxing bodies filled the room before he cleared his throat and spoke.

"Just now I have been told the ghetto is completely quiet," Gens said. Some people smiled and nodded. Others continued to watch Gens with eyes that revealed none of their thoughts.

Zenia felt an almost imperceptible touch on her elbow. Leizer was standing beside her. She had learned by now that Leizer was a very private person, not comfortable with even the smallest intimacies in public, so she settled for a quick exchange of hellos and gave him a furtive smile.

Everyone was listening to Gens, who had just finished extravagantly praising his own management of the ghetto and now spoke so softly and genuinely of its sorrows that telltale sniffling and even the occasional muffled sob could be heard in the room. Gens too seemed to be choking a bit as he remembered the dead.

Gens was closing his speech, and many pulled their attention back. If only the Jews would behave in a way that pleased the Germans, Gens was saying, they would have a safe year. And, he continued, there was a good chance that if they could have a safe year, they would be free by its end.

"Let us celebrate this night next year as free people," he called out, raising his glass. The crowd roared with approval.

• • •

As the first signs of spring began to break through the cold gray of winter, there seemed to be some truth to Gens's self-promotion. Things had remained relatively calm in the ghetto for many months. No organized *Aktionen* had terrorized the people, and though the Nazi appetite for Jewish suffering and blood required constant feeding, the meals had been smaller.

Zenia rarely wanted to look at her face anymore in the small hand mirror they had mounted on the wall of the bedroom. She was so gaunt she thought she looked more like a twelve-year-old boy than a woman now out of her teens. By that point hardly any young women had regular menstrual periods, and many had stopped menstruating altogether. Though they tried to laugh and say that was one good thing about the ghetto, many secretly worried that something might have gone seriously and permanently wrong with their bodies.

A constant dull ache had settled into their stomachs after the first few months of inadequate food, but few would describe the ache as hunger pangs. Those pains seemed like an indulgence now, a fretful but almost pleasant anticipation of satisfaction soon to come. Now their stomachs simply felt as though they had caved in and had given up sending signals that they ought to eat.

At the end of March 1943, residents of Vilna were told there was room being made in the Kovno ghetto for any who wished to go there. Hundreds of ghetto residents began preparing to leave for Kovno, then Lithuania's capital. Some families were anxious to reunite with relatives there, and others signed up for the transport in hope it was true that they would find better living conditions in Kovno. The Nazis claimed they were preparing places for them to live, and underground reports said it actually appeared to be so.[1]

The Nazi-sponsored relocation to Kovno meant a little more room in Zenia's apartment building, but also brought with it a great deal of temporary chaos. Many of the families leaving Vilna were in a frenzy trying to figure out how to get their meager possessions to the train station and then onto the crowded train. The Kovno transport would not actually begin in Vilna, but in the smaller villages in the surrounding area, as part of the Nazi effort to rid the countryside of what they considered to be the potential for a large-scale Jewish partisan effort. If every last Jew was surrounded by ghetto walls in Kovno, Vilna, or elsewhere, they would be easier to keep track of, control, and eventually eliminate.

Salek Dessler and Meir Levas had personally selected a cadre of police to go in advance to organize the evacuation of these smaller ghettos. Those who were not selected for deportation to labor camps were to be loaded onto trains that would then head to Vilna to pick up anyone else who volunteered to join them. Those taking the transport from Vilna would be waiting in closed boxcars to be added to the end of the train when it arrived in Vilna.

In the early evening on April 4, 1943, a crowd of approximately four hundred Jews was milling around the ghetto gate waiting to be escorted by Lithuanian officers along with the ghetto police to the Vilna train station. The gate guards watched from the gate as the residents lined up with their suitcases and were marched out of the ghetto.

Since members of the ghetto police would be taking the

train all the way through to Kovno with them, the Jews joining the train in Vilna trusted everything would be all right, and they paid little attention to the barbed wire that had been added around the windows of the six boxcars waiting for them on the track. Approximately sixty people and their possessions would have to fit on each boxcar, and it was clear there was not enough room for everyone who wanted to join the transport. Scuffles broke out, and the jostling and shoving intensified to open anger and hysteria as the train to which they would be attached pulled into the station.

Once the cars were connected to the train, all the doors were closed up and locked from the outside. Gens, who had quelled anxious passengers' worries by accompanying the train himself, was told to go with the other ghetto policemen to a separate compartment in the front of the train. The train pulled out of the station after dark and moved slowly through the night. About an hour later, the brakes began to squeal, and the train slowed down to an unexpected stop. The door to the police car was thrown open to reveal half a dozen Gestapo and Lithuanian police waiting for them outside.

Ordered to get out, the ghetto police jumped down off the train and looked toward small pools of garish light reflecting on a thin layer of snow a hundred feet or so from the tracks. They could see uniformed men standing at the edges of the spotlights. The glow of cigarettes dangling from their mouths disappeared into clouds of breath on the cold April night. Beyond them, the outline of the forest was even blacker than the night sky. The locomotive belched a huge cloud of vapor into the night. It took the policemen only a few seconds to realize they were at Ponary.

Nazi Security Police Superintendent Martin Weiss, in charge of exterminations at Ponary
COURTESY OF LEYZER RAN'S
JERUSALEM OF LITHUANIA

Nazi Security Police Superintendent Martin Weiss greeted Gens and pulled him aside. Gens was clearly outraged. This was not Kovno, and this was not the plan.[2] He returned to the huddled group of police and told them in clipped syllables that they were returning immediately to Gestapo headquarters in Vilna.

At headquarters, the returning police were ushered into a dining room, where a table was spread with more food than anyone had seen since the opening of the ghetto. They all sat down and began piling their plates, but after a few bites some could not swallow, thinking about what was happening to the Jews. Would the soldiers wait till morning, or had the boxcar doors already been thrown open? Did the people already know their fate, or were they still wondering aloud in the darkness when the train would start moving again toward Kovno? Or perhaps, the stunned police realized, they were all already dead.

Word that something terrible had happened to the transport had electrified the ghetto by the time the police got back, late the following morning. Over the course of the day, a few Jews on the transport found their way back to tell the tale of what had been a near total slaughter of everyone on the train.

These few survivors had managed to lie motionless until the rifle squads left, and then had been able to escape. They told how at dawn the cars had been opened up and the Jews had been herded to large pits. They had been forced to strip and then to dance before they were shot. Later a train from another village ghetto had arrived. When the cars were opened up and the Jews saw bodies on the siding, they swarmed out in a desperate attempt to escape, or at least fight back. Dozens fell on the soldiers with their fists, or with knives or other small weapons they had hidden on their bodies, until they were mowed down. A man who had seen the slaughter said there must have been at least five hundred bodies lying on the platform before the Nazis reestablished control.[3]

Stunned, the ghetto waited to see how Gens and the other ghetto officials would react. Later that day, Gens and Dessler summoned all the ghetto policemen for a meeting. Gens told them what they already knew to be true: Four thousand Jews on the two transports were dead.

Shame was written on Gens's patrician face as he looked at them. The events had been terrible, he acknowledged, but it was important not to overreact. As usual, he had been reassured by the Nazis that the Jewish population was at a supportable size at that point and there were no further actions planned.

He went on. "I have been ordered to send officers to the site to bury the bodies." He paused to clear his throat again, and they saw his hands were trembling. "It is the sacred and honorable duty of any Jew to fulfill the obligation to bury the dead," he said. "You." He motioned to two dozen policemen.

"I know I can count on you for that. Dessler will accompany you." Gens then turned and abruptly left.[4]

Leizer had not been among the two dozen police swept up by Gens's gesture. While his unlucky colleagues were getting into vehicles that would take them to Ponary, Dessler went to talk with Weiss, and instead of returning, he jumped into a waiting car. The driver turned it around and sped off, but not in the direction of Ponary. As the others rode away toward Ponary without Salek Dessler, it seemed clear that none of them would ever return.

Eight

A FIRE INSIDE

Inside me a fire demands.
And in the fire, my days.
But in cellars, in holes
The murderous silence weeps. . . .
—FROM "UNDER YOUR WHITE STARS,"
SUNG IN THE VILNA GHETTO

Much to everyone's surprise, all the Jewish policemen returned safely from Ponary. In bits and pieces, their story emerged. Their truck had stopped a few kilometers from Ponary, and they were ordered to begin marching. They saw Polish villagers walking toward them on the road, and as they passed, the police realized they must be carrying the clothes and other possessions of the Jews on the transports. As they looked around the bare fields, they saw dozens of other villagers making their way to and from the forest directly ahead. Those on their way in were empty-handed. Those coming back were bent over with their loads.

Entering the forest, they had begun to smell a faint, almost sweet odor, like the smell of a wet, rusty knife. It was the smell of blood, still fresh in the dark woods. The pathway was strewn with empty liquor bottles, and they could hear the loud voices of drunken Lithuanian riflemen. They reached a small clearing next to the train tracks and saw the soldiers laughing and smoking amid the strewn corpses and body parts of Jews, caked with dirt and covered with flies. Unprotected by the shade of the forest, the flesh was already beginning to give off a gassy, rancid smell.

Half of the Jewish policemen were ordered to load bodies onto carts, and the other half were told to follow a German officer into the woods. They walked down a slope toward another open area in the center of which was a huge, deep pit, about fifty yards long, twenty yards wide, and three feet deep. More than a thousand bodies lay sprawled and spattered with blood. Hundreds of arms and legs stuck out like sticks in a leaf pile. The German officer gave out shovels and said, "Cover them."

Ponary   COURTESY OF LEYZER RAN'S *JERUSALEM OF LITHUANIA*

While one of them recited the Kaddish, the traditional Jewish prayer said by mourners, they started shoveling dirt from the embankment onto the corpses. To reach the middle, they had to roll wheelbarrows full of dirt across the bodies. The sun was out, and by midafternoon the corpses had begun to stink, and the workers were all weak from hunger, exhaustion, and shock.

When they finished, Weiss took them to another pit, where there were even more bodies than in the first one, and he told them to cover those as well. He spoke with no more feeling than if he were giving routine orders to a household servant. From time to time he would laugh, as if the whole thing—not just the killings themselves, but the hapless policemen's reactions—gave him immense pleasure. Weiss pointed out where the Jews of the Yellow Pass Aktion were buried, and the Pink Pass, and the Yom Kippur Aktion. Every one of the rumors about Ponary, the policemen realized, had been true.

Even when the burial party sent to Ponary surprisingly came back unharmed, few Jews continued to hold on to hopes that the Germans did not intend to kill them all. After all, who shows the evidence of their crimes unless they are sure no one will live to tell? More and more people started to believe that Gens was a fool to think Jews would be kept alive because they could work for the Germans. Hingst and Murer had let anyone go to Kovno who wanted to. They didn't tell the young and strong to stay behind, nor did they direct the sick and the weak to go. It was clear they didn't really care at this point who died when. It would all be the same in the end.

Support for Gens waned with every month that passed. As

the arsenal of weapons smuggled through the gates continued to grow, hopes of those in the underground also grew that a successful uprising could be mounted in Vilna. In Poland, the Warsaw ghetto uprising, which began on April 19, 1943, was not suppressed by the Nazis for six weeks, and as April drew to a close, a small band of Jewish heroes had emerged. The two Warsaw fighting brigades, the ZZW (Zydowski Zwiazek Wojskowy, the Jewish Military Union) and the ZOB (Zydowska Organizacja Bojowa, the Jewish Fighting Organization), and leaders such as Mordechai Anielewicz and Yitzhak Zuckerman had assumed legendary status in all the ghettos of Europe.

To Abba Kovner and the FPO, Anielewicz, Zuckerman, and the others were an example of the FPO's main premise: There was a way, if not to survive, at least to die with dignity. To Gens, the Warsaw ghetto uprising was a nightmare. If the underground decided to fight back, the Vilna ghetto would be reduced to rubble and corpses, as the Warsaw ghetto had eventually been. Though Gens had long said that if the ghetto faced imminent liquidation he too would fight with the resistance,[1] he had no intention of letting things get to that point. He kept close track of the progress of the war and still believed liberation would come in time to save many of Vilna's Jews if they could keep appeasing the Germans.

But more and more of them, young men and women in particular, were willing to follow the path of the heroes of Warsaw. The FPO now had three hundred members, and the Yechiel Struggle Group close to two hundred, drawn both from the original ghetto population and from those who had been transported to Vilna or escaped when their own communities were liquidated. These newcomers had little patience for the subtleties of ghetto politics when it came to appeasing trigger-happy Germans, and they had no loyalty, or even grudging respect, for Gens. The leaders of the Yechiel Struggle Group and the FPO were respected, however, and the bitter irony of it, Gens realized, was that people like Isaac Wittenberg and Abba Kovner, not he, were keeping peace in the ghetto. Gens, whether from a sense of internal conflict or doubt, or because it was in his best interest to hide the existence of an underground rather than reveal how it had grown on his watch, continued to look the other way while the resistance movement went on training and collecting arms.

Gens's view of those wanting to escape to the forests was considerably less sanguine. He could pretend that the underground did not exist, but there would be no way to hide from the Nazis the disappearance of substantial numbers of people. If groups began escaping, Gens feared, the Nazis would react the way they had elsewhere, by moving in quickly to liquidate the entire ghetto.

In April a few emissaries from partisan camps outside Vilna slipped into the ghetto to try to persuade FPO leaders to take the entire group to a partisan camp in the Narocz forest northeast of Vilna. The FPO's response was chilly, suggesting instead that the partisans join them to fight for the Jews in the ghetto. However, the offer to leave the ghetto fell on more receptive ears outside the FPO. Moshe Shutan, a Jewish member of a Soviet partisan group led by Fiodor Markov, was able to collect and escape with a small group of Jews who, like him, had fled the town of Swieciany when it was liquidated by means of the Kovno transports.

No one was terribly sorry to see these Jews go. Having no roots or family loyalties in Vilna, outsiders often behaved more like gangs, threatening and attacking the beleaguered Jews for what little they still had. Those who wanted to fight the Nazis endangered the underground's efforts to keep the Germans in the dark about the existence of arms in the ghetto and the growing strength of the movement. Gens was even more pleased to get rid of them because they undermined his efforts to keep the ghetto quiet, peaceful, and productive. When Shutan was arrested with the names of those escaping in his pocket, Gens could have simply turned them over to the Gestapo. Instead, pleased to look supportive of the underground and the partisans while simultaneously having his own needs met, Gens secretly facilitated the Shutan party's escape from the ghetto.[2]

As groups began to leave for the forests, divisions grew within the FPO over whether to leave while they still could, rather than staying to defend the ghetto. None of them expected to live out the war, but in the ghetto they could really do nothing except wait for their moment to die in a hopeless cause. Some in the FPO were beginning to think along the same lines as the Yechiel Struggle Group, that escaping to the forests was a better use of the remainder of their lives. The FPO command even began discussing the idea of having a parallel strand within the FPO to accommodate these views. The escape of some of their members would enable them to establish uniquely Jewish partisan camps for the survivors of Vilna's armed revolt to join. However, it seemed to make more sense to try to form one unified resistance group in the ghetto, rather than work at cross purposes while the

Nazi Security Police Officer Bruno Kittel, Vilna ghetto liquidator
COURTESY OF LEYZER RAN'S
JERUSALEM OF LITHUANIA

ghetto did not seem to be in imminent danger of liquidation. Perhaps, Kovner and the other FPO leaders thought, they and the Yechiel Struggle Group might be able to unite around a common set of principles.

Indeed, it seemed as if solidarity were more important than ever in the spring of 1943, when Bruno Kittel became the Nazi Security Police officer for Vilna. Kittel, one of the most innately sadistic of the German officers, gave orders to liquidate the work camps surrounding Vilna, which, in the view of the Germans, were riddled with potential partisans. Kittel began enforcing a policy that for every Jew who escaped, ten would be shot in the presence of the other prisoners. In one camp, sixty-seven were shot for six escapees— just a little bonus, Kittel had laughed. While some camps were shut down by bringing the workers back to Vilna, wherever partisan activity had been uncovered, the preferred way to ease the threat was to kill all the workers. This Kittel achieved by such means as setting a building in which they were trapped on fire, or luring them to the mess hall by special treats like jam and bread he claimed he had brought as a reward for their hard work and productivity, and then ordering them shot as they sat there.[3]

As word of Kittel's actions trickled back to Vilna, the ghetto was thrown into spins and counterspins of opinions and speculations about what the renewal of the vicious wholesale slaughter meant for Vilna's Jews. Two things were clear. It was impossible to know what any Nazi's words or actions meant. An offer of a spoonful of jam might be just that one time, and the barbed hook that lured Jews to death the next time. It was also clear that any attempt to outwit the Nazis would bring down terrible retribution. A confiscated weapon, an escape to the forest—any act by which a Jew showed his or her unwillingness to go meekly along with the Nazis' plans unleashed a flurry of death and suffering among those still clinging to existence as their lives sagged and sank in the deteriorating conditions of the ghetto.

Giving in to Nazi intimidation and threats was not an option for the underground. In June, ten members of the Yechiel Struggle Group, led by Borka Friedman, one of Leizer's friends on the police force, left the ghetto to join the partisans in the Narocz forest, about eighty miles south of Vilna.[4] Friedman and the others had been chosen in part because they were being closely watched after having been arrested for one reason or another, and their lives were felt to be in imminent danger. Though Gens had been supportive of removing potential problems from the ghetto by allowing certain individuals to escape, the fact that there were two police officers among the ten was embarrassing to Gens, and he reacted with fury and bitterness toward the underground.

Leizer was summoned to a meeting of all the ghetto police. A shaken Gens addressed them.[5]

"People are faced with whether to stay here or leave for the forests," Gens said. "And it's a good question. Why should I stay here?"

He looked around the room. "The ghetto exists by virtue of twenty-five hundred strong young men. What if five hundred escaped? What retaliation would you expect? It's a question of a few individuals, or all of the Jews still alive here. Put yourself in the Germans' place—would you let a nest of partisans grow under your noses?"

He held the gaze of a few officers long enough to make it difficult for them not to squirm. "I wouldn't. I would wipe out the entire ghetto to protect my interests." He turned to leave. "You have not heard the last of this," he said, then strode from the room.

Indeed they had not. Several policemen were dismissed, but Leizer apparently was not suspected of involvement with the underground. Gens's retaliation focused on two people: Leon Bernstein, a leader in the Yechiel Struggle Group, and Joseph Glazman of the FPO. Glazman was arrested in his apartment in late June. When he resisted, he was handcuffed and beaten with rubber truncheons as he was marched through the streets to Gens's office.

Though the Jews were used to beatings, Glazman was one of the most respected men in the ghetto, and the Jews took it personally, as if this one beating were an assault on the dignity of each person in the ghetto. The FPO had tailed Glazman as he disappeared into the police headquarters, then set up observation posts and developed a plan to rescue him if he was being marched out of the ghetto. Indeed, a few hours later, they saw him, still manacled, come out from 6 Rudnicka Street in a horse-drawn wagon escorted by ghetto policemen, and head toward the ghetto gate.

As passers-by looked on in shock, a small cadre of FPO fighters led by Shmuel Kaplinsky surrounded the wagon and knocked the driver to the ground. During the commotion, Morton Shames pressed a gun to the policeman in charge, who was walking alongside Glazman on the wagon. "If you want to stay alive," he said, "remove your guards immediately. You are surrounded and we are armed." The policeman was terrified, and the guards quickly dispersed. Kaplinsky cut Glazman's chains with a hacksaw, and they whisked him to safety.[6]

It was the first time that the ghetto population was aware that there was an organized resistance within its walls. Gens was so unnerved and angry that he went to the FPO head-quarters and told them his credibility as ghetto leader would be so tarnished by this act of rebellion that he would resign and put them in charge of running the ghetto if they did not turn over Glazman. He promised that Glazman would be sent to a labor camp and not be deported or sent to Ponary, and that his release could be negotiated within a few weeks.

Reluctantly, the FPO complied, because they took Gens at his word that he would resign and force them to take a public role as ghetto authorities. Glazman left the ghetto for the Rezca labor camp, but two weeks later he was back when the entire camp was sent back to Vilna. Whether Gens would have lived up to his promise was not clear, but Glazman had survived.

Gens's bitterness toward the underground grew as a result

of the Glazman affair, and from that point forward he looked for ways to undercut or even dispose of the movement's leaders. Many in the ghetto agreed with Gens that a few hotheads and would-be heroes jeopardized them all, but others whispered with pride about the "Glazmanists" among them. Even Gens, however, had little idea how advanced the underground had become.[7]

Efforts to prepare for the defense of the ghetto were proceeding well in the middle of 1943. The Nazis had dumped thousands of books they had looted from various libraries and synagogues in a few storage rooms. The ghetto administration had supplied them with several workers known to have strong backgrounds in foreign languages, among them FPO members Abraham Sutzkever and Schmerke Kaczerginski. The Nazi official in charge knew nothing of Jewish culture, and he reasoned that the most attractive books must be the most important. The ones with impressive bindings were ordered to be forwarded to the Frankfurt Institute, and the rest were to be sent to a paper mill for recycling. The Jewish workers assigned to the task were given the nickname of the Paper Brigade. Their job was to catalog the books and identify anything that might be of interest to the Nazis, but instead the FPO members spent most of their days finding hiding places for the most culturally valuable texts and combing the rest for information of use to the group. In one Finnish text they found explicit information about how to make small, handheld explosive devices. In another work, a Soviet munitions manual, they gleaned information about how to make Molotov cocktails and land mines.[8] Piece by precious piece, not only guns and ammunition, but critical bits of information as well, were making their way into the hands of the FPO.

It was far easier to stockpile weapons than to agree on what to do with them. As the weather warmed, and as partisan bases began harassing and sabotaging the Germans behind the front lines in the spring of 1943, the leaders of the Yechiel Struggle Group and the FPO began to negotiate for a merger of the two organizations. This was accomplished in May, by a fragile and largely illusory incorporation of the Yechiel Struggle Group as an autonomous group reporting, for the purpose of coordination, within the administrative structure of the FPO.

That month, Abba Kovner invited key leaders of the Yechiel Struggle Group to attend a meeting to discuss the bylaws for the now united group. It was the first time the commanders and other key figures of both groups had met together. Though there was a risk in being seen, for many it felt good to be in a room crowded with people who had for a long time been making their secret contributions to the cause.

Wittenberg called the meeting to order, and everyone stood silently, listening. As Kovner had told the FPO participants to expect, the debate over the bylaws was heated almost to the point of blows. But most of the concerns were practical and reasonable, and Wittenberg was peppered with questions. There had been major *Aktionen* before that looked like the end and weren't. How would they decide when to give the order to fight? Who would give the order to mobilize? Once mobilized, how would they get their orders? What could they do and not do on their own initiative? Wittenberg knew that behind the

Yechiel Struggle Group's questions lay a fundamental lack of confidence in the FPO to act aggressively enough. Everyone wanted to be a hero in his or her own way—some in the streets of Vilna and some in the forests—and that element of individuality would undermine the reliability of any defense plan. But he was looking into the faces of those who wanted to fight, and that was the way it was. He would have to work with what he had.

He did his best to answer each question and waited for the most contentious question of all: When would they abandon the ghetto and escape to the forest?

Wittenberg was firm. They would go to the forest only after the battle for the ghetto had been lost.[9] Then, survivors would escape, taking as many as they could with them. In the forests they would regroup and continue the battle against their enemies.

The Yechiel Struggle Group's leader, Ilya Scheinbaum, nodded a somewhat uneasy assent. The combined fighting group had passed its first challenge. The defense of the ghetto was to be strong, focused, and unified.

By late spring, Vilna's Jews had other, more immediate concerns than resisting the Germans. By this point they had been imprisoned for well over a year and a half, and the ghetto was being sapped one death at a time. Though crowding had eased greatly because of the number of dead, daily life, as winter turned to spring, was an ongoing saga of empty stomachs, complaining bowels, chattering teeth, tattered clothing, hacking coughs, and dwindling hopes.

The health of ghetto residents had taken a turn for the

worse as a result of a shift away from employment outside the ghetto, which sometimes afforded the opportunity to bring in additional food. Along Rudnicka Street in particular, the ground floors of buildings had been turned into workshops. Now, if the army needed boots, or socks, or any other items for soldiers on the front, an order would be placed with the ghetto administration and the finished product would be delivered to the ghetto gate for pickup. In some cases Jews were moved to worksites such as Heereskraftfahrpark 562 (Vehicle Repair Park 562, known informally as HKP), which had been set up at the eastern edge of Vilna on Valkovsky Street, near the Cheap Houses where Leizer had stayed when he first came to Vilna.

As people's health became more and more undermined by poor nutrition, stress, and exhaustion, the funeral wagons of

Heereskraftfahrpark 562 (HKP)   COURTESY OF DEATHCAMPS.ORG

the Chevra Kadisha, the Jewish burial society, became more and more of a presence in the ghetto. No one was allowed to accompany the wagons beyond the ghetto gate except the wagoner and the undertaker, who took the corpses for burial in the Jewish cemetery. Unknown to the Nazis, they also often brought in weapons and other FPO contraband under the floorboards of the wagon and inside the coffins themselves.

The funeral wagons had to pass by All Saints Church, located across the street from the ghetto's main entrance. Those coming to and from church would have seen the sign posted by the gate: "Danger of Epidemics in the Jewish Quarter. Entry to Non-Jews Forbidden!"[10] The parishioners for the most part ignored the obviousness of the lie. Work parties do not march out of quarantined areas six days a week, nor do highly infectious diseases remain contained by wooden gates and boarded-up windows. The vast majority of the congregation of All Saints, along with the other Christians of Vilna, simply ignored the ghetto as much as they could—except for those who could find some way to profit from it—coming once a week to the church next door to pay their respects to a God who had made humans in his image and watched over them with love.

The closing down of workplaces outside the ghetto corresponded to a significant increase in the availability of work inside. Even Bluma had been caught up in Gens's effort to turn the ghetto into a captive factory town where everyone worked. She, Zenia, and Rose had been assigned as seamstresses in a uniform repair shop.

Despite Bluma's productivity as a worker, she had no illusions about her security in the ghetto. The few remaining elderly would be the first to have their lives bartered away by Gens if the situation worsened. As a result, Bluma was greatly upset each time she saw flyers posted by the underground. Zenia tortured herself with the knowledge of Leizer's involvement because it was not like her to keep such a secret from her mother or grandmother. But Zenia was by then keeping an even bigger secret: She was in love.

Though Rose and Bluma might have been suspicious of any suitor, Zenia saw how they stiffened at the mention of Leizer's name. Zenia was a cultured, educated girl from a well-to-do family of Vilna, a city known as the Jerusalem of Lithuania and widely viewed as the heart of European Jewish culture. Before the war Zenia would have chosen her husband from among the doctors, professors, or successful businessmen in Vilna. Zenia and her family spoke Yiddish with the Vilna accent, a mark of prestige in and of itself, whereas Leizer's Yiddish revealed him for what he was—a poor Jew, raised in a small town in Poland. Zenia was a Litvak, a Lithuanian Jew, and to Bluma and Rose there was simply no comparison between a Litvak and a Polish Jew.

To make matters worse, he was one of the ghetto police. That might make all of them a little safer because he cared about Zenia, but what did it say about him? Sure, they had heard some stories about police who tried to help the Jews, and Zenia had said he was one of those, but who joins the police in a ghetto?

And then there was the matter of Leizer's involvement with

Ha-Shomer ha-Tzair. It wasn't that Bluma and Rose thought there was anything wrong with getting involved in youth groups, and besides, who would disagree now that the Zionist groups had a better idea than the ones who said Jews should stay put in Europe? But Ha-Shomer ha-Tzair was so far left. Most of Zenia's school friends were more the type to join Joseph Glazman's group, Betar. Zenia herself had leaned that way before the war, and had even gone to a few meetings, but more out of sociability than true interest in politics.

And besides, Bluma frequently asked Rose, what kind of a Jewish name was "Bart" anyway? No, Leizer Bart would never do as a husband for her granddaughter.[11]

In other circumstances, Rose might have given Zenia more typical motherly advice about the importance of keeping a boy at bay, of preserving one's virtue, but in the ghetto things were different. There, having the time and energy it would take to go about ruining one's reputation was almost impossible to imagine. And where would boys and girls find the privacy in which to wander into trouble? Bluma and Rose kept a watchful eye, but said nothing, while Zenia tried deliberately to downplay Leizer's importance to her, shrugging her shoulders and calling him just one of her friends. Having Leizer in her life had somehow made her feel more secure, but in other ways she had never felt lonelier, because she did not have Bluma or her mother with whom to share the strange new emotions she felt.

Zenia and Leizer's budding relationship was genuine, though it was common in the ghetto for people to fake relationships, on paper at least. A Jew with no spouse or family on his or her *Schein* would feel the pressure to pretend to be married and to claim two minor children. In this way, more Jews would have rations and a means to avoid being rounded up by the Germans. People who had managed to find their way into the ghetto after their communities were liquidated or had escaped from a work camp were in particular need of quick cover. It was another example of the old rule—Jews needed to help Jews—and many in the ghetto were swift to respond.

There were risks in this form of kindness, however. In the spring of 1943, a young woman Zenia's age made the mistake of helping a young Jewish man by adding him as her husband on her *Schein*. Soon after, he was caught smuggling contraband. The Nazi authorities then demanded the arrest of all of his family members as a means of deterring others in the ghetto from similar acts. Not only the young woman but also the rest of her immediate family had been picked up because she was registered as his wife. They were kept for several days at the small jail inside the ghetto, while friends held out hope that the fact that they had not been taken to Lukiszki Prison was a good sign they would be released. Their hopes were in vain. Leaving work one day, Zenia heard that the young woman and her family had just been escorted through the gate by two ghetto policemen.

Zenia and the others in the ghetto knew by that point what such an exit meant. She had seen it many times, but for some reason this time it struck her with particular ferocity. Perhaps it was because the young woman and her family had simply been trying to do their best to live honorably in such horrible circumstances by helping someone else, or perhaps it was because she was Zenia's age, or perhaps it was something else altogether, but picturing the young woman walking through the gate with her doomed family caused something to rise up from

Zenia's belly. It was anger—anger at the Nazis, at Gens, at the naïveté of the young woman, at the ghetto, at everything. She stood near the gate, stiff with rage, until Leizer went off duty.

He had never seen her show such intensity before. "I am so tired of waiting to die," she said. "I want to join you in the underground." Leizer was not sure what had led to Zenia's startling outburst. In a world of such injustice, it was easy to imagine any number of possibilities. She would explain later, he was sure, and for the moment all he could think about was how frightening her words were.

"Zenia, no. It's too dangerous," Leizer said. "You know what happens. You see it."

"No, Leizer, I don't care anymore. If I'm going to die, I want it to be with you." Words kept tumbling out, and she was sobbing. "If I'm only going to live for a short time, I want my life to matter for something."

Leizer took it in silently. Then, out of the blue, Zenia blurted out, "I love you."

It was the first time she had said it. The phrase drifted into the space between Zenia and Leizer and hung there, as if time could not begin again until he had taken it in.

"I love you, too," he said. Despite the fact that it was difficult for him to show his feelings in public, he pulled her to him and held her for a moment, not caring who saw them.[12]

"Will you marry me?" he asked, then wondered where those words had come from, because he wasn't even sure he had thought them. Immediately the doubts flooded in. Marriage simply didn't happen in the ghetto. Were there even any rabbis left?[13] He might die at any moment. She would be a widow. She might follow him out of love into a situation that would leave her dead. He couldn't do it. Marriage was for better times. He would simply add "after the war," and hope she thought that was what he had meant all along.

He opened his mouth to explain, to take it back, and to run from the emotions making him say crazy things. Tomorrow they could make plans for if and when they survived the war. She would see it his way. She would have to.

His unexpected proposal was like a break in the clouds, clarifying the scenery as far as Zenia's mind could see. She kissed him lightly. "Yes," she said. "Yes, I will. We need to speak to my mother and ask her for permission. We may not have much time."

Nine

LOVE AS FIERCE AS DEATH

Let me be a seal upon your heart,
Like the seal upon your hand.
For love is as fierce as death . . .
Its darts are darts of fire
A blazing flame.
—THE SONG OF SONGS 8:6

No! Absolutely not!" Rose said. "How can you even think such a thing?"[1]

Leizer stood inside the tiny, sheet-lined cubicle in Zenia's apartment. Of course Rose was right. He should not be asking this.

They also should not be here. They should be in their homes minding their own business. She and Bluma should be making *cholent* and challah for Shabbos. Zenia should be going to parties. Michael should be going to school. But they weren't. This was the only life they had.

Rose found herself drawn to this solemn young man standing before her asking for her daughter's hand. His accent was Polish, but his words were respectful. A Jewish mother had clearly raised him well. He was not what she had expected for a son-in-law, but what of any of this had she expected?

Her daughter was in love. Only a foolish mother could fail to notice. But what did Zenia know about such things? How would she be a wife here? How could he be a husband? It was hard even to comprehend what getting married would mean in the ghetto, where there seemed to be no future for anyone. But then again, of what value were her misgivings when there might be no marriages, ever, for either of her children? This was her daughter's whole world. She would have to make her way in it.

Rose grilled Leizer about how he would feed Zenia, house her, clothe her. Leizer's answers were as good as anyone in the ghetto could give: He did not know. But he would, he promised, try with everything he had to keep her safe.

They couldn't even live as normal newlyweds used to before the ghetto. Zenia would move to the room where Leizer lived, but setting up a household or even private quarters was impossible. Such things would simply have to wait. If they survived the war, Leizer was sure he would win Rose over because she would see what a good husband he had turned out to be. As it was, he could offer her no reassurances now except to say that Hitler planned to kill them all, and Leizer intended to do all he could not to let that happen to Zenia, or to him, as her husband and protector.

He did not say anything about belonging to the underground. He did not say anything about Zenia's expressed desire to fight alongside him. Rose would not have allowed her daughter to see him again if she knew that—no mother would. There would be time later to explain their chosen path.

It was settled. Rose would go to make arrangements with the rabbi.

On Sunday, May 23, 1943, the rabbi arrived in the quiet back quarters of the Jewish ghetto administration buildings. It was Lag Ba'omer, an important event in the Jewish year. Traditionally, the fifty-day period known as the Omer, between the Jewish holidays of Passover and Shavuos, commemorates the lives lost in a great plague in Roman Judea during biblical times. Because weddings do not mix with mourning, observant Jews do not get married until the thirty-third day, Lag Ba'omer, when the plague is said to have ended.

Only a few guests had been invited. Isaac Alter, who lived in the same ghetto building as Zenia's family, and Abram Dimitrowski, who was a senior official in the ghetto police, along with Michael and one other man, made the traditional chuppah by holding the tallis over Leizer and Zenia's heads as the rabbi began the ceremony.[2]

It was a speeded-up affair. The rabbi bobbed rhythmically as he leafed quickly through the prayer book mouthing words here and there, with only a few recognizable phrases of Hebrew breaking through his murmured prayers. Then he asked for the ring.

Leizer reached in his pocket, and pulled out a tin-colored band he had serendipitously found on the cobblestoned street only a few weeks before.[3] As he put it on her finger, the rabbi guided him through the blessing. *"Harai at mekudeshet lee,"* Leizer said, "be sanctified to me with this ring."

Moving to the seven blessings of the Jewish wedding ceremony, the rabbi counted the male guests and realized they were short of the minyan, the ten males needed to proceed. The rabbi thought for a moment. Then he said, "There has never been such a thing as this ghetto. We shall proceed. I am sure God will understand." He shut his eyes and began. "Blessed art Thou, O Lord God, King of the universe, who created everything for his glory . . ."

Zenia was more upset than she let on about the absence of a minyan. What if that meant they were not really officially married? But what could she do? At the end of the blessings, a glass was wrapped in a headscarf. "We break this to symbolize the destruction of the temple and the presence of sorrow amid happiness," the rabbi said. Leizer brought down his heel with all his might, and a crunching sound brought the room to applause and muted cries of "mazel tov."

The rabbi smiled and said, "Kiss your bride."

Leizer shifted his weight and looked at the floor, embarrassed that there were so many people watching, but Zenia lifted up on tiptoes and brushed his lips without further prompting. Rose beamed. Bluma and Michael beamed. The rabbi and the guests beamed. It was, they all said, the nicest day they could remember in the ghetto.[4]

Weapons were so difficult to get, it was hard for anyone to be accepted as part of the underground unless he or she could also bring a gun to add to the arsenal.[5] Often a sufficient amount of money or valuables was substituted, so the underground could purchase a weapon itself. Leizer and Zenia had a few pieces of gold jewelry to use for this purpose. It was one half of Rose's remaining coins and jewelry sewn into the seams and hems of her clothes on the night before they went to the ghetto. Rose had brought it out and divided it between Michael and Zenia just before the wedding.[6] A gun would not be Rose's idea of a wedding present, and they would never tell her that her last asset would be used for such a thing, but Leizer and Zenia agreed in the end it could be one of Rose's two greatest gifts to her daughter. The first was the gift of life, and the second was the possibility to keep living it.

Despite Leizer's friendship with and respect for Abba Kovner, Leizer and Zenia joined the Yechiel Struggle Group. Its members were divided into five groups. Nathan Ring was the leader of the group to which Leizer, along with two hometown friends, Shlomo Brand and Israel Weiss, and several other members of the ghetto police were assigned.[7] Ring was a police commissar, one of the highest-ranking members of the ghetto police, and this enabled him to purchase weapons in the city. Leizer's key role was to help smuggle these arms into the ghetto while he was on duty at the gate. Once the weapons were inside the ghetto, they were hidden in Ring's office, on the theory that it was unlikely to be searched.[8]

Leizer had clearly found a good fit within the Yechiel Struggle Group,[9] and Zenia would as well. Several of the members, including Ilya Scheinbaum himself, were married. The influential women in Kovner's FPO tended to serve in risky and daring roles as scouts, saboteurs, spies, and couriers, and unlike the Yechiel Struggle Group, the FPO did not simply accept people with no specific skills just because of whom they married. Zenia would have been superfluous, in their thinking, and Leizer's value to the group would have been undermined by the commitment he had made to her.

More importantly, Leizer and Zenia agreed that going to the woods gave them their only real chance for survival. If they were to stay in the ghetto, the likelihood was that they would never have the opportunity to build a life together after the war.

Leizer was determined to see his family again, and he hoped that he and Zenia would be able to follow through on his goal to go to Palestine. Both of these were further reasons to choose the forest. But personal survival was not the main motivating factor for those committed to the resistance. Leizer and Zenia would accept whatever happened to them, life or death, just to be part of the fight against the Germans. From time to time in the weeks following her wedding, Zenia would shake her head in wonderment at how much her life and priorities had changed. She had gone from a naïve and carefree teenager to a married woman and a member of the resistance, from idle daydreaming about the future to skepticism as to whether there would be one, all within the scope of two years.

Get up! Liza is calling!"

It was a little after midnight on July 16, 1943. An FPO scout was calling out the code word for immediate action that had been adopted to honor FPO member Liza Magun, who had been shot trying to warn the Jews of Oszmiana about their imminent liquidation.

The message "Liza is calling" pulled the entire FPO membership from its beds. They quickly learned that Isaac Wittenberg and Abba Kovner had been called to a meeting in Gens's office in the middle of the night. A few others had also been

Chiena Borowska, political commissar
COURTESY OF VILNA GAON JEWISH
STATE MUSEUM

summoned to the meeting, including Zenia's cousin Chiena Borowska, who was one of the leaders of the Young Communists in the ghetto. Anticipating the possibility of betrayal of their leaders by Gens, the FPO mobilized all over the ghetto, waiting with their units for further directions.

Within minutes several members of the FPO stood watch in the shadows of the *Judenrat* courtyard. Soon Salek Dessler was observed leaving the building and going out through the ghetto gate. Within a few minutes he was back, talking animatedly with two SS officers as they hurried toward the entrance to Gens's office.

After ten minutes, a solitary man emerged, guarded by the officers. His feet were shackled, and the dragging chains sent grating echoes across the courtyard. The man stumbled forward, prodded by a gun barrel, and Isaac Wittenberg's face became visible in the courtyard lights.

The FPO members watching there, and from vantage points in the street as Wittenberg was led toward the ghetto gate, knew how serious this arrest was. Wittenberg was the chief of the FPO, an organization already far larger and better organized and equipped than the Germans could have imagined. If they knew who Wittenberg was—and why else would they have come to get him in the middle of the night?—he would be tortured, and if he broke, it could mean the destruction of everything they had worked for.

The soldiers moved toward the gate, prodding Wittenberg in front of them. As Wittenberg passed a side street, an FPO fighter leapt out and disabled one of the guards with a few quick punches.[10] The other soldier reacted, but he was jumped from behind by several more fighters before he could draw his weapon. The attack was so silent and so swift that not a single person sleeping in the apartments above even got up to look out the window. By the time the Jewish police arrived, all that remained was two SS soldiers sitting in the street rubbing their heads.

By early morning, news of the arrest and escape was making its way across the ghetto. Clusters of people milled around sharing facts and rumors, marveling at how, just as with the Glazman affair, the rescuers had seemed to come from nowhere. As they talked among themselves, a young woman held an older woman by the elbow to guide her through the street. The old woman's dress was pulled unnaturally tight across the shoulders, and her headscarf was coming loose. Unnoticed, Wittenberg was being smuggled across the ghetto to another safe house.[11]

The next morning Abba Kovner told FPO members what had happened at the meeting with Gens. Only hours before, Wittenberg had been denounced as the leader of the ghetto Communists by a party member under prolonged torture. Gens had tried to explain to Kovner's delegation that he wasn't betraying Wittenberg as leader of the FPO, but as a Communist. Gens claimed he had no choice but to give him up, because if he refused, the Gestapo would sack the ghetto looking for him.[12]

True or not, Gens had duped them all. He had made small talk with them in his office knowing the Gestapo was outside the door with Dessler. There would be no more cooperating with Gens.

Within hours of Wittenberg's escape, German authorities announced that if Wittenberg were not handed over by six that evening, German war planes stationed in Kovno would bomb the ghetto and set it afire. Gens, sensing a chance to restore his image as the overlord of the ghetto, came in his police uniform to the *Judenrat* courtyard, to which all Jewish men had been summoned.

"Wittenberg is being hidden by a few foolish hotheads who call themselves the underground. They threaten us all!" Gens told the residents of the ghetto.[13] His voice once more soared over the crowd. "We must stamp out this evil in our midst," he said. "Wipe them out, or otherwise your lives and those of your wives and children are at risk. The Gestapo wants only Wittenberg. As soon as they have him, there will be peace again. Otherwise it will be the end for all of us."

He paused. "Which shall it be? Wittenberg or the ghetto?"

The crowd roared, "Wittenberg! Wittenberg!"

"Then go find him," Gens replied.

The sound of shattering glass disrupted the meeting at the FPO headquarters on Strashun Street. "Give us Wittenberg!" the crowd chanted. Inside, Abba Kovner and Joseph Glazman watched as several FPO members who had been beaten in the street by *Starke,* ghetto thugs who worked for Dessler and

Gens, staggered in. The crowd outside was yelling, "Why do you want us to die? Why do you choose him over us?" Wittenberg himself was not there, but hiding in a location deliberately unknown even to Kovner and Glazman. It was clear that neither intended to bow to the crowd, or to Gens, who had personally come to try to persuade them to cooperate. One of the last remaining rabbis in the ghetto also came to try to convince them to give up Wittenberg.

His message was highly unusual for one steeped in Jewish law: The Jewish people came first, and they could save many by giving up one. The Torah says no Jew should ever betray even a single other, but the rabbi urged them to consider the damage they would do to the suffering people of the ghetto if they did not surrender their leader.

Kovner never dreamed that the ghetto would not be on the side of the resistance when a time such as this came. Worse yet, the violent mood in the street indicated that the FPO might have to resort to violence against fellow Jews just to protect themselves. This was not at all the idealistic scenario Kovner had built the organization's hopes around. The ghetto was not going to rise up and resist the Nazis—that much was clear. In fact it had shown more energy that day than ever before, and that fervor had been directed at resisting the resistance.[14]

"If blood is to be spilled," Kovner said, "it cannot be by us against fellow Jews." They would have to go to Wittenberg and persuade him to give himself up.

Wittenberg did not want to do it, but as they thought through every possible alternative, it seemed apparent that nothing short of his surrender would keep the Nazis from shedding blood in the ghetto. Escape, even suicide, were considered.

Once the decision was made, Wittenberg surrendered within the hour to Gens, after making it clear to the FPO that Kovner was his choice to be its new leader. He was immediately arrested and led from the ghetto. He approached the gate alone, guarded at a short distance by armed police. A crowd had gathered. A few called out words of encouragement, while others were silently relieved that a man they believed to be a threat to their safety was being removed. Wittenberg's head was high and he looked straight forward as he marched through the gate. On the other side, Nazi officer Bruno Kittel moved forward to take him into custody and drive him away.

Gens had been negotiating to get Wittenberg released even before he was out of the ghetto. Such a release might have been possible, if in fact Wittenberg was arrested for being a Communist and not because he was known to be the head of the FPO.[15] Gens's efforts failed, however, and within a day Wittenberg was dead from a poison capsule Gens had supplied to him, in case he could, in the end, offer Wittenberg nothing more than an easier way to die.[16]

Ten

INTO THE FREE FORESTS

From the ghetto's prison walls
Into the free forests,
Instead of chains on my hands
I carry a new rifle. . . .
Jews are storming from beneath the earth . . .
Bringing sunshine to the night—
Jews! Partisans!
—FROM "JEWS, YOU PARTISANS"
BY SCHMERKE KACZERGINSKI

The FPO entered a maelstrom of recriminations, guilt, and anger as a result of Isaac Wittenberg's death. To some, Joseph Glazman and Abba Kovner had shown themselves incapable of true leadership, because they should have refused to turn over Wittenberg even if it triggered Nazi retaliation. Such retaliation would start a Jewish revolt that would cost lives, but after all, some reasoned, what had they been preparing for all this time? Why, in the twilight of the ghetto, were they still waiting, still letting the Germans call all the shots? To others it was equally clear that starting a revolt and jeopardizing other people's lives would not have been justified when it was so clearly against the wishes of the rest of the ghetto. From that point forward, however, controversy and second-guessing dogged the leadership of the FPO.[1]

Even though Joseph Glazman was more seasoned in underground warfare and leadership of fighting units, Wittenberg had seen him as too risky a choice to be the new FPO leader. He had already been arrested and imprisoned several times by the Nazis, and he was being closely watched. When Wittenberg appointed Kovner head of the organization instead of Glazman, many were surprised and some were deeply displeased. Kovner was magnificent with words, but he had little practical experience as a fighter and even less as a combat commander. Would he be able to give the call that would escalate the bloody end of the ghetto? And if he did, would he truly be able to coordinate and command the fighters so that they inflicted as much damage as possible but still had a chance to survive and go to the forests to continue the struggle? As the battle for the ghetto loomed, the fact that Kovner was not adequately tested in the capacity he now held was a source of great concern.

The Yechiel Struggle Group, also known as the Second Fighting Organization, had agreed to continue coordinating its resistance activities with the FPO after Wittenberg's death, but the union was more strained than before. Kovner preferred to keep the resistance a closely knit group of people who had worked and trained together, rather than a larger and more amorphous collection of individuals and groups. He preferred to make decisions in consultation with only a small circle of longtime friends,[2] and this may have resulted in a flattering but not necessarily always helpful form of loyalty. Unaffiliated individuals, some of whom even had managed to get weapons, were told they were on their own and could not join the FPO. This created disgruntlement among people the FPO would sorely need when the time came to defend the ghetto.

The FPO and the two groups that had merged into the Yechiel Struggle Group had their roots in long-standing friendships and ideological affiliations before the war. The reality at that point was that the typical young person in the ghetto who wanted to resist the Nazis was likely to be a newcomer, having been forced into the Vilna ghetto after his or her own town had been liquidated, or, as time passed, a person too young to have been part of their group before the war. Others had no affiliation because politics simply didn't interest them. The Yechiel Struggle Group recognized this and was more accommodating, but the FPO remained clannish and inflexible, and though there were legitimate reasons to be secretive, their attitude stood in the way of forming a truly ghettowide effort to resist the Nazis.[3]

Although he had affiliated himself with the Yechiel Struggle Group, Leizer maintained his friendship with Abba Kovner and others in the FPO. His straightforward and cautious nature, his long-standing ties with Ha-Shomer ha-Tzair, and his levelheaded work as a gate guard made Leizer able to bridge the psychological and ideological gap between the two groups in a way that was rare in the tense atmosphere within the ghetto resistance. Serious and quiet, Leizer was hard to get to know well, but people agreed he was easy to respect and to like.

Abba Kovner was having increasing difficulty not just with the membership, but also with keeping the underground's focus on resistance within the ghetto itself. Kovner's strongest argument had always been an ethical one: Jews should not abandon fellow Jews even if it was to fight against the Nazis elsewhere. The ghetto's response during what became known as the Wittenberg Affair seriously undercut that argument. Vilna's Jews had made it clear that they did not support the resistance movement, and, as a result, many members of the underground had concluded that if the ghetto did not want to resist the Germans they were under no further obligation to do so on its behalf.

A second problem also faced Kovner. When he issued his first manifesto on New Year's Eve 1941, resistance within the ghetto seemed to be the only option. No organized partisan effort existed in the forest, because the invasion of the Soviet Union was still only a few months old. By mid-1943, however, the forests of Lithuania, Byelorussia, and other occupied parts of Europe were riddled with underground camps of various sorts. Some groups calling themselves partisans emphasized personal survival, terrorizing villagers for food and supplies but rarely if ever carrying out acts of sabotage against the Germans. Some didn't use the name partisan at all, but formed what were known as family camps, made up of people who had gotten to the forest and were simply trying to live out the occupation. But there were a growing number of partisan units, some formally associated with the Soviet army, whose reason for being was to disrupt German supply and communication links with the front. There was now a viable alternative to a heroic death in a doomed ghetto.

For more and more members of the underground, including Leizer and Zenia, escape to the forests made far better sense than staying to fight. The FPO did not try to stop members of other groups from leaving, because Kovner understood the critical role these first escapees would play in forming Jewish partisan units and preparing a forest base for those who followed. Scouts and messengers from the Vilna underground regularly traveled between the ghetto and the Soviet partisan camps, and Soviet liaisons frequently made secret visits to the ghetto. Kovner insisted there would still be a strong and heroic defense of the ghetto when the time came, but by the summer of 1943 even some FPO members, particularly those who were in imminent danger of being arrested or deported to labor camps, began to join the exodus to the forest, with the blessings of the FPO leadership.

During August, armed fighting units began to leave for the Narocz forest. By the end of August, little ammunition and few arms remained in the FPO arsenal, but despite that fact, the group decided to put up armed resistance with the remaining weapons.

The chance to do so arose when the ghetto was suddenly surrounded by Nazi troops around sunrise on September 1, 1943. Largely in reaction to the increased number of escapes and the growing partisan activity around Vilna, the Germans had decided to speed up the liquidation of the Vilna ghetto. The first step was mass deportation to Estonia, where mine workers were required. In the early hours of daylight, soldiers began roaming through the ghetto, abducting any Jew they laid eyes on, to round up a quota of five thousand for deportation to Estonia.

The FPO issued a mobilization order to begin its much-anticipated revolt, but before one of its battalions could even reach their weapons cache, they were captured and marched away for the transport to Estonia. Later it was learned that they had probably been betrayed. Someone had been so certain a showdown would be disastrous for the Jews that he had told the Germans where to intercept the battalion, jeopardizing the lives of seventy-five to one hundred resistance fighters. The capture of what amounted to about a third of its trained members was a disaster for the FPO, for it not only seriously reduced the ranks but also showed that the group was not nearly as well prepared or coordinated as it needed to be to defend the ghetto.

When the call-up came, Leizer rushed to join the fighters near FPO headquarters on Strashun Street. It had never been the plan to initiate the battle there, but rather to keep enemy soldiers out by defending the ghetto at its entrance. It was too late for that, as soldiers were already marching through its streets. Kovner quickly went to a backup plan of defending the headquarters by preventing the Germans from entering Strashun Street. Kovner ordered the fighters from both groups to take up positions at the entrance to the street and at several other points. These included Kovner's own apartment, which had been heavily fortified for some time so it would be ready on a minute's notice to serve as a stronghold for the FPO if they were cornered in the ghetto.

There they sat, waiting for several days to hear the sound of soldiers' boots coming toward them, but none came. Unknown to them, Gens had promised the German officials their full number of deportees if they would leave the ghetto and allow the Jewish police to handle the matter. But the Jews who had survived to this point were capable of hiding so quickly that the crowded streets and apartments of the ghetto could look like a ghost town within a few minutes. A few hundred unwary Jews were caught or volunteered, but the roundup for deportation was clearly not going to meet its quota.

By midafternoon, Kovner had written a new manifesto, which was duplicated by the clandestine press and distributed across the ghetto. "We will not stretch our necks for the slaughter!" he wrote. "We have nothing to lose. The hand of the hangman will fall on everyone. Do not cower in the hideouts! Get out into the street. Use hatchets, if you have them, or pipes and sticks or whatever you have! For our fathers! For our murdered children! Strike at the dogs, fellow Jews."[4]

Kovner looked down Strashun Street hoping he would see the street full of Jews who had finally heard what he had been saying. Soon he had to acknowledge that the residents of the ghetto weren't coming. It didn't matter what he tried to tell them. The ghetto Jews would just keep hiding, and hoping that once again it would not be their turn to die. He had done all he could. The FPO would only fight now if the Nazis came for them.

By nightfall they had. When only six hundred Jews had been collected for the transport by early evening, the Germans and some Estonian troops reentered the ghetto, working their way slowly toward its farthest corner, Strashun Street. Eventually, the Estonian soldiers turned the corner onto Zumkzka and began marching down the street. Soon they were banging rifle butts on the door of each building, and calling on the Jews to come out or be blown up where they hid.

In one building, where a sizable number of Jews were hiding in *malines,* an explosives specialist went in to set mines. A last call to come out was issued, and when no one responded, a deafening roar followed. Debris flew through the air, shattering nearby windows and rattling walls all the way to the end of the street. The building lay in ruins, its occupants dead or dying underneath the rubble.

Ilya Scheinbaum of the Yechiel Struggle Group, along with his wife, Pesia, and FPO members Ruszka Korczak and Motl Gurwitz, was stationed closest to the entrance of Strashun Street. Located in the front position on the second floor, the group had rifles and various types of explosives, and was ready to fight.

Another group, commanded by Morton Shames, took the middle position at 6 Strashun Street, in a large second-floor apartment near the library. With a view of both sides of the street, Shames held in his hands the only machine gun possessed by the FPO. As the Nazis and Estonians marched through the ghetto rounding up any Jews they could find, Shames stood on the balcony camouflaging the machine gun. Earlier, Abba Kovner had explained to Shames the importance of this middle position, since the group stationed there had most of the FPO weapons and ammunition remaining in the ghetto—a few loaded guns, some grenades, homemade Molotov cocktails, and bottles filled with sulphuric acid.

Kovner and a third group of fighters were barricaded at the bottom of Strashun Street, a dead-end street artificially created when the Nazis walled in the ghetto. He told Shames to keep in continual touch with him and act according to orders, but if circumstances required quick decisions, Shames was to use his own best judgment.[5]

The FPO had been in position for several days, and tensions were rising from lack of action. Then, late in the day, before the underground positions had been discovered and attacked, the Estonian soldiers began to march away from Strashun Street. Motl Gurwitz and Ilya Scheinbaum, both in the forward position, were among the first to realize this. After a minute Ilya Scheinbaum leaned slightly forward to see if the soldiers had gone. A sniper's bullet caught him under the chin and traveled up through his skull, killing him instantly.[6]

It was so quick, and no sign of a wound was immediately apparent, so it took a minute for the fighters to understand what had happened. The leader of the Yechiel Struggle Group, one of the most admired and well-liked personalities in the resistance, was already dead, minutes into the revolt. In the confusion, someone shouted that the building was being mined and they needed to escape. Leaving Scheinbaum's body behind, they went down the stairs and leapt from the windows of the second floor, some escaping only seconds before the building exploded.

Then suddenly, when it seemed that only the rubble blocking the street could keep the soldiers from marching down to the FPO headquarters and making a quick end to the resistance movement, they turned around and left. Perhaps it was because they knew they had the upper hand and did not need to engage in a firefight, or perhaps it was because night was falling, and they were afraid of being caught in the streets of

Strashun Street after demolition of the buildings by Nazi explosives
COURTESY OF LEYZER RAN'S *JERUSALEM OF LITHUANIA*

the ghetto after dark. It was not a foolish fear, despite being fully armed. In the Warsaw ghetto uprising, soldiers trying to find their way back to the gate in the crooked and unfamiliar streets of the ghetto were often found the next morning beaten to death or with their throats slit.

Ilya Scheinbaum's body was found in the debris. The battle that had killed him was to be the only armed resistance in the Vilna ghetto. The feeling of defeat was made even worse in the aftermath of the shoot-out, when thousands of Jews came out of hiding and signed up for the deportation. In all seven thousand Jews went to Estonia, most of them voluntarily, leaving only eleven thousand in the ghetto, approximately one-third of its original population.

Jews signed up for deportation because they simply wanted to get the hiding and waiting, the fear and the misery, over with. Their energy had been drained by constant hunger, lingering illnesses, incessant torment from bedbugs and scabies, and a thousand other problems big and small that wasted their human spirit. Their nerves were rubbed raw by harsh invectives in German, and what seemed like an incessant crackle of bullets, splintering wood, and breaking glass. They had seen too many Jews sprawled dead in the streets, and spent too many nights wondering about the fate of those they had last seen disappearing through the ghetto gates.

In short, they finally realized they were broken beyond fixing and were willing to throw their fate to the armed and menacing men who this time might be telling the truth about not intending to kill them. Even if they weren't, it would only cause them to join the dead, who had often been the envy of the suffering ghetto. In the end, the decision to leave saved many of their lives. Of the Vilna Jews who survived the Holocaust, many were liberated from the same Estonian labor camps to which this final group of deportees was sent.

The remaining Jews were told they would be relocated soon to various labor camps around Vilna, but for the time being they were left alone. Since the shoot-out, the *Judenrat* had ceased to function. The police force had been disbanded,[7] but even before that many of them had simply stopped showing up for work when it became clear that no one really cared anymore if there was order in the ghetto.

In the FPO headquarters on Strashun Street, the unusual quiet gave the members a chance to think about the next step.

There was nothing more to fight for in the ghetto, and Kovner wanted to use the period of calm to plan the FPO's escape carefully, and to minimize the risk of losing any fighters through simple mistakes.

Kovner swallowed his pride and went to Gens, who agreed to help the FPO escape as long as they did not take nonmembers with them. Gens still feared that a mass exodus might trigger immediate liquidation, whereas the planned transfer to work camps at least gave some Jews a chance of surviving the war. Kovner gave his word that the FPO would take only members with them, and in return Gens supplied the underground with new means to escape, including the key to one of the side gates used by the authorities to go in and out of the ghetto.[8]

Whereas in the past many people had escaped by posing as work parties, there were few such groups leaving the ghetto at this point. Escapes would need to be made at night, and weapons would have to be smuggled out as well. To help with this, Gens arranged jobs as gravediggers for some FPO members, and as bodies were taken from the ghetto, the FPO cache of weapons was smuggled out in the same way much of it had been smuggled in, and then buried in a Jewish cemetery on the outskirts of town.

Little by little, groups began sneaking out through the side exit. After they were outside the ghetto, they went first to the cemetery to retrieve weapons, and then headed off to join others already in the forests. One of their first actions was a ceremonial removal and burning of the yellow stars on their jackets. Their relationship with the Germans had changed. They would now be the hunters rather than the hunted, and if there were to be a symbol on anyone's chest or back, it would be an imaginary bull's-eye on every German or collaborator they saw.

During early September it was possible to move around the ghetto without fear of abduction, and the lack of harassment in the now half-empty streets was an eerie contrast to the violence of only a few weeks before. Zenia took advantage of the calm to visit Rose and Michael daily. Rose's health had deteriorated, and she clung to Michael with the grip of a spectre, her now entirely gray hair clumped carelessly at the nape of her neck.[9] She looked older than Bluma, who had shrunk into a bony but still vigorous-looking frame. Zenia worried about her mother constantly, and about Michael even more. It was amazing that a twenty-year-old man had not been taken away already, but there they were, all four of them still alive.

After the shoot-out on Strashun Street, Leizer and Zenia agreed it was time to tell her family about their involvement with the underground. No longer working, Leizer came with Zenia one afternoon to the substantially less crowded apartment where Rose and Michael still lived. From the beginning of the ghetto, he told them, he had been part of the resistance. Rose was amazed that a gate guard could have undertaken such a role, but the news that Zenia was involved was even more of a shock.

Hardest of all was what they had to say next: Leizer and Zenia were leaving the ghetto. They did not have an exact date, but they were scheduled to leave soon to go to the forest to fight with the partisans. Michael begged to go with them, but they had to turn him down due to Kovner's promise that no one other than members of the resistance would be allowed to leave the ghetto for the forests. The leader of any escaping group would have refused to allow Michael to go along, and there was no point in getting his hopes up.

There were no good choices anymore, only the necessity to choose between bad ones, and over the course of the afternoon, the family came up with a plan they thought gave Rose and Michael their best chance for survival. When liquidation came, no one would be spared, and it was best for them to go in advance to one of the camps outside the ghetto where essential war labor was still being done. At Bluma's age she had no hope of being chosen for transfer to a work camp, so she would go to live with her other daughter, Lizzie, when Rose and Michael left.[10] There was hardly anyone left in Lizzie's apartment, and they had a good *maline* if there were any further opportunities to hide. The deaths of so many Jews when buildings were blown up had left few Jews with any real confidence that the *malines* could help them any further, but it was best to talk as if there were still options, still hope, for those who had no choice but to stay in the ghetto.

Leizer had heard that HKP, the labor camp that repaired automotive equipment, was expanding its workforce. Major Karl Plagge, who had a reputation for treating Jews fairly, ran HKP. New work camp assignment lists were being completed by the ghetto administration, and Leizer used his contacts to help Rose and Michael get on the HKP list. Once he and Zenia left for the forest they could do nothing further to help them, but at least Rose and Michael would be in the safest possible place to wait out the war.[11]

Within a few days it had all been arranged. On the night before Rose and Michael were to report for transfer to HKP,

The remnants of Rose's wedding silverware
BART FAMILY COLLECTION

Zenia slept at their apartment. Rose pulled out a small box in which there were two spoons and a fork. They were the remaining pieces of silver they had brought from home, the rest having been either sold or bartered to stay alive during the two years they had been in the ghetto. Rose wanted Zenia and Leizer to take them. They were small enough to carry, and she imagined they could use them in the forest. "Carry these with you, as my blessing," she said.[12]

The next morning Zenia went with them to the makeshift station in one of the ghetto streets where processing for HKP took place. A number of other ghetto residents were also saying their last good-byes near the processing tables. Those who were leaving were assembled in one part of the street, while Zenia and the others milled around nearby waiting to watch their family members and friends go through the gate.

Suddenly an order was issued to round up all the Jews in the area where Zenia was standing. As Rose, Michael, and the others began to march toward the gate, soldiers began forcing everyone else in the opposite direction, pushing Zenia along with them. As the group approached the ghetto jail, it became clear that the Nazis intended to take advantage of the HKP departure to rid the ghetto of this other group as well.

A soldier stood just inside the entrance to the courtyard, and as Zenia approached him, she was suddenly overcome with panic. "I can work!" she said as she reached out for him. "I can work!"[13]

But work would not save the ghetto Jews anymore. He lifted his rifle butt and struck Zenia on the back of her head so hard it slammed into an iron gate. She fell forward and her head struck hard on the courtyard stones, knocking her unconscious.

Zenia's legs and arms lurched and she was awake. A crust of dried and oozing blood covered a split in her scalp that was now beginning to curl around a massive bump. She pulled herself up to sit, and as her eyes focused, she looked around the courtyard. The soldiers were gone, leaving the gate to the jail open.

It took a moment for her to understand what was in front of her eyes. All the Jews who had been herded in with her were dead, their bodies lying where the soldiers had mowed them down. Zenia sat for a while as the enormity of what had happened sank in. They had left her for dead. She was the only one who had survived.[14]

Zenia had no idea how long she sat in a daze before she rose to her feet. Then, tracing her hand over the sides of buildings for support, she took one dizzy and unsteady step at a

Ghetto jail at 6 Strashun Street/7 Lydos Lane
COURTESY OF GHETTO FIGHTERS' HOUSE, ISRAEL

time toward the underground headquarters. Leizer, frantic with worry, found her about halfway there. He reached up to cradle her bloody head and felt her wound. His fingers sprang back, and as he pulled away to look at her, Zenia fainted in his arms.

A ghetto nurse diagnosed Zenia with a concussion, and for the next few days she stayed in bed, in a world where dreams were concocted out of the noises and activity surrounding her. As soon as she was able to concentrate and was steady on her feet, she and Leizer met with Shlomo Brand and a dozen other Yechiel members to make their final plans to escape the ghetto and join the partisans. Zenia was still feeling dizzy and had searing headaches, but she tried to keep this to herself, because

The entrance to the jail. Through the back door at Lydos Lane, prisoners were led to Ponary.   COURTESY OF LEYZER RAN'S *JERUSALEM OF LITHUANIA*

she knew the time to escape had come, and she didn't want Leizer to hold back out of concern for her. Besides, if the others knew how sick she felt, they might think she couldn't keep up, and would make them wait for another group to depart.

Late in the evening of September 15, 1943, Leizer and Zenia escaped the ghetto with Shlomo Brand.[15] At the side gate on Jatkowa Street, to which Gens had earlier given Kovner the key, the group stopped to listen for signs of life outside. Even though the patrols around the perimeter of the ghetto had been greatly reduced, the risk was still significant. Any German passing by would shoot them on sight, and many residents of Vilna were likely to run for the police if they saw a bedraggled party of Jews outside the ghetto.[16]

Zenia could hear that the streets of Vilna were silent on the

The ghetto jail USHMM, COURTESY OF WILLIAM BEGELL

other side of the small gate. Someone cracked it open, and the first of their party made a foray out to see if the Lithuanian policeman that Leon Bernstein had bribed was waiting for them with his truck. He signaled that he was there, and one by one they ran through the gate and into the back of the truck.

As Shlomo Brand's party drove through Vilna to the arranged drop-off point just outside the city, the streets once so familiar to Zenia were menacing and nightmarish. Only as long as the truck kept moving would they be safe, and each block they covered felt like an act of defiance.

Getting out of Vilna was only the first obstacle. They had been ordered to go to the Rudnicki forest by the Soviet partisan command, rather than to the Narocz forest, a more established partisan stronghold and a route with which underground scouts in the ghetto resistance were more familiar. To reach

One of the underground members, Dr. Leon Bernstein
USHMM, COURTESY OF YIVO
INSTITUTE

the edge of the Rudnicki forest, Leizer and Zenia's group would need to cross approximately fifteen miles of mostly flat farmland on foot, skirting a number of small villages as well as several German army posts and checkpoints. Where they were at any given moment and what lay ahead was a mystery, and mysteries of this sort could cost them all their lives.

When morning came they were outside the city,[17] and Zenia and Leizer took their first look in years at an unobstructed sky and horizon. The wet fields sparkled like a jeweler's tray of unset emeralds, and the woods beyond glowed gold and amber in the fall light. Zenia felt tears spring to her eyes at such beauty, not just because she hadn't dared to hope she would ever again witness it, but because Rose and Michael were still working in the gray and dreary HKP camp and Bluma was still trapped inside the ghetto with Lizzie. Much as Zenia's heart tried to lift, it was still shackled to that reality.[18]

Every stream, every field, every road, every village posed a potential threat for escaping Jews, and Shlomo Brand's party was slowed down by the need to send scouts out to see if the next stretch of the journey was safe. Their plan was to walk all night in the general direction of the forest, and then rest in the fields during the day. Wherever possible they would have to avoid the roads, for fear of running into Germans, Lithuanians, or local Polish residents, who if not openly collaborating with the Germans were generally hostile toward Jews.

It took two days to cover the distance between Vilna and the edge of the Rudnicki forest. At that point Brand's party faced a new kind of dilemma. The Rudnicki forest was so thick that little light penetrated to the ground. Its muddy trails more often than not ended in a swamp within a few hundred yards. There would be no choice but to stay on roads or trails, even if others used them as well, and the partisan camps were so well hidden they would have to hope to be found rather than do the finding themselves.

Brand's party spread out into smaller groups as they went cautiously along the slightly elevated road, ready to dive into the muddy brush on either side of the path at the first hint of danger. Birds sang from trees to which signs were nailed saying, "Beware of the Partisans." They were still so far from safety, and the trials of life in the forests lay ahead of them, but they were free, and for once the only smells were those of life.

Suddenly Leizer heard the sound of sticks breaking underfoot a few yards away. He froze, grabbing Zenia's elbow. Then he saw three men coming out of the woods, their weapons drawn. He shoved Zenia into a shallow depression by the side of the path and threw himself over her. He felt the men's shadows fall over him and tensed his body, awaiting the bullets.

Underground member Mitia Lipenholz COURTESY OF LEYZER RAN'S *JERUSALEM OF LITHUANIA*

A rifle butt prodded his back. "Get up," he heard one of them say, and he was partway to his feet before he realized they were not speaking German, or even Lithuanian or Polish. The man with the rifle was Russian. Leizer whispered to Zenia, "I think they're partisans. Stand up slowly and put your hands in the air."

"Who are you?" the man asked, when they were both on their feet. Leizer answered him in Polish. "We are escapees from the Vilna ghetto. We are trying to reach the partisans." The man's lips parted in a smile that revealed a gold tooth in a row of tobacco-stained ones. "Come with us," he said.[19]

Leizer helped Zenia to her feet, and immediately their attention was distracted by shouts from farther up the road. It was other Russian partisans, who had found the rest of their group and were calling down the road for no one to shoot.

The path to the camp was barely visible, skirting the edge of standing water a few inches deep. Anyone who strayed at all from the path spent the rest of the journey squishing along in mud- and water-soaked boots. A few more steps and they would have sunk up to their waists in swamp water. Frogs jumped from rotting logs as they walked by, and large ants crawled across the path.

After an hour, the canopy of trees blocked the morning sun, and the forest grew darker. They could smell the smoke from campfires and could see what looked like another shoreline on the other side of an oily-looking lake that was the color of grass. They turned off the path and jumped from one carefully placed log to another over a marsh.

Within a few hundred yards they reached a bridge of lashed tree trunks spanning the water. On the other side they could see and smell the smoke from several campfires. As they made it across, they found themselves in a clearing full of small campfires, each with a group of men and almost as many bottles of vodka.

The Soviet partisans seemed disinterested in Brand and his group. They were, however, warmly greeted by other members of Yechiel who had arrived a week before. Zenia's cousin Fania Bulkin-Wolozni and her new husband, Meyer, had come with the earlier group.[20] Among the first Jews to arrive in the forest, Fania and the others in her party had been received with the same lack of warmth from the partisans as Leizer and Zenia's group had been.

But there they were, and there was no turning back. They had arrived deep in the forest, with only the clothes on their back. They slept that night in the open, with a primeval forest looming just beyond the glow of the campfire. Wolves howled in the distance. They were safe enough within the partisan camp to get some sleep, but they were all a bit disconcerted by the cool and indifferent welcome.

Was there not a common enemy to defeat? Was there anyone who wanted to hurt the Germans more than the Jews did? They were ghetto-toughened, and they had survived a perilous journey to get where they were. Would they be just as unwelcome there as elsewhere? Zenia and Leizer shivered through the night, wondering what winter would bring.

Eleven

VANISHED LIKE SMOKE

For my days have vanished like smoke
and my bones are charred like a hearth.
My body is stricken and withered like grass;
too wasted to eat my food;
on account of my vehement groaning
my bones show through my skin.

—PSALM 102:4–6

The liquidation of the Vilna ghetto could not have been more different than Abba Kovner had envisioned less than two years before. On the morning of September 23, 1943, Nazi officer Bruno Kittel appeared in the courtyard of the *Judenrat* and told the remaining ghetto residents that they all would be deported to Estonia and Latvia. The deportation could take place violently or peacefully depending on them, Kittel said. All Jews were to pack their bags and be ready to leave by noon that day.

Jacob Gens was not with him. A few days before, he had been arrested and charged with not reporting the existence and activities of the underground. He had been warned his arrest was imminent, but he had refused to escape while he

Shmuel Kaplinsky
COURTESY OF LEYZER RAN'S
JERUSALEM OF LITHUANIA

could, fearing that other Jews might pay the price for his desertion. In respect for his station, he was told by the chief of the Gestapo, Rolf Neugebauer, that he would have the honor of being shot by him personally.[1] He stood at the edge of a freshly dug hole, felt the barrel of Neugebauer's pistol against his head, and fell dead as the bullet crashed through his brain. Salek Dessler had fled the ghetto with his family after hearing the news.

At FPO headquarters, Kovner was a bundle of nerves. He had received word a week or so before that a number of FPO fighters had been ambushed and killed by German scouts in the Narocz forest.[2] He was advised to take his last group to the Rudnicki forest instead, but because previous groups such as Shlomo Brand's had only been going there for a few weeks, the route was still unfamiliar. He had sent scouts to figure out the best way to get to the forest and to find the base there, but they had not returned.

By September 23, 1943, Abba Kovner had between sixty and eighty FPO members left in the ghetto. The ghetto was being actively cleared of its residents, and Kovner could not wait any longer for the scouts to return. Months before, Shmuel Kaplinsky, a former sanitation department engineer for the city of Vilna, had mapped the sewers for the FPO so they would have one last means of escape if they needed it. Now they did.[3]

Rain had been intermittent, with more expected that day, and because pipes filled and emptied with rainfall, Kaplinsky needed a little time to find a feasible route. A few hours later, he reappeared, black, slimy, and stinking. Rain had raised the water level so much that some pipes were impassable, and it was too risky to stick to the original plan of coming out on the river at the main outlet, near the edge of the city. The new route Kaplinsky had figured out would allow the fighters to keep their heads above water while traveling along a circuitous two-mile route. It would take as long as six hours and would leave them outside the ghetto, but unfortunately well inside the city limits.[4]

It was the only option remaining to the FPO. The ghetto was surrounded and squads of soldiers roamed the streets. By late afternoon, lines of Jews were being driven from the ghetto in the cold rain, amid the sounds of explosions of the buildings in which they had been living. Members of the FPO had been told to make their way to a workshop on Rudnicka Street, across from the *Judenrat*. There, a ladder led to a crawl space that connected to the sewer pipe under the street. Kaplinsky had already entered to guide the group, followed by Morton Shames, with the FPO's only machine gun attached to the inside of his coat, along with two grenades and a loaded gun in his hand. Several dozen more people were in the pipes behind him.[5]

Abba Kovner roamed among the fighters, giving encouragement and last-minute instructions. Once everyone had

A typical Vilna sewer entrance (postwar photo)
BART FAMILY COLLECTION

entered, he would go last, to ensure that any lost or disabled fighters were not left behind. One by one, the remaining members of the Vilna ghetto resistance put their feet on the rungs of the ladder and descended below the main street of the ghetto. Above them, soldiers were prodding the rest of Vilna's Jews toward the ghetto gate. There were mothers, sisters, uncles, cousins whose destiny from that day on the FPO could not change or help to shape. There would be no heroic last gasp of the Vilna ghetto, only this clutching and crawling in the darkness toward the chance to fight again.

The stench of ammonia and sulfur slammed into their nostrils as they reached the bottom of the ladder. They had to feel for the opening to the narrow, ten-foot-long tunnel leading to the main collector pipe, then tuck their heads and shoulders in and begin to crawl. The viscous slime coated their hands and soaked their coat sleeves as they brushed the brick sides of the three-foot-diameter pipe.

Many of the fighters heaved in paroxysms of dry gagging. They shook their heads, squeezing their eyes shut in a frozen gesture of disbelief, and then began moving forward. It was so dark they could only tell the level of the water by the sensation around their legs. The sewer narrowed even more as they slithered along pipes barely larger than the width of their body. Their fingers, numb from the cold, grazed the slimy grit lining the pipes.

In front of them they heard the echoes of choking moans and cries to God. Occasionally, on a long straight stretch they could see the flicker of portable lights that had been distributed among the fighters going through the sewers,[6] but most of the time they crawled in total darkness. Eventually they reached a place where sewer lines crossed, and the space was wide enough to stand up. Trembling with cold and shock, their legs shook so violently that many could barely stand.

A small group had collected there, and several members who had fainted had to be revived after being dragged through the pipes by those in front and back of them. The air in the intersection of the pipes was slightly better, and they all rested for a few minutes, knowing the only way to survive was to go on again into the darkness and the unknown. Kaplinsky had warned them that the pipes would fill if it started raining heavily, and there was still a distinct chance of drowning if they did not finish the journey quickly.

Above them they could now hear the faint rumble of toilets flushing and sinks draining in the Gentile side of Vilna. They knew they were close to the surface, and almost free. The fighters pushed on toward a now visible light and low voices in the distance. When they got closer to the light, a dark figure loomed next to them. "Quiet, you're almost there," a hoarse voice said, motioning to a ladder.

One by one they put their numb feet on the rungs, and with thighs trembling from exposure and fatigue they began to climb. Cool, fresh air seemed to be flowing downward, and then suddenly their faces were in the wet, clean drizzle of the world.

Sonia Madejsker, an FPO scout living on false papers outside the ghetto, helped pull them out and get them on their feet. They stumbled down Ignatowska Street, toward an open door where another woman was beckoning them. More fight-

Ignatowska Street
COURTESY OF LEYZER RAN'S *JERUSALEM OF LITHUANIA*

The road to Rossa Square
COURTESY OF LEYZER RAN'S *JERUSALEM OF LITHUANIA*

ers emerged and stumbled across the cobblestones, the street-lamps forming golden circles in the heavy mist, making halos to light their escape.

Not too far away, the Jews who had been driven by Estonian guards from the ghetto that day, including Bluma and Lizzie, who had already been separated from her three sons, stood all night in the courtyard of a church on Rossa Square, awaiting whatever fate the Nazis chose for them. The last groups marched from the ghetto earlier that month had been safely transported to labor camps, so they waited without undue alarm, expecting that in the morning they would find themselves on the way to Estonia or Latvia.

Perhaps Bluma and Lizzie were glad they decided not to

resist deportation, considering they were still alive. Perhaps they discussed how fearful they were for Leizer and Zenia, and how glad they were that Lizzie's sons had not been part of the resistance. Earlier that evening three members of the FPO, caught as they fled from the sewers toward a safe hiding place at the Kailis work camp, were hung from lampposts in full view of the Jews gathered in Rossa Square.[7]

To Bluma and Lizzie the steady cold rain could only have added to the misery of the last day of their two hard and unhappy years in the ghetto. To the bedraggled and exhausted cadre of members of the FPO, however, the rain felt like a blessing, rinsing the worst of the mud and sewage from their clothing as they made their way through the deserted streets toward their designated hiding places.

Within a few hours of their arrival, most of the fighters were at least somewhat clean, in a change of clothing and jackets without yellow stars, brought by Sonia Madejsker. Bluma and the others who had stood in Rossa Square were not so fortunate. Madejsker and Zelda Treger, another FPO scout, brought news that the last ghetto residents had been herded into a ravine near the train tracks, where some had been ordered into groups for deportation to Estonia and Latvia, and some had been put on trains headed in the direction of the Majdanek death camp in Poland. The rest had been taken to Ponary. Bluma, Lizzie, and her sons were anonymous among the thousands, and Zenia would never learn for certain about their fates except that none survived the war.[8]

Abba Kovner had other things to worry about besides the last of the ghetto Jews. He and about fifty other members of the underground were hiding in the basement of the German Security Police Headquarters on Subocz Street. Two by two, the escapees had left the manhole in the middle of Ignatowska Street and walked through the streets of Vilna, either to the Kailis labor camp or to the hideout on Subocz Street. But the scouts they had waited for in the ghetto were still not there. Now they were more vulnerable than ever, hiding in forbidden territory outside the ghetto.[9]

They could hear the sounds of the German police in the courtyard and above them in the building, as they waited in silence for two days. What might have seemed like a poor choice of a hiding place was, to Kovner's way of thinking, the opposite. They were hiding in one of the few places the Nazis would not think to look. But the longer they stayed, the more inevitable it became that something would give them away. Kovner pored over maps of the area, and when two days had passed with no sign of the scouts, he announced that he would lead them to Rudnicki himself.

On September 26, 1943, shortly after nightfall, the FPO fighters went up a back staircase of Security Police Headquarters, leaving through the same side door through which they had entered, disheveled and exhausted, two days before. A light rain was falling. Spacing themselves so they could see those immediately ahead of them, the fighters began heading for cover a safe distance from the police building. Then, two by two, they stepped out into the streets of Vilna.

Some of the pairs acted like they were on a date, the girl's head resting casually in the hollow of her partner's shoulder, his arm around her back. Others, hands shoved deep in pockets, walked quickly on the forbidden sidewalks. As they walked past brightly lit cafés, and the last merchants locking up their shops, they dared not speak even a word, for their Yiddish would give them away as quickly as the yellow star would have. Now, missing from their chests, it still felt like a phantom presence.

As they neared the bridge leading out of Vilna, they scrambled across the road and down the riverbank. Using the trees as cover, they found a hiding place where they could watch the bridge entrance, which was guarded on both ends by German soldiers. After an hour, approaching midnight, the guards on the far side of the bridge got into a military vehicle and drove off. A few minutes later, the hardest rain of the night began to fall in sheets blown by the wind along the street facing the river. The two soldiers guarding the near side of the bridge ran for cover in a guardhouse that only had windows facing the street. Once inside they could not see the bridge at all.

The first of the fighters scrambled toward the end of the bridge, crawling up over the railing behind the guardhouse. Then they ran, slipping and stumbling on the wet pavement. When they reached the far side, they headed toward a clump of trees. Several more pairs were now running across the bridge. Others were coming out from their hiding places along the riverbank, sliding over the railing and sprinting behind them. Unobserved, the last members of the FPO had made their escape from Vilna.

They spent the rest of the night at their rendezvous point, trying to dry out in front of a small fire. Couriers had brought weapons from hidden caches in the Jewish cemetery, and for most of the night the fighters, too keyed up to sleep, cleaned their guns with meticulous care, without saying a word.

Lithuania's newest partisans left their hideout shortly before dawn. They walked out of sight of the main road, skirting
local villages, until by midday they were weak from hunger. A
few of them raided a farmer's yard, coming back with chick-
ens that they cooked over an open fire. Abba Kovner continued to consult his map, and sent out a few people to scout for
the location of the partisan bases. They came back grim-faced.
They had found the body of one of the missing guides who
had not returned from the scouting mission on which Kovner
had sent her.

Soon they could see a forest immediately ahead. They waited
while the scouts went on to search the woods for signs of the
partisan camp. Instead, they found a patrol specifically waiting
for Kovner's group to arrive. They took them to the camp, but
when they arrived, Kovner's group got no warmer welcome
than Brand's had. The other Jews were no longer there. Having
sensed the hostility of many of the Russian partisans, they had
gone off to set up their own temporary camp nearby, while they
waited for the rest to arrive.

The Soviet partisans themselves had only been in the Rudnicki forest a little while. Since the Nazi invasion of the Soviet
Union, Byelorussia and not Lithuania had served as the stronghold of the Soviet partisans, particularly in the region of the
Narocz forest, just east of the Lithuanian border. It was to
Narocz, approximately seventy miles east of Vilna, where the
first groups of escapees from Vilna and other ghettos had fled.
The Soviet partisan movement in Lithuania had been close to
nonexistent before the middle of 1943, and the partisan camp
in Rudnicki had been established only that summer by a group
of parachutists doing surveillance, developing supply links,

and building a camp in anticipation of the fall arrival of partisans of the southern division of the Lithuanian Brigade. The first Russian partisans arrived at roughly the same time as the first Jewish escapees from Vilna, in early September 1943.

The parachutists' leader, known as Captain Alko, had been willing to absorb only the men in the Jewish groups, and of them, only those with weapons. The Jews who had escaped the ghetto were not about to go along with what amounted to a forest version of Gens's selections. To lose any people or any resource at that early stage might easily have been fatal to them all. Getting food from nearby villages would be an undertaking as risky as any sabotage mission, and it would require weapons and nerves of steel. Villagers were also hungry and afraid of the coming winter, and while they might share more willingly with Lithuanian partisans, whom they perceived as heroic fighters against the German occupiers, Jews were a different story. Why help the few who, at least so far, had escaped their intended fate? No, the first Jewish partisans decided, getting the food they needed would be like fighting a small war every time. Even with all their weapons and all their people it would be hard enough to make it through a Baltic winter.

Furthermore, the idea that women were not equally capable fighters was offensive and inaccurate. In the ghetto, all resistance groups had many female members. Men and women were both involved in combat, espionage, and sabotage missions against the Nazis. Some women, such as Sonia Madejsker, achieved legendary status for their many risky intelligence missions between the various ghettos and the forests. Others, such as Liza Magun, had already died on missions for the underground. Scouts such as Zelda Treger and Dina Grinwald regularly conducted groups escaping the ghetto to camps in the forest.[10] The two women closest to Abba Kovner, Ruszka Korczak and Vitka Kempner, personally took on some of the riskiest assignments. In July 1942, only five months after the FPO was formed, Vitka had led a small group out of the ghetto on the FPO's first mission, blowing up a German train. Vitka herself lashed the pipe bomb and detonator to the track. It was one of the first such acts of Jewish sabotage in all of occupied Europe. The tracks were destroyed, the train was smashed, and two hundred German soldiers going to the front were killed.[11]

The first Jews to reach the Rudnicki forest had been stunned to see how little the Jews' potential contribution was valued. But the reality was even worse than they first thought. All of the first Jewish arrivals at Captain Alko's camp quickly sensed the underlying anti-Semitism among many of the partisans.[12] Lithuanians, including Poles living in Lithuania, were partisans for different reasons than Jews were. Their villages were occupied, their brothers and fathers were shipped off to the front, and their mothers and sisters were frightened and hungry at home, or in some cases deported to Germany for labor. They wanted the Germans out of Lithuania because it was their country, and the Germans had no right to be there. Many of them, however, felt the same way the Germans did about the Jews.

Some partisans were motivated by genuine patriotism, but the ethics of a significant number of them were little different from those of the Lithuanian Snatchers, who had plagued the Jews even before the ghetto. Many people had joined the partisans for no reason at all other than to save their own skin. Some were deserters from the army, and others were wanted by the German authorities for crimes ranging from theft to murder. Few had any claim to the status of hero. To these self-interested partisans, the greater the chance of being shot, the more sense it made to send a Jew out first. Perhaps, these partisans thought, the Jews were good for something after all.

In many partisan camps in Rudnicki and elsewhere, women were usually welcomed, on the assumption that in the face of probable death they would have few qualms about being casual sexual partners for the men. In some cases this was true, adding to the problem for those women who felt otherwise. In the Jewish camps, a stricter sense of morality prevailed, but nevertheless, any Jewish woman caught alone in the woods risked sexual assault from non-Jewish partisans.

If Leizer, Zenia, and their fellow ghetto survivors had come to Rudnicki expecting to be part of a unified effort to defeat the Germans, they saw quickly that they would be disappointed. Would they have to look over their shoulders even when they went into the woods to relieve themselves? How could they march in front of a partisan they knew might be ready to claim his weapon had accidentally misfired into the back of the Jew in front of him? Such things had already happened in Narocz. Life in the forest would be riskier than they had first thought. Clearly, they all decided, it would be best to establish only the necessary connections with other groups, and live and function as far away from them as possible.

Furthermore, though they shared a desire to push the Germans out of Lithuania, the Jews' motivations went beyond that. They had genocide to avenge, brought down to a personal level for each of them by the names and faces of parents, siblings, relatives, and friends beaten, murdered, or simply vanished. They wanted to strike back at the Germans for all the Jews they had already killed, and act preemptively to keep them from killing the rest. Recognizing the importance of establishing their own terms and their own methods for resisting the Nazis, within a few days the Jewish partisans had left Alko's camp and set up their own, a little over a mile away.

The arrival of Kovner's group was followed within a day by the second group of sewer escapees, led by Vitka Kempner. More were sure to be coming from Kovno and elsewhere, and it was already necessary to move the camp to a location more suitable for their growing numbers and for a longer stay. Leizer and others had gone out scouting for a new site deeper in the forest, and when they located another island in the swamp, the Jewish partisans, who continued to arrive daily and numbered close to two hundred in early October, set out to build their new base.

Once the base was nearing completion, Zenia, carrying supplies, left the old camp and followed the scouts across several miles of muddy forest. Pesia Zlotnik-Scheinbaum, the widow of Ilya Scheinbaum, the founder of Yechiel who had been killed in the shoot-out at Strashun Street, was similarly laden just behind her. The two of them were among those assigned to cooking duties for the base.[13] Zenia had gotten to know and like Pesia very well, and was pleased that they were assigned together as camp cooks. The term was often a bit misleading, because the typical fare was nothing more than a soup known as *balanda,* made from unsalted, boiled swamp water, thickened with rye flour. Thin as most of the partisans were, one bowl was almost always enough.

When they got to the log bridge the others had already constructed to cross the swamp to the island, they had to struggle to keep their balance, like intoxicated diners trying to reach the door of a restaurant. Each person on the bridge sent contrary signals to the logs, making them pitch and roll as they took one lurching step after another until they reached the other side. From time to time someone would not be so lucky, and the result was an unintended trip into the swamp.

Leizer was already there, living with the others in tents. Isaac Alter, who had been one of the witnesses at his wedding to Zenia, was now charged with designing and overseeing the building of the Jewish partisan camp. It needed to be well camouflaged both from the ground and from the air, and it had to be well enough built for the partisans to survive the ferocious Lithuanian winter. Their primary tools were shovels and axes, and the swampy ground made exhausting work of moving the sticky and heavy mud.

For each bunker, the partisans dug a ditch and then erected log walls to buttress the earthwork. After standing the walls up, they cut logs for the roof, and once it was in place, they covered it with branches and dirt. In the spring, swamp grasses would sprout, making each bunker look just like a little hill in the forest.

Inside there was room for little more than sleeping space and an oil drum that served as a stove to keep them warm. The bunks were no more than long, wide shelves stretching the length of the bunker on each side, stacked three deep from floor to ceiling. At the beginning, Zenia, Leizer, and the others simply crawled up into any available spot and fell asleep, but over time, people established their personal spots and would find the same little bit of space available for them whenever they went in to sleep.[14]

Kovner was to have his own command headquarters, where meetings would be held and he and his closest advisers would sleep. A separate bunker with a traditional bathhouse and sauna would be constructed as well. After the bathhouse was completed, they placed stones over dried wood, and then started a fire under the stones. When the stones became hot, they poured water over them, creating steam. Not only would the steam from the sauna help them keep clean, but it warmed

The Avengers' camp in the Rudnicki forest, where 108 Jewish partisans lived, consisted of five bunkers and a bathhouse (postwar photo).
BART FAMILY COLLECTION

them in winter and helped them control lice, a constant aggravation in the camp. Every time Leizer and Zenia and the other partisans entered the sauna, lice would fall from them in such numbers it was impossible not to be amazed that anything in that quantity could have been hiding in their hair and the creases in their skin.

The building of the camp left some of the more impetuous among them grumbling that they had not yet seen any action against the Germans. But Kovner was firm. The enemy counted ammunition by the crateful. For the partisans, bullets were so scarce the inventory always included an exact number, in the dozens, and they had only thirty to forty rifles in the whole camp. Kovner had been told they could get explosives more easily than guns, and their efforts would be focused on blowing up German trains and sabotaging their communications and supply lines. If guns and food didn't make it to the front for the other soldiers, they would feel the hands of the Jews on their throats just as surely as if they had killed them directly. But for now, they needed to finish the camp or none of them would survive the winter.

The bunkers were finished in less time than predicted, their completion coinciding with the arrival of a Soviet officer known as Yurgis, who was the head of the southern division of the Lithuanian Brigade. Kovner and the leaders of the various groups living in the camp spent the day in meetings with Yurgis. The camp was abuzz. Now that Yurgis was here, what would happen? Would the Soviets recognize them as a part of the Lithuanian Brigade and begin supplying them with weapons and ammunition? What would they want in return, and who would call the shots about missions? How many Soviet resistance fighters would come to join Yurgis, and would that be good or bad for the Jews?

The day felt odd and rather disorienting. The familiar crashes of falling timbers and banging logs from the building campaign had ceased. Birds sang again and dust hung in the shafts of sunlight, but few of the partisans noticed, they were so busy speculating, debating, and wondering.

The camp was called together the following morning to hear the results of the discussions with Yurgis. The question of whether to keep the Jews together or incorporate them in small numbers into other divisions had been the most divisive aspect of the negotiations. The Soviets wanted the Jews to be as invisible as possible, because they knew that neither Communists nor Jews were popular in Lithuania, and that the Nazis would be able to fan feelings of a Jewish-Communist conspiracy if it were obvious how many of the partisans were Jews. In mixed units, the Jewish presence could be more or less hidden, whereas separate units would only flaunt the existence of Jewish partisans.

Kovner would have nothing to do with that position, arguing that experience had taught that the few Jews in any unit would find themselves discriminated against, weaponless, and servile. Yurgis, who was actually a Jew who had disguised his roots for his own reasons,[15] knew firsthand that Kovner was right, and he eventually conceded. The Jewish partisans in Rudnicki would be part of the Lithuanian Brigade, but they would be allowed to remain in predominantly Jewish units rather than be absorbed piecemeal into other divisions.[16]

Rudnicki's Jews were to be divided into detachments based

on the ghetto from which they had come. The FPO and the Yechiel Struggle Group would all be part of the Vilna detachments. Within the brigade these detachments would bring the groups down to a reasonable size, to make the logistics of camp life easier and to create more cohesive fighting units. The structure would be a military one, with Abba Kovner serving as commander of all Vilna's Jewish partisan detachments. Kovner would remain in the present camp with one of the detachments. The others, with their new leaders, would find sites nearby to build their own camps.

Kovner had drawn up a list of who would belong to each unit. Shmuel Kaplinsky, who had led the FPO through the sewers, was appointed leader of Za Pobedu (To Victory) battalion. Zenia's cousin Fania Bulkin-Wolozni and her husband, Meyer, and Zenia's cousin Chiena Borowska, who later became Shmuel Kaplinsky's wife, were also assigned to Za Pobedu. The Smert Fashizmu (Death to Fascism) battalion would be headed by Jacob Prener, and the Struggle unit by Avrasha Rasel. Kovner continued reading names, and eventually Leizer and Zenia heard their own.[17] They were staying with him. They would be known as Nekamah, the Avengers.

Twelve

SUMMON THAT ELUSIVE HAPPINESS

Sing, accordion—and the blizzard be damned!
Summon that elusive happiness.
In the cold dugout, your inextinguishable love
Keeps me warm.
—FROM "DUGOUT,"
A RUSSIAN PARTISAN SONG
POPULAR WITH THE VILNA PARTISANS

Since the German invasion, the Jews had been prey, and being in the forest did not change that. They had escaped the hunters but were still the prey. For more than two years, Leizer and Zenia and all their partisan companions had been imprisoned by people who treated them as if they were infected with some terrible genetic contagion bringing down the human race, and they carried the psychological damage of this experience with them into the swamps of Rudnicki. Just surviving was not enough for the Jews of the Lithuanian Brigade. Being in Rudnicki was a chance for redemption.

In the ghetto they had been forced to live in a way that made it difficult to stand up and shout that they were not dogs, oxen, or vermin, not scared rabbits or scurrying mice, not lice or plague or any other similar invectives that had been hurled at them in the streets, printed in the newspaper, or whispered loudly enough to make sure that they heard. Leizer, Zenia, and the others had their basic humanity to reaffirm, a statement to make not just to the Germans, but to themselves, to the sky, to the stars, that what had been done to them was so wrong that it had imbalanced the universe.

But they were now living on an island in a swamp, without electricity, running water, a steady food supply, or even, for some, a change of clothing. And winter was clearly coming. The green shoots that had begun to grow on the roofs of the bunkers had gone limp and brown from the morning frosts, and still the partisans had many fewer guns than fighters, and more mouths to feed than there was food. Tension was growing, as it seemed less and less likely that the spectacular acts of revenge that could have in some fashion begun to set things straight psychologically would be forthcoming any time soon.

Kovner's group, however, was not named the Avengers out of some childhood sense that a brave name is a substitute for real bravery. They and the other Jewish detachments could not wait to begin fighting back against the Germans, and on October 7, even before the camps were entirely built, the first groups had gone out to do whatever damage they could with a few tools stolen from the barns of nearby villages. That night, fifty telegraph poles were felled near Vilna, their wires cut and their insulators broken, disrupting military communication between the city of Grodno and Vilna. Four nights later the same operation was repeated along another route, destroying seventy more poles, followed by a third operation within a few days. When the Germans put up road barriers into the Rudnicki forest to try to stop the sabotage, a fourth operation destroyed the barriers.

By the end of October, the Avengers had gotten hold of several English mines from Russian partisans and wanted to use them in the most spectacular way possible. Four partisans, two men and two women, led by Vitka Kempner, penetrated into the heart of Vilna, where the women set timing devices on four electrical transformers while the men put the last device on a mechanical conveyor that delivered water throughout the city. Afterward, Kempner and her partner collected sixty Jewish prisoners from the Kailis fur factory to bring back to the forest.

Kempner had warned the two young men who had blown up the water conveyor to escape with her while they could, because once the mines blew, the Germans would be out in force to find them. They had decided instead to stay in Vilna to rest, and she had clearly been worried about them all the way back to the camp. That night the mood around the campfire was somber. If the men had left Vilna the following morning, as they planned, they should already have arrived.

When news came a few days later that they had been captured by the Gestapo, conversation did not hinge on where they might be or what might be happening to them. There was little point in pretending that the Jews of Rudnicki had not suffered their first fatalities. There would be many others. By the time the war was over, the Avengers and the other Vilna detachments would lose more than one hundred of their fighters, more than a third of the total casualties among the Lithuanian Jewish partisans.[1]

That October they were not yet ready to begin inflicting casualties of their own, but by late fall the situation had changed somewhat. Links to the Soviets had provided the Jews with better access to explosives, though their weapons cache remained small, and many of the partisans were still unarmed. The Russian partisans had no such problem, and they often carried more than one weapon at a time. When new shipments came from Moscow, however, they did not want to give any weapons to the Jews, and initially they even made outrageous demands that Jews give up some of the few weapons they had.

This form of discrimination was similar to the injustices the Jews had faced from the beginning of the Nazi invasion. We despise you, the logic ran, so we will take away what you have, and then we will despise you even more for not having it. In the eyes of the Russian partisans, Jews had never been known as fighters and therefore their weapons could be put to better use by those with more experience in partisan warfare. However, once a Jew no longer had a weapon, he or she was viewed as being of no worth whatsoever. It was a no-win situation, and faced with such contempt, the Jewish partisans took matters into their own hands and began stealing weapons by any means they could.[2]

The Avengers decided to maintain the same policy they had followed in the ghetto regarding possession of weapons. People with their own guns gave them up so that an armory could be created, from which weapons were checked out as needed. One evening Leizer was part of a group of twenty men and women from two Jewish detachments who picked up rifles and rounds of ammunition from the armory and set out for a village about four hours away. Taking turns carrying

Rudnicki partisans marching on assignment
COURTESY OF LEYZER RAN'S *JERUSALEM OF LITHUANIA*

bundles of explosives, by the middle of the night they had crept past the village, avoiding barking dogs and the German sentries in the barracks at the edge of town.

A few days before, Jewish scouts had found a perfect spot just beyond that village for a dramatic sabotage mission against a German supply and troop train. When planning such a mission, partisans would look for a slope or a sharp bend in the tracks, so that a derailing locomotive would bring the train cars down with it. Just outside the village, the railroad tracks ran along a ridge leading down to one of the many small rivers in the area. Two of the fighters secured one mine to the first location selected on the tracks, and then laid a fuse up the slope. Farther down the track, they selected an additional location and repeated the process.[3]

Every night up until then, several trains had crossed that

Jewish partisan setting explosives on the railroad
COURTESY OF LEYZER RAN'S *JERUSALEM OF LITHUANIA*

stretch of track, carrying food, soldiers, and ammunition; when nearly an hour had passed without a train passing, the partisans began to worry that their mission might accomplish nothing that night. They could blow up the tracks and disrupt future transports, but there would be no casualties or loss of equipment unless a train was passing by. If one didn't come soon they would have to give up, for it would take several hours to get back to the forest, and it was too risky to be anywhere else in the daylight.

The sound began low, and then grew distinct and louder before the headlights of a locomotive finally cast a glow down the tracks.

The timing had to be exact. The train had passed over the first mined location and was nearing the second. Then, simultaneously, two deafening explosions ripped the tracks apart. The locomotive appeared to keep going as if it had no need of a track, but the cars behind it created such torque that it careened back, jumped the track, and slipped toward the slope. Behind it, an undulating force pulled a few of the middle cars over the edge in a cacophony of screaming wheels and crumpling metal. The last few cars had been directly hit by one of the bombs and had been lifted in the air, landing on their side. The two cars in front of them jackknifed as they smashed into a car still partly on the track; then they dropped down again with a crash as loud as the sound of the explosives.

Within a minute or two of the wreck, the door of one of the jackknifed cars opened. Not all on board had been injured or killed, despite the ferocity of the crash, and several dozen soldiers were spilling out and opening fire. With bullets whizzing by them, Leizer and the others ran up and over the top of the

Derailed Nazi train COURTESY OF LEYZER RAN'S *JERUSALEM OF LITHUANIA*

ridge and into a thicket along one of the streambeds. They stumbled over fallen branches, slipping on the loose, slimy rocks as they ran from the scene.

Within half an hour they had traveled far enough to rest briefly in the cover provided by a small stand of trees. On the nearby road they could see the headlights of military vehicles racing to the scene where the Avengers had made their first big impression on the enemy.

That night also marked the beginning of what would be a series of losses on such missions. As they approached a local village on their way back, shots rang out, and two of the partisans fell to the ground, where they lay wounded. The rest used precious bullets to drive back the local villagers, who had been patrolling their fields waiting for any partisans who happened to come by.

As partisan numbers grew in the forest, the Germans had stepped up their courtship of the local Polish villagers, offering them food and protection throughout the war if they would help them fight the partisans. Villagers that agreed were given arms and ammunition and encouraged to be as aggressive as they wished in tracking down and killing partisans. The villagers were easily able to figure out where the partisans were going in and out of the woods, and though they didn't venture in after them, they could simply monitor the nearby fields, taking a few victims at a time.

The mission that night had accomplished the intended result, but because of the casualties, it could only be called a qualified success. Kovner disappeared into his bunker the minute they returned to the camp and did not come out until the campfire embers were dying down that evening.

Leizer and Zenia were among the small group still sitting by the fire when Abba's lanky figure came out of the shadows, and he sat down by the fire. The group had come back with soggy boots and had their feet propped up near the coals. They watched until the soles of their boots began to smolder, then pulled them back to cool. Abba propped up his own feet and accepted a cigarette from another partisan. It was an acrid concoction made from newspaper and forest leaves, and after a puff or two, he put it out on the fire ring.

Kovner eventually spoke his mind. Some of them were going to die, and others would be hurt. After all, it was a war. But the partisans were going to need to do something about those villagers who were shooting at them. They had blown up the tracks and derailed the train, but dying going to and from a mission was a waste, and it needed to stop.

The fire in an oil drum that served as their heater had died down to a few embers, casting a faint glow over the sleeping partisans inside the bunker. Zenia and Leizer crawled into what had become their place among the two dozen partisans sharing the bunker, halfway down on the left side. They stared into the darkness, with thoughts of the casualties keeping them awake until nearly dawn.

The next day Leizer went out again. His life had settled into a routine of going on all-night sabotage missions or forays in local villages in search of food, with days of rest scattered in between. He and the other fighters were on the upper end of a pecking order that divided the camp into those who fought and those who did not. The camp included a doctor and a nurse, gun repair specialists, radio operators, and even a

printer who forged pa-
pers and prepared leaflets
on a small press, but no
one else held the stature
of those who went out at
night and came back with
tales of dynamited tracks
and narrow escapes from
ambushes.

Still, life even within
the camp was not with-
out its risks. The biggest
problem for units like the Avengers was other groups roaming
the area, most notably the AK (Armia Krajowa), or Land Army.
It operated under the aegis of the Polish government in exile in
London and was extremely anti-Semitic. Chance encounters between Jewish partisans and the AK members stationed in two
outposts in the Rudnicki forest were almost certain to lead to violence. Shortly after Leizer and Zenia's group arrived, Shlomo
Brand was attacked by a member of the AK. For the rest of the
time they spent in the forest, Brand wore the man's army jacket
as a proud message about who had won the fight.[4]

Food and other resources were scarce, and encounters with
Soviet partisans also had the potential to turn ugly, especially
when it came to sharing with Jews. From time to time Soviet
planes dropped supplies, and the Jews had to struggle with

other Soviet partisans for their share of these drops. The partisans usually knew when and where to expect drops, but the supplies rarely landed exactly on target. When this happened, whichever group arrived first would commandeer all or most of the supplies. For that reason, any Jewish partisan who could be spared would hike through the woods to await a drop, grab quickly whatever he or she could, and hurry back to camp.

When the Russians got there first, they rarely shared equitably. On the other hand, when the Jews were first on the scene, they were accused of interfering with the war effort if they did not turn over much of what they had found.[5] On one occasion Abba Kovner was taken into custody by the Soviet partisan leadership for his refusal to give information about the contents of several crates, still attached to their parachutes, that had been found high in the treetops a few days after a drop. It cost him his formal role as commander of the Jewish detachments, although the Jews continued to call him "Commander" and his replacement was wise enough both not to object and to share the leadership role with him.

Disagreements with Soviet partisan units were rarely violent, but the AK was another matter. One day in January 1944, Zenia stood in a clearing and watched small parachutes dropping from Soviet planes through a pale gray sky.[6] Earlier, the AK had been spotted nearby, so the pickup had to be done swiftly. Zenia and several dozen others ran toward the containers as they fell, and within a few minutes they had scooped up almost everything. Behind them they heard gunfire and saw a small group of AK trying to drive them off from the last of the supplies. She tucked a small box of medical supplies into a bag she held under her arm and carried another in front of her as she rushed along the path back to the camp. Bullets nicked trees a few feet from her, sending splinters of wood into the air, but the AK fell back and did not follow them.

Zenia arrived back at the camp unharmed but shaken. She took the supplies to the medical bunker, and she sat down to calm her nerves as a nurse unpacked the little box Zenia had tucked under her arm. The nurse held up a delousing comb. "Would you look at this," she said. "I've never seen anything like it."

"What?" Zenia said, taking the comb. There, caught in the bent and broken teeth, was a bullet.

"You were carrying that box under your arm?"

Zenia nodded, speechless. She had cheated death once again.[7]

Leizer worried about Zenia back at the camp almost as much as she worried about him out on missions. Smoke from their campfires could not be disguised, and the swamp was now frozen, making access to the island easier and increasing the chances of ambush while the fighters were away. Their thoroughly camouflaged bunkers and the disorienting density of the forest made discovery unlikely, however, and Leizer's worries about Zenia were mostly of other sorts. As fighters were injured, captured, or killed, and as the pace of missions stepped up with fewer fighters to carry them out, camp personnel, including Zenia, had begun filling in as couriers between the units.[8]

More and more often Zenia would spend her days going through the Rudnicki woods to one or another of the Jewish camps. To be a fighter took a certain kind of personality, and

Fania Jocheles slept across from Leizer and Zenia Bart in the bunker.
COURTESY OF VILNA GAON
JEWISH STATE MUSEUM

Zenia had always been con-
tent to support the fighters by
doing her job well back at
camp. But she greatly admired
the women partisans, including Fania Jocheles, who slept
just across from her in their
bunker. Fania went out on
several missions with her husband,[9] and Zenia had hoped there
might be some way that she herself could play a more significant role beyond the boundaries of the camp. Despite the potential for danger posed by the AK, hostile partisans, and
German scouts, as well as the scattering of bandits and rene-
gades who prowled the forest, when Zenia was needed as a
courier she took on the assignment with pride.

As January dragged on, dark and cheerless, other problems
plagued the partisans. They began to suffer from gum disease,
scurvy, and other ailments caused by poor nutrition.[10] Bread
was a luxury, to be given to the sick and wounded in single bite-
sized pieces. Most days there was at least *balanda,* but from
time to time there was not even that.[11] Other times there were
potatoes and meat, or at least a bit of lard and some onions to
vary their diet, but it was still so imbalanced that many of them
simply accepted their chronic coughs, sores, and skin conditions that would not heal. Those who went on food missions

213

brought back what they could, but the truth of it was that most of the people they raided were eating poorly as well.

Food missions were extraordinarily dangerous—much more so than sabotage.[12] Blowing up a train, if everything went smoothly, was one-sided, except for the occasional ambush, firefight with soldiers, or problem with armed villagers on the way to and from the mission. The partisans had learned to set their explosives and then get away as fast as they could. Suppressing their desire to watch their handiwork, they listened in the darkness on their way back to camp for the explosions in the distance, and then sent scouts back to survey the damage later.

Food missions were another matter, for they involved farm families and villagers who were afraid of starvation and willing to protect what little they had with all the means at their disposal. A few times, shortly after their arrival in Rudnicki, the Jews had been able to simply promise payment after victory for supplies from a few local people wishing to help with the resistance,[13] but even then they discovered that most villagers disliked the Jews and the Nazis about equally. However, as time passed and the peasants grew poorer and the number of partisans grew, the Avengers, like everyone else, were forced to turn to thievery and coercion to get what they needed to survive.

The Jewish detachments tried wherever possible to target villages and farms that were known for collaborating with the Germans to harm Jews. For this reason, in the beginning they often went much farther afield than they would otherwise have had to, bringing back food over great distances on foot or using wagons that broke down, got stuck in the snow, or sank in the muddy ruts of dirt roads. Once inside the forest, they had to be careful to cover their tracks back to the camp. This was far easier to do with footprints than wagon wheels, so most missions ended by packing in the new supplies on foot.

The time it took to bring food to the edge of the forest often gave those who had been robbed the chance to alert the Germans, and food parties sometimes had to scatter without their booty even before reaching the woods. They solved this problem either by resorting to villages or farms closer to the edge of the forest so they could escape quickly, or by taking a member of the targeted house hostage and forcing him to use the family wagon to take the supplies to the edge of the forest. The family of the hostage was told that if the Germans were sent after the departing partisans, the hostage would be shot. If not, he would return home unharmed.

By early 1944, missions to procure food, tools, and the occasional weapon and ammunition from local farmhouses had resulted in many partisan casualties, and Leizer and the other Avengers were constantly at risk. The targeted house had to be surrounded so no one could escape to alert the authorities. While some partisans went inside to handle the occupants, others stood watch. The more people who came along, the more hands could carry the booty back to camp, but more lives were endangered as well.

Leizer had gone on so many missions it had become routine, so Zenia was not particularly concerned when his group did not come back as expected from a farmhouse raid. Scouts had been sent out to look for them, and Zenia and the other cooks began to warm water for the meager soup they could prepare if the mission had been unsuccessful. By the time the pots of water were boiling, the scouts had run into camp.

"We have a casualty," she heard one of them say to a group by the campfire. One of the scouts looked momentarily at Zenia, then looked away as the others got up and began running in the direction the scouts were going. Zenia's heart began to race. She felt someone's strong arms wrapped around her to keep her from running out of the camp after them. "Wait here," she was told. "You can't help out there."

Then she saw him, his shirt covered with blood, being helped into camp by another partisan. His blue eyes were narrow and unfocused with pain and loss of blood. She stepped into stride beside him, putting her arm around his waist as they took him to the infirmary.

Zenia had been sitting beside her bandaged and sleeping husband for several hours when one of the fighters came to check on him.

"What happened?" she whispered. Quietly, so as not to waken Leizer, he told Zenia the story.[14]

That night they had approached a farmhouse owned by an anti-Semitic family known to have collaborated with the Nazis. This farmer and his family, the Avengers agreed, were the perfect candidates to be forced to share their winter store of food with the Jews of Rudnicki.

The raid by Leizer and the others on the farmhouse itself had gone well, but the owner had told them, at gunpoint, that there was a stockpile of food hidden in the barn. When Leizer and a few others went to check, they walked into a trap. One of the owner's sons was guarding the barn. When he heard voices speaking in Yiddish, he fired off several rounds, hitting Leizer in the side.

Leizer was carried back to the edge of the forest on the wagon containing the haul of food and weapons, and then had walked with assistance the rest of the way to the camp. Though he had lost a great deal of blood, he had not been hit in any vital organs. Basic but skilled medical care kept his wound from becoming infected, and he was back to his regular duties within a few weeks.

Sabotaging the Germans, getting food, and maintaining the camp required around-the-clock effort, and even in that short recovery period Leizer watched several groups march out on missions without him. One successful food mission brought back several jugs of homemade grain alcohol called *samagon.* Few of the Jewish partisans in Rudnicki drank alcohol, although they took whatever they could get from the farmhouses in the event they needed something to barter with. *Samagon* was popular with the Russians and other non-Jewish partisans, but it was notoriously hard to predict. The percentage of alcohol varied widely. Some of it was so harsh it could barely be swallowed, but occasionally a jug would taste like surprisingly good vodka. Some batches left more vicious hangovers than others, but as with most cheap, homemade spirits, its advocates claimed it was only the first few sips that tasted truly awful.

One of the jugs of *samagon* had been brought out the evening after the mission, although few had taken more than small tastes. The weather had been brutally cold, one of the coldest winters on record, but little snow had fallen and the ground was bare and frozen. That night the stars disappeared and the air grew heavy with impending snowfall. Low clouds were finding their way through the bare branches to the clearing where the Avengers sat smoking and passing the *samagon* around the campfire.

The farmhouse had been well stocked with food preserved for the winter, which the group was happily consuming. The raiding party had also found a hand-cranked gramophone, which they had carried back, along with the only four records they could find.

"Put on Vertinsky," one of them said.

While one cranked, another placed the needle. The muffled crooning sounds of the famous singer seemed to come from somewhere far away as the record crackled and skipped. Rather than going to the next one, they savored the first, playing it again and again until everyone had learned all the words and was singing along. Fania Jocheles and a few of the others had gotten up to dance.

"What else do we have?" someone finally said.

"We have 'Blue Rhapsody,'" one of the women said, looking through the remaining three black discs. She put it on and placed the needle.

They were safe. They were happy. Their stomachs were full. As the familiar notes wafted into the night air, the firelight illuminated the grins on the dancers' faces.[15] Suddenly, just as the record ended, someone said, "Look!"

Snow was falling, enveloping the woods in a rare and precious silence. A few of the partisans moved away from the fire ring to feel the snow falling around them. Zenia put her head on Leizer's shoulder. As the heat from the fire rose, the snowflakes formed a dome over their heads, evaporating into the still air without touching them.

Thirteen

UNDER THE LOFTY, SILENT HEAVENS

We shall remember the day,
The day in its brightness, the sun that rose
Over the bloody conflagration,
The lofty, silent heavens.
We shall remember the mounds of dust
Beneath the gardens in bloom.
The living shall remember their dead
For they are forever before us.

—FROM "YIZKOR FOR YOM HASHOAH" BY ABBA KOVNER

By April 1944 green shoots and the earliest spring flowers poked through patches of snow around the base.[1] These tiny but insistent messages of renewal were largely lost on Zenia and Leizer and the rest of the Jewish partisans, whose camp had turned into one large mud puddle. Emotions swung between loathing the endless squish and slog of wet boots and muddy clothing, and elation at being able to take off the coats they had worn day and night for months. The days were growing longer and warmer, but the mosquitoes and flies seemed to have noticed this as quickly as the partisans had, and soon swats and curses mingled with the forest sounds of nesting birds.

The momentum of the war had turned irrevocably against the Germans over the course of the winter, and this usually settled any discussion among the Avengers as to whether the arrival of spring was something to cheer. The only questions at that point were how long it would take to push the Nazis out of Lithuania, and how much damage Hitler was prepared to do in the process. What he claimed would be a Thousand Year Reich would rise and fall in scarcely 1 percent of that time, and it was not difficult to envision what revenge he might exact on those he perceived as thwarting his plans. Cities leveled, villages burned, farmland scorched—whatever happened, the path to the end of the war would be a painful one for everyone in Lithuania.

And there were still some Lithuanian Jews left alive—a few thousand in the labor camps of Vilna, and a few thousand more deportees in Latvia and Estonia. The survivors tormented Hitler and his followers. The last few Jews were the strongest, the Nazis thought. Had the Final Solution winnowed down the Jews only to accomplish their genetic improvement? It was enough to raise the Nazis' murderous impulses to a fever pitch.

As long as Jews were imprisoned in work camps, there would still be victims on whom the Germans could take out their anger and frustration, still Jews to take out of the equation of the future. When the partisans thought about the Jews in captivity, they feared for them, but most thought there was no new evil to invent. In the middle of April, Abba Kovner and the Jews of Rudnicki found out that they were wrong. There had still been one unimaginable degradation to inflict

Ponary, 1944
COURTESY OF USHMM

on the Jews of Vilna. This time, it would be a sacrilege against both the living and the dead.

It involved Ponary, and the bearers of the story were five men, escorted into the Avengers' camp one afternoon by a group on a reconnaissance mission who had discovered them trying to find their way across the swamp to join the partisans.

Their story was so harrowing that, little by little, the Jews in the camp forgot about the nauseating stench emanating from the five ragged and filthy men. They had been part of a work detail of approximately seventy-six men and four women,[2] assigned to Ponary in the fall of 1943 to destroy the evidence of the slaughter there. They had lived in a covered pit, surrounded by barbed wire and guards with dogs, and worked every day exhuming dead bodies and cremating them.

The remains were not called bodies, or corpses, or even "the dead." The Nazis at Ponary simply referred to them as "figures." Some of them still had their identification papers on them, and from time to time the work crews would find someone they knew. One of them, Isaac Dogim, found the bodies of his mother, wife, three sisters, and two nieces in the middle of one of the pits, and carried them to the bonfire for cremation.[3]

The names of the roles the Jewish captives filled were stunning euphemisms. "Figure pullers" had to take a hook and pull out bodies that the "uncoverers" had found in the pits. "Dentists" checked the uncovered, rotting corpses for gold fillings, which were pulled and given to the German officers.

Jews were forced to dig up bodies of victims who were shot at Ponary.
COURTESY OF LEYZER RAN'S *JERUSALEM OF LITHUANIA*

"Pyre builders" alternated a row of bodies with a row of logs, building an access ramp as the pyre grew higher, and not stopping until three thousand five hundred bodies were ready for burning. "Fire masters" ignited the pyre by soaking it in oil and gasoline, then lighting it with fire bombs and monitoring it to make sure it did not go out. It took four days for the fire to burn sufficiently to cremate the bodies, after which "gold diggers" sifted the ashes for gold and other valuables, such as swallowed gems, that might have been missed. After giving the valuables to the Germans, they broke up any remaining bones with hammers, then mixed the ashes with dirt, to be distributed throughout the forest to complete the cover-up.[4]

Below the top few levels the bodies were unrecognizable. Some of them had been there for two years, and they fell to pieces when they were touched with the hook, but the captives

Pyre builders built rows of bodies and cremated them.
COURTESY OF LEYZER RAN'S *JERUSALEM OF LITHUANIA*

223

had to go down and make sure they got every piece. Sometimes skin slid off the bones, and they had to shovel that up, too.

Life was ruined for them, they said. What had motivated them to escape was not so much the will to survive but the desire to witness, to make sure the world knew what the Nazis were trying to hide.

The prisoners had uncovered and burned nearly sixty thousand bodies in about six months.[5] Unknown to the Nazis, they had also started to dig a tunnel leading from a little storeroom in the back of the hole where they lived. Every night they dug, using spoons, plates, whatever they could find. When they found a handsaw inside the pants of one of the corpses, they used that as well. At times they would shovel into a burial pit

Prisoners (seventy Jews, nine Russians, one Pole) lived in an underground bunker inside this pit, surrounded by two rows of barbed wire, mines, and SS guards. USHMM, COURTESY OF INSTYTUT PAMIECI NARODOWEJ

they hadn't worked on yet, and body parts sagged into the tunnel. Every morning they would fill their jacket pockets and pant legs with dirt and let it out as they worked. Guards would climb down a ladder into their pit to check on them at night, but they never figured out what they were doing.

On April 15 there was a new moon, so they knew it would be darkest then. They had dug beyond the perimeter of the fence surrounding the pit, and after breaking through a foot or two of earth, they would be ready to escape. Because the first few had the best chance of getting out without being discovered, they went out in order of how much digging they had done. They sawed off their shackles and crawled to the end of the tunnel, where the first of them broke through into the night air.

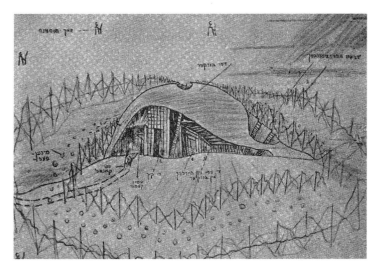

Underground bunker located inside the pit
COURTESY OF LEYZER RAN'S *JERUSALEM OF LITHUANIA*

When they saw the forest ahead of them, they just started running. Suddenly one of them stepped on a dry branch, which snapped underfoot. The Germans heard the noise and threw on a searchlight. Most of the escapees were caught in the glare and were mowed down by machine guns. Those who had already made it to the woods eventually found a river and floated down it, because they could hear dogs barking and knew the animals could pick up their scent better on land. Eventually, when they could no longer hear dogs, the men started hiking toward where they had heard there were Jewish partisan camps. Stopping at night, they buried themselves in manure piles at farmhouses because it was the only thing they thought would mask the stench of rotting and burning human flesh in their clothing, skin, and hair.[6] Their journey had taken five days, without an opportunity to bathe and with almost nothing to eat.

Leizer and the other partisans went through their meager belongings to find a full change of clothes for each of the men, while others went to start a fire in the bathhouse. They created a sauna with hot rocks from the campfire, and handed the men a pail of water and a bar of harsh lye soap. While they bathed and sweated the toxins out of their skin, their old clothing was burned.

The men came out dressed in their new clothes, with raw red skin that glistened in the embers of the dying campfire. Each was assigned a place to sleep, and one of them, Motl Zeidel, settled into Leizer and Zenia's bunker.[7] By the middle of the night, the smell began to emanate again from the five men, and the partisans sleeping near them in the various bunkers had moved as far away as they could to avoid it. The next morning Zeidel and the others were told they must bathe several times a day, and their hair was cut close to their scalps. Their new clothes already stank and had to be washed again and again.

In a few days, they began to smell normal. Within a week, as they sat smoking around the campfire, they were indistinguishable from the other partisans with whom they had just returned from a mission. Indistinguishable, except perhaps for their voices and faces, which reflected the elixir of their first act of well-deserved revenge.

Even before the arrival of the escapees from Ponary, tensions had been unusually high in the Jewish detachments because of the increasing attacks by Polish villagers whenever the partisans left the woods. While returning from a recent mission, villagers had shot and seriously wounded one of the members of another Jewish detachment. Many of the Rudnicki Jews had already fallen in battle against the Nazis and their collaborators. In March of 1944, Abba Kovner wrote and distributed a missive to the *shomrim*.[8] In it, Kovner wrote a *yizhor* to the fallen partisans, "In Memoriam":

> Each one of us, we are the last ones. [Let us remember] our dead that fell in battle and sanctified their names and the honor [of] their people. On its altar they gave the prime of their lives.
>
> Let the movement remember.
>
> Its loyal members, heroes of the destruction, that in the hour of catastrophe and death raised up the banner

of battle and of revenge for the catastrophe, and even with the last of their might, carried it to the very end!

Let the homeland remember.

The memory of its zealots, the last that fell on foreign soil, soaked in the blood of millions of our brethren, and the cry of revenge was on their lips.[9]

After he wrote the missive, Abba Kovner began meeting with other Jewish, Russian, and Lithuanian partisan leaders to plan a response against the Polish villagers who had attacked them. One particular town, Koniuchi, was notorious for its enthusiastic support of the Nazis against the partisans. The Germans had helped the residents fortify their village by building defense trenches and lookout towers, and organizing the men of the town into an antipartisan militia, armed with German rifles and even machine guns.

One day in April a scout returned from Koniuchi. Because he looked "Aryan" and spoke unaccented Polish, he had been able to enter the village posing as a member of a pro-Nazi militia from another village. In the village he had seen the corpses of two Jewish partisans, who had been killed and afterward placed on public display.

When Kovner heard this, he reported the event to the Russian partisan commander, with whom the leaders had already been discussing retaliation against hostile villages. The commander ordered an unprecedented call-up of all available fighters from the various Jewish and non-Jewish brigades in Rudnicki for an attack on Koniuchi.

Leizer and the other Avengers would be part of a small

army of well-armed and trained partisan fighters. They would surround the town from all sides and destroy it. No building was to be left standing. All residents who resisted in any way were to be killed. Only those who surrendered would be spared. They were not to take anything from Koniuchi—no food, no livestock, no valuables. It needed to be clear that they had come for one reason alone, to make the other villages think twice about turning them in or shooting at them as they passed by on their missions.

The fighters disappeared down the path with rifles slung over their backs while Zenia and others at the camp began an edgy and sleepless wait for the fighters' safe return.

By dawn the strike force had surrounded the three land-locked sides of the village and taken control of the river on the fourth side. Several partisans had torched houses, stables, and granaries on the outskirts of the village, while the others began riddling the town with gunfire and incendiary bullets.

The people of Koniuchi returned fire from their houses and defensive positions. The straw roofs burst into flames, and within minutes the German ammunition hidden inside homes began to explode. Soon the whole town was ablaze.[10] Half-clothed villagers, roused from their sleep, jumped out of windows and escaped across the river. Anyone in the town who surrendered was told to leave, but those who fought back or ignored calls for surrender were killed. Within two hours the mission was complete. The town had been leveled, three dozen people were dead, and another dozen had been injured.

Leizer and the other Avengers came back safely from Koniuchi. All any of them had to say was that it was done and that Koniuchi would not be a problem anymore. Once other nearby villages saw the price to be paid, they would most likely not be problems either. Kovner had once said that, unlike the Nazis, the Jewish partisans didn't kill because they wanted people to die. Making an example of Koniuchi had been necessary for their survival, and the validity of their cause made the choice between their survival and that of the people of Koniuchi a defensible one. After the war, when recounting their exploits, Koniuchi was rarely spoken of.[11]

From that point forward, the threats to the Avengers came less from local residents than from the general chaos caused by the German retreat. Though facing defeat and increasingly on the run, German troops were still well armed and more than willing to attack the partisans, whose effectiveness was a humiliation to the Reich and its claims of German invincibility.

By the spring of 1944 the Soviet army had come to see the Rudnicki partisans as more than brave people on the sidelines, willing to create distracting nuisances for the Germans. Now they were strategically located in the path of German retreat and could be used to incapacitate the troops and to form a pincer that would hem in those left behind to defend Vilna. The Soviets began supplying the partisans with more and better weapons and large amounts of explosives. Using these, the Avengers and other Jewish units destroyed miles of train track and critical sections of highways to and from the front in the spring and early summer of 1944.

The Germans, however, were determined to remove the partisan menace from their path of retreat. Troops were diverted from the war front to patrol train tracks and highways, and this made missions far more dangerous than they had been when there were only local villagers to worry about. Other German troops surrounded and laid siege to the Rudnicki forest, conducting meticulous sweeps to find and kill the partisans and destroy their bases. Many in the camps had at that point not been trained to put up a strong defense if they should be discovered while the fighters were gone, because the weapons were continually in use on missions. When arms and ammunition became more available, Zenia learned to fire a rifle and a pistol, as did the others who generally stayed in the camp.

Some of the German patrols in Rudnicki came very close to locating the Avengers' camp. For one week, the danger was so great that the partisans left for a place deeper in the swamp, a temporary camp they called Long Island. But luck was on their side when the German patrols assigned to Rudnicki received a sudden change in orders. Reinforcements were needed after a major loss of German troops on the front, and the patrols disappeared from the forest. The relieved partisans were able to return to their base, finding it intact and undiscovered.

The Red Army was advancing steadily across the occupied parts of the Soviet Union in the late spring, and by June 1944 it was nearing Vilna. It was moving so fast—covering as much as twenty miles a day—that it often went beyond a city or German stronghold without pausing to fight. As it passed beyond, thousands of Germans were trapped inside enemy lines. The

AK and some of the units of the Lithuanian Brigade began patrolling fields and country roads, shooting German soldiers who were trying to find their way back to safety.

The Jewish partisan units, however, were not roaming the countryside in that fashion. They had received orders to participate in the liberation of Vilna, and Soviet officers had arrived in June to brief them about their role. "You are now fighting with the Soviet army," they were told, and some of them received at least parts of a Soviet army uniform. Machine guns and automatic rifles were given out to the seasoned fighters, and for the first time, each partisan's weapon was his or her own to hang on to during the fight for Vilna. A year after giving her mother's jewelry to the underground to help buy a weapon, Zenia finally had one to keep with her in the camp, a hand-me-down rifle from the Avengers' armory.

On July 7, 1944, the Jewish battalions left the Rudnicki forest and marched in plain view in broad daylight along the roads leading north to Vilna. As they passed by villages and farmhouses, some people cheered, but those who had collaborated with the Germans frowned and closed their windows. Their faces were grim for good reason, for already anger against collaborators was rising, and their choice to help the Nazis would be one for which they would pay dearly.

Hundreds of partisans were coming down paths that led out of the Rudnicki forest. Over the course of the day, the road to Vilna would swell with several thousand, Jews and non-Jews alike. Though they were all briefly united, the Jews had learned in their time in the forest that there was little true commonality among them. Even after all the Jewish partisans had done to help liberate Lithuania, many other partisans still would view Jews as unwanted outsiders. They would have no place for the Jews in their thinking once the victory was won.

But for now, as they crossed the Biala Waka Bridge, heading closer to Vilna, spirits were high, and it was time for Zenia to allow herself to hope. Word had reached the camp about a mass execution of HKP workers a week or so before, but Zenia had been told that Rose and Michael were still alive. Rose had been working with most of the camp's other women in a large sewing workshop handling damaged military clothing. Day after day, they washed, sterilized, patched, and restitched the uniforms into usable condition for the next young conscripts. As soon as Vilna was liberated, Leizer and Zenia had decided, they would immediately head for the Cheap Houses.

Partisans marching in liberated Vilna
COURTESY OF GHETTO FIGHTERS' HOUSE, ISRAEL

Perhaps she had not lost everything back in Vilna after all. When the partisans began to sing their camp songs, she joined in heartily. As they reached one of the major crossroads and saw a sign for Vilna, the group burst into the familiar partisan hymn.

"Never say that that you are walking your last road," Zenia and Leizer sang, "the hour we have longed for with all our might is coming. Our step will beat out like a drum—we are here!"

The battle for Vilna lasted over a week, and was fought street by street and house by house. The German *Wehrmacht* was determined to hold on to Vilna and inflict maximum damage on the city. Soviet soldiers, using artillery and armored vehicles, did most of the heavy fighting. In the last phases of the battle, partisans familiar with Vilna led groups of soldiers to places where Germans might still be hiding. Leizer participated in skirmishes with German soldiers ambushed while trying to escape the city. As in the forest, Zenia made herself useful helping in the infirmary and cooking for the partisans.[12]

Michael Lewinson's signature on a list created at HKP work camp
between January and February 1944

FROM THE LITHUANIAN CENTRAL STATE ARCHIVES

Leizer Bart is in the back, wearing a cap.
BART FAMILY COLLECTION

Finally, on July 13, 1944, it was over. Eight thousand Germans had been killed, including a number who had parachuted into the city in a desperate move to reinforce the troops. The Germans were in full retreat not just from Vilna, but from all over Lithuania. Vilna was in shambles. The center of the city was badly damaged by artillery and tank shells, as well as from air raids.

At last, people in the temporary partisan camps outside Vilna were told they could enter town. They would have to be cautious, they were warned, because of unexploded bombs and shells, undetected mines, and unstable buildings. From that point on they were not really part of any army but simply civilians going home; nevertheless, they were told to remain in whatever military clothing they possessed. Though that might make them targets for the isolated

An article published in Soviet newspapers Pravda *and* Red Star *written by well-known Soviet journalist Ilya Ehrenburg about the Jewish partisans liberating Vilna. Ehrenburg, a Jew, was intrigued by the Jewish partisans and wrote several articles about their heroism.*

BART FAMILY COLLECTION

German snipers who were still holed up in town, for the most part announcing their status as veteran fighters in that manner would give them a measure of safety as they walked the streets.

Zenia and some others were driven in the direction of the ghetto, down one of the streets that had once been sealed off. She found Leizer standing silently on Rudnicka Street, near the entry to the *Judenrat*. The ghetto was bare and deserted, except for a few people who had moved in after the last Jews had been marched away. Small groups of partisans wandered around the streets, looking oddly lost in a place they had known intimately for two years.

"Let's go," Leizer said. Zenia did not have to ask where.

A few minutes later, they were part of a group of anxious partisans heading down Subocz Street toward the Cheap

Houses.[13] Upon their arrival they saw a huge mound of fresh earth between the two buildings, and small clusters of bodies lying in the shadows.[14] As they got closer, Zenia saw her mother. She was lying on her side, her face turned toward the wall, wearing an old, frayed sweater Zenia remembered from the ghetto.

"Mama!" Zenia said, as she dropped to her knees beside the body. A wail burst from her and she threw herself down on her mother's neck, taking in great, husky gulps of air as she sobbed.

"Zenia?" Leizer said from a few yards away. She looked up. He had rolled over another body, and she saw Michael, staring with blank eyes at the sky. Zenia toppled to the ground, keening with the passion not just of mourning but also of dashed hopes, of sickness of life, of wishes for blackness to envelop her and take her away. Leizer knelt beside her and lifted her up, holding her in his arms. He rocked her as she wished for death, as she screamed in anger, as she spat in hate, as she surrendered to reality.

"I don't know what to do now," she said, after her tears had subsided. She picked up a handful of dirt and sprinkled a little over her mother's sweater. "How will we bury them?" Leizer held her silently, not knowing what to say.

Zenia got up to go to Michael. "He would have gone with us," she said, as she sprinkled soil on his body. "We said we were going to the forest, and he wanted to go."

Leizer remembered Michael in the kitchen of the ghetto apartment, making his bid for freedom. He had said no to him. Emphatically. No discussion. They were under orders.

There was Rose to think of also, and besides, Michael always seemed too delicate and mild for the path he and Zenia were taking. And now, however necessary and valid their decisions, the consequences lay there in front of them.

It was growing dark. "We need to get back," one of the partisans said to them. "We don't know what the city will be like at night now."

"Yes," Zenia said hollowly. She and Leizer walked arm in arm toward Subocz Street, where the partisans flagged down a passing truck and asked for a ride back to the camp. As they rode through Vilna, the streets were filled with Poles, drinking from bottles of liquor the Nazis had left behind,

Soviet journalist Ilya Ehrenburg (wearing a tie) pictured with a group of partisans. To Ehrenburg's left is Isaac Alter (wearing a cap); behind Alter is Motl Gurwitz; to Alter's right is Israel Weiss.
COURTESY OF LEYZER RAN'S *JERUSALEM OF LITHUANIA*

The Avengers, photographed by Soviet journalist Ilya Ehrenburg on July 14, 1944, one day after Zenia and Leizer found her mother and brother dead. Included are Gedalia Kovner, Yochanan Mersik, Bluma Markowicz, Zelda Treger, Abba Kovner, Ruzka Korczak, Zenia Lewinson-Bart, Leizer Bart, Vitka Kempner, Elhanan Magid, Morton (Motl) Shames, and Abraham Perlstein. USHMM, COURTESY OF YIVO INSTITUTE

shooting guns in the air, and singing songs at the top of their lungs.

The two of them watched the spectacle blankly, as they left Vilna behind and rode in darkness and silence to the camp.

Fourteen

A WORLD WAS HERE

We knew what the hazards were—
to cross the soft earth,
to pass the still glowing iron
and to say to a stranger
—a world was here.

—FROM "MY LITTLE SISTER" (1968), BY ABBA KOVNER

Though the rest of Vilna celebrated the liberation, the Jews did not. For several years the Jewish resistance had concentrated on what was immediately in front of them—a chance to rescue Jews here, a chance to harm Nazis there, chances to survive and chances to avenge. Now there was nothing to fight against and no one left to save. The future yawned, empty, in front of them.

For the Jews, freedom brought with it the opportunity to walk openly in the streets, but the streets were full of ghosts. It brought the power to go home, but offered no home to go to. Boisterous Soviet troops swung around corners on trucks and jeeps, and after a few nights of celebrations, broken liquor bottles filled the gutters where Jews wearing yellow stars had once walked. It felt to the Jewish liberators like the desecration of a cemetery.[1]

And in that cemetery they were still burying their dead. Whenever possible, Jews are buried within twenty-four hours of their death, and the deep burden of leaving Rose and Michael lying in the courtyard of the Cheap Houses had kept Zenia from sleeping. The partisans had told the others in their camp what they had found, and the following morning, a group of them set out with shovels for the Cheap Houses. Several other Jews were already there, looking for their own dead, when Zenia and the others arrived. Working as one, they gathered up the bodies, and buried them as they had died—all together.

They stood over the soft mound when the burial was complete, and followed along as one of the men led them in the mourner's Kaddish. *"Yisgadal v'yiskadash sh'mayh rabo,"* Zenia

Memorial at the Cheap Houses, where HKP prisoners lived—and died (postwar photo) BART FAMILY COLLECTION

and Leizer whispered. "May His great name grow exalted and sanctified."

"May there be abundant peace from heaven, and life upon us and upon Israel," the group murmured. But there was no life there, no peace. The only abundance was death. "He who makes peace in his heights, may He make peace upon us, and upon all Israel." As the group said the final "Amen," Zenia buried herself in Leizer's arms.

No one spoke for a moment, until one of the Jews who had been there when they arrived asked them how they had known the bodies were there. When she heard Zenia's story, she asked, "What was your mother's name?"

"Rose Botwinik," Zenia replied.

"I knew her," the woman said. "She had a son, Michael."

The woman knew the whole story. On the first of July Major Plagge told the inmates of HKP that the German army was leaving Vilna and that the camp was going to be evacuated by the SS. The Jews knew this was not a good sign, as the SS was more likely to kill them all than take the trouble to move them anywhere. The camp was by that point lightly guarded, and as soon as it got dark, some of the inmates hid in sewers and *malines* within the camp, and others ran away to *malines* all over Vilna to save themselves.

The woman had heard some young men talking that afternoon to Zenia's brother, trying to convince him to go with them. They kept saying how he wouldn't listen, how stubborn he was, how this was his last chance to join the partisans and finish off the Nazis. But he wouldn't go. He said, "I'm not going to leave my mother. I will die with her."[2]

Rose and Michael had been part of a group hiding in a well-disguised *maline* in a portion of the basement. With the camp empty of Germans, they had decided the safest course was to remain in hiding there rather than risking the chaos of the streets of Vilna.

The woman had been among those who had left, and she had come back to see if the remaining Jews were still alive. She had gone to the *maline* and found it open and empty. Rose and Michael were among the last few dozen of Vilna's imprisoned Jews to die.

It was only the first of several funerals. A mass burial was held the next day at Zaretche, the Jewish cemetery, for all those, civilian and partisan, who had been killed during the battle for liberation. As more and more Jews arrived in Vilna, either as former residents or as refugees from places that no longer existed, it became clear that a formal memorial for all those who died was an important initial step in moving on.

On September 5, 1944, Leizer and Zenia were part of a procession of several hundred who left the site of the Vilna ghetto for Ponary.[3] A short time later, they arrived in the cool shadows of the forest. People walked quietly along the paths to a central clearing and gathered for a memorial service staged from the flatbeds of army trucks. Words of speeches floated above the sobs and murmured prayers of those who came to honor the nearly sixty thousand Jews whose remains still lay somewhere nearby, or whose ashes floated in the shafts of light filtering through the trees.

Those present rocked and swayed to the words of Yizkor,

The first memorial at Ponary. S. Katcherginski reads "A Letter from Ponary" from the car platform.
COURTESY OF LEYZER RAN'S *JERUSALEM OF LITHUANIA*

asking God to remember the souls of their parents, siblings, and friends, all their aunts, uncles, and cousins they would never see again.

"Ayl molay rachamim shochayn bam'romin," the rabbi chanted. "O God full of mercy, Who dwells on high, grant proper rest on the wings of the Divine Presence, in the lofty levels of the holy and pure ones, who shine like the glow of the firmament . . ."

Millions of memories.

"Let us say amen," the rabbi called out.

The murmured response rose up through the clearing. At the end, a few people turned to walk away, taking each other's arms and bending their heads together. Zenia put her arm around Leizer.

"I need to go to Hrubieshov." Leizer's tone was blunt and simple. The yellow leaves of the aspens shuddered as they walked back through the long shadows of Ponary.

Leizer could not go to Hrubieshov, not then at least. The Soviet army had not liberated Poland, and travel into occupied areas was forbidden. At Auschwitz-Birkenau Jews were still being murdered at a furious pace, and even if travel had been possible, it would have been the height of insanity for any Jew. For Leizer, the journey there was unfinished business, but for the time being, he and Zenia waited, anxiously and unwillingly, in Vilna.

It was clear that liberation had not had a positive impact on Zenia's health. In the forest, the headaches from the concussion she had gotten in the ghetto had abated. In fact, many

Another photo from the memorial at Ponary
COURTESY OF LEYZER RAN'S *JERUSALEM OF LITHUANIA*

of the partisans had made the same comment about their chronic medical problems, and several asserted that they had never had fewer sick days in their lives. Many years later, Jewish partisans would say, with a bit of puzzlement at the oddity, that they had been happy in the forests of Rudnicki.[4]

Eventually, Leizer was able to locate a Russian nurse who treated Zenia for nerves and depression.[5] "Everyone in my family is dead," she told the nurse. "My husband doesn't even know about his. We want to leave Vilna, and I have uncles in the United States that might be able to help us, but I can't write to them because I don't know English."

The nurse had studied English for a while and told Zenia that if she came back with a blank postcard, she would help her fill it out. The next day Zenia waited for her to go off duty, and they found a quiet place to sit.

Zenia told her to address it to her uncle and tell him that she was the only one in the family left alive. "My dear uncle," the nurse wrote in broken but adequate English. "I am to inform you that I, your sister Rosa's daughter left one from the whole family."

The nurse had a suggestion. Zenia's postcard would have to go through Soviet censors, and giving them some good publicity would help ensure the postcard got through. With Zenia's permission the nurse wrote, "I was a Russian partisan and was saved by the glorious Red Army." It wasn't true, but that wasn't important.

There wasn't much room left on the card, so the nurse summarized. "Please inform all the relations about the sorrowful state. I look forward to your answer."

Her uncle's family wouldn't even know she had gotten

married, but there was only a small space in which to mention him. "My husband sends his best wishes" would have to suffice. The nurse finished writing and turned the card over to address it.

"They live in Springfield," Zenia said, "on Belle Street number 91."

The nurse wrote "America Springfeld," and below that the street address, adding Zenia's uncle's name where she could find room. The two of them studied her handiwork, and after the nurse pronounced it ready to send, she asked Zenia, "Do you want to go to America?"

It had been a subject about which she and Leizer had differed all along. Leizer still dreamed of going to Palestine. The idea of what some called "muscular Judaism," working with his hands and his body to build a Jewish homeland, greatly appealed to him. But the conditions under which the settlers lived were very primitive, the work of clearing fields and irrigating the parched land was backbreaking, and relations with the resident Arabs had grown very tense and often violent. For that reason he had acceded to Zenia's wishes to try to build

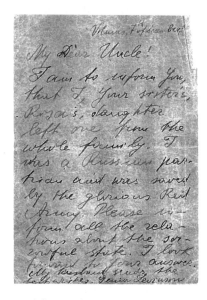

what would be a more stable and comfortable life, more like the one she had before the war, in the United States.

The postcard she held in her hand was the compromise she and Leizer had reached. If things worked out for them in the United States, they would stay. If not, they would leave America for Palestine. But there were still two big "ifs." First, the postcard would have to get to her uncle. Second, Zenia and Leizer would have to get visas, which would require sponsorship by Zenia's American relatives. She took the postcard from the nurse. "Thanks for helping," she said. Maybe her uncle wouldn't write back. She guessed that would settle it.

Whatever happened in the future, they both knew they wanted to leave Vilna as soon as possible. Some Communist partisans such as Chiena Borowska were planning to rebuild their lives there, because the liberation by the Soviets meant that Lithuania would once again be under Communist rule. At the moment, however, they and the other partisans had good reason to try to get out of Vilna as quickly as they could. Some military officials had wanted to conscript the Jewish partisans into the regular Soviet army. This would have meant that after all the hardships of the last few years, and after all the help they had rendered in the liberation, Leizer and the others would have been sent to the front to risk their lives yet again. Within a few days of liberation, many of the partisans found themselves in hiding once again, to avoid being drafted. Another view eventually prevailed, however. The Soviet military command decided there were now so few Jews left, it would be indefensible to do anything that would further reduce the number of survivors. The Jewish partisans were once again safe to come out into the open.

The war was still going on, however, and for the time being, Leizer and Zenia had no choice but to stay in Vilna. Leizer was quickly able to find work under one or another branch of the Soviet bureaucracy, because, as the joke ran, the Communists would hire any Jew on the spot because they were the only ones they could be sure hadn't been collaborating with the Nazis. But Leizer and Zenia agreed that the work was only temporary. Zenia wanted to leave Vilna, now a town of ghosts and heartaches for her, as soon as she could.

By July 1944, the Polish city of Lublin had been retaken by the Red Army. It became the temporary Polish capital and a gathering point for Jews and other refugees. On January 17, 1945, the Germans retreated from Warsaw, and ten days later, the death camp at Auschwitz was liberated. For Polish Jews like Leizer, the wait in Vilna was at an end. Using transit papers hastily procured from a Jewish partisan working for the Soviet administration in Vilna, he left with Zenia at the end of January.

As their train stopped at each checkpoint along the route to Lublin and their papers were checked, they saw the chaos around them. People were on the platforms, sitting by all their possessions, and drunken soldiers staggered by children begging for food. Wedged in his right boot, Leizer had a pistol he had gotten from the Soviet forces during the battle for liberation. When the partisans had been asked to turn in their weapons, he had produced Zenia's rifle and his own, but Leizer was a Polish Jew and no fool. He knew his countrymen. Though Poland was glad to be rid of the Nazis, there were still many Poles who wished Hitler had finished the job on the Jews first. All over his country, Jews returning home were being shot by people who were not going to let the "Jewish problem" go unsolved.

When they reached Lublin, they walked, each carrying one of the two small bags containing all they owned, to 58 Vishinsky Street, where the Vilna partisans who had arrived before them had told them to come. The apartment was already crowded, not just with people Leizer and Zenia knew but with Zionists who had spent the war in the unoccupied parts of the Soviet Union, and those who had survived ghettos and partisan camps all over Europe. In Lublin, the Red Cross and the Joint Distribution Committee had begun a database of survivors, and had begun collecting information from them about others whose fates were known to them. Lublin was a magnet for survivors, and though the streets around the Red Cross and JDC headquarters were crowded with displaced Jews, their numbers were deceptive, as they were, in effect, a small part of the sad remnant of Jewish Europe.

In February, Leizer and Zenia traveled from Lublin to Hrubieshov. Before the war, Hrubieshov had been a town of over ten thousand people, approximately half of them Jews. As they walked through the streets toward Leizer's home, he saw a few people he recognized, all of them Poles.[6]

He called out to one of his neighbors, whom he remembered being a decent man. The neighbor approached him, obviously shocked to see Leizer alive. Leizer had little time for pleasantries. "What happened to my family?" he asked.

With coaxing, he said what Leizer had hoped against hope he would not hear. There had been two pogroms in 1942, one in June and the other in October. Three thousand Jews were taken to the Sobibor death camp. A few days later the Germans took a few hundred more and shot them in the Jewish cemetery. The neighbor did not remember seeing Leizer's mother, father, or brother after that point.

"And my sister?"

"Your sister had already been taken to the woods by some men from the town. She never came back."[7]

Wordlessly, Leizer began to walk at a near run up the street. Zenia, who had never been in Leizer's hometown, was not sure where they were going, and as his pace quickened, she had to struggle to keep up.

He stopped in front of a modest house on a frozen dirt road. "This is it," he said. He heard the urgent barking of a strange dog and saw the familiar curtains in the front window being pulled back. A man looked out at him; then the curtain dropped and he disappeared back into the house.

Leizer opened the gate and walked up to the door. Reaching up instinctively to touch the mezuzah, which Jews place on their doors to remind them of their covenant with God, he saw a splintered hole where it had been pried away. He banged on the door.

The man opened it and asked, "Who are you?"

"I am Leizer Bart and this is my house."

The man stood blocking the doorway. His expression, at first a glare, passed beyond that into a mosaic of hatred and spite. "This is my house now, Yid."

Suddenly Leizer was pointing an army pistol at the man's chest. "This is my house," Leizer repeated. "You have forty-eight hours to get out."

He turned, walked out into the road, and started back toward town. They passed a neighborhood church, where a priest sweeping the steps recognized Leizer and asked what he was doing in town.

"I'm here to take back my family's house and possessions."

The priest set aside his broom. "Do not try to do that," he said, emphasizing each word. "No one will give you anything. There will just be two more dead Jews in Hrubieshov."

Over Leizer's angry protests, the priest went on. "Leave now," he told them. "Leave while you have a chance. Don't even spend the night."[8]

They returned to Lublin after nightfall. Leizer went out alone the next day, wandering around Lublin to clear his head. Zenia stayed in the apartment, curled up in their bunk. When Leizer came back, he told her he wanted to leave Poland as soon as he could. Some of their partisan friends were going to Bucharest to meet up with people who intended to run the British blockades to get into Palestine. He and Zenia had an agreement to try to go to America, and he wasn't going back on it, but they would be able to go with the group only if they claimed they had decided on Palestine. Bucharest seemed to be as good a place as any to be until the war ended. At the very least, it would put a little more distance between them and the scene of so many bad memories. In Poland, it seemed there was nothing to think or talk about but death.

Zenia had lost hope that the relatives in America would write. After all, she hadn't had an address to give them other than Zenia Lewinson in Vilna. She was Zenia Bart in Lublin, or Bucharest, or wherever else homeless Jews might find themselves. Zenia's head injury still plagued her, and it may have contributed to the deep depression into which she had sunk after the liberation of Vilna and the loss of her mother and brother. She didn't care where they went. In fact, she didn't care about much of anything at all.

In less than a month they were in Bucharest. Traveling for the most part without valid transit papers, the Jewish partisans of Vilna rode on the tops of trains and in the freight compartments through areas where the Soviet army was in firm control.[9] Soldiers would board the trains, and when they saw groups of beleaguered and tattered refugees they would ask *"Zhid?"*[10]

In answer, some travelers would simply roll up their sleeves and show their concentration camp tattoos. Where lack of papers might be a problem, or where Jews had continued to be victims of violence, they walked, guided along mountain paths and valleys by Jewish scouts.

Leizer and Zenia rarely spoke unless they needed to. Leizer had always been quiet and shy, so his introversion was not as noticeable as Zenia's. She, who could make everyone smile when she entered a room, who even in the ghetto had lifted spirits, had become listless with severe anemia and had grown so silent and withdrawn he sometimes thought if he pushed her even slightly she would fall over.

In Bucharest they found a doctor to consult about Zenia's health.[11] "I don't have the equipment I need for the right tests," he said to both of them one afternoon in his office. "Still, it's clear you have a significant head injury." He pulled his chair closer to his desk and leaned over it to look at them. "But that isn't what I want to say."

He looked at each of them, waiting until he could get them to look back at him. "You are, in my estimation, seriously de-pressed," he said to Zenia. "That doesn't just mean you are sad, which God knows you have a right to be. It means you are sick with sadness, and the cure is to be less sad."

"How can I be less sad?" Zenia said, shrugging her shoul-ders.

"I am not a Jew, so I won't pretend to know how you feel. But you know our experiences affect us in a way that can make us very, very sick."

He leaned back in his chair and crossed his arms, waiting for her reply. When there was none, he said, more softly, "The war is almost over. If you want the Nazis to finish the job, I just want you to know you're helping them."[12]

The war was indeed almost over. On May 7, 1945, the Ger-mans surrendered. Bucharest was a blaze of light and a roar of sounds as thousands celebrated in the streets. Zenia and Leizer stood in the window of their apartment looking down at the revelers.[13]

"We need to put this behind us," Leizer said, his voice almost drowned out by the sounds of church bells and the pop of exploding tracer shells in the sky. "You know Abba and the others are talking about keeping the Avengers alive and getting revenge against the Germans."

Zenia pulled back to look at him. "The Avengers?"

Leizer nodded. "Six million Jews are dead, they are saying, and he wants the Germans to pay."

Zenia laid her cheek back down against his chest. "I don't think that's a good idea." After a moment she added, "I want to find my family. I think that's the best thing to do." But that was a matter of them finding her.

Soon after, Leizer and Zenia went to Rome, where they settled temporarily in a displaced persons camp known as Cinecittà set up at a site that after the war would become famous as Federico Fellini's studio. By the time they arrived, the weather in Rome was warm, but they had only the winter clothing they had been wearing for months. Zenia was given a light summer dress and cloth jacket, but the only clothing for Leizer was a striped uniform left over from one of the concentration camps. Undaunted, Leizer found work with the Joint Distribution Committee, which was helping Jews reconnect with surviving relatives and resettle in Europe or elsewhere.[14]

Two weeks after they arrived at Cinecittà, Leizer came rushing back to the shelter where he and Zenia slept.

"Look what I have!" he said, waving a letter.[15]

She took it from his hand and stared in disbelief. The post-

Leizer Bart (center, left photo; right, right photo) at Cinecittà DP camp in Rome BART FAMILY COLLECTION

mark was Springfield, Massachusetts. It had taken eight months for Zenia's postcard to arrive in the mailbox of Aaron Fineberg (born Aaron Balcwinik). "What do you need?" Aaron had asked by return mail. "How can we find you? How can we bring you here?"[16]

It was settled. They were going to America. Soon after, they rented a room from the Ferraro family on Via dei Serpenti in Rome and settled in for the long wait to complete the immigration process. Despite the frayed sheets and sagging mattress, to Leizer and Zenia, it was a luxury beyond belief—a place of their own.

· In their married life they had lived in the ghetto, a partisan bunker, crowded apartments in Lublin and Bucharest, and a

Despite the improvements in their living conditions, Zenia and Leizer show the strain of their ordeal.
BART FAMILY COLLECTION

Former partisans gathered for a seder in Rome, 1946. Leizer Bart is pictured at bottom center. COURTESY OF GHETTO FIGHTERS' HOUSE, ISRAEL

camp for displaced persons. Though they had little money and few possessions, life in Rome could not have offered a starker contrast. While many of their partisan friends who had left Vilna were already on their way to Palestine, Isaac Alter and a few others were in Rome, and together they began to construct a more normal life, including, in 1946, celebrating Passover together. Life began to have elements of fun— dinners with new and old friends at a Jewish restaurant on Via Palestro; opportunities to visit tourist attractions, to swim in a local pool, and for Leizer to ride a motorcycle. Most important, the Italians treated their Jewish refugee population with respect, and often with affection. Leizer would often comment later that he had never been treated as well by anyone, other than fellow Jews, as he was by the Italians during his stay in Rome.

Left and center: *Zenia and Leizer Bart in Rome*   Right: *Leizer Bart with friends in Rome*   BART FAMILY COLLECTION

But Zenia had something nagging at her. As a Jew, it was important to her to know that her wedding ceremony had been conducted validly under Jewish law. She knew there were a few things that had been different about it. They didn't have a minyan, and some of the details she remembered from other weddings had been skipped. She hadn't been overly concerned before that point, because for their whole marriage they had slept in their clothes, crammed in with others into ghetto rooms and forest bunkers, but now that they had their own bedroom, she found herself wondering whether she was living with someone to whom she was not properly married.

To Leizer it seemed like an odd thing to worry about, but he could see that Zenia was truly bothered. Two of their witnesses, Isaac Alter and Abram Dimitrowski, had settled temporarily in Rome as well, and he asked for their help. On January 3, 1946,

Leizer Bart, on the motorcycle, pictured with friends
BART FAMILY COLLECTION

they all appeared before the Chief Rabbi in Rome, who, after talking with them, certified that the wedding had been performed in accordance with Jewish law and thus had been valid since that day long ago in the ghetto.

Exactly two years later, on January 3, 1948, Leizer and Zenia stepped onto the *Marine Perch,* a former troop ship leaving from Naples for New York. It had taken that much time to complete the process of getting letters of support from Zenia's American family, securing visas to travel, and working with the Joint Distribution Committee to get a place on a ship leaving Italy. It was scarcely a honeymoon cruise. While Zenia had been

Zenia and Leizer Bart BART FAMILY COLLECTION

COMUNITÀ ISRAELITICA DI ROMA

UFFICIO RABBINICO

CERTIFICATO

N. _____   *Roma,* 3 Gennaio 1946
                                                     Rosc Hodesc 5706

        Noi sottoscritti dichiariamo di esser stati presenti
al matrimonio celebrato in Vilna(Ghetto) nel giorno di Lag Baomer
1943 fra il Sig. Eliezer Barth nato a Hrubiescuif il 15 Giugno 1915
e ora abitante a Roma Via dei Serpenti N°170/13 e la Sig.na
Genia Löwinson nata a Vilana(Ghetto) il 5 Giugno 1922 e ora abitante
a Roma come sopra.
Izsak Alter via Alessandria 25/3 *Izsak Alter*
Abram Dimitrowski via Regina Margherita 206/8 *Abram Dimitrowski*
Sulla base della testimonianza di cui sopra è stato da questo
Ufficio Rabbinico convalidato il matrimonio fra i coniagi sunnominati
secondo l'antico uso vigente ancor oggi in Erez Israel.

        Abram Dimitrowski   *Izsak Alter*

Marriage certificate prepared by the Chief Rabbi in Rome, in which two surviving witnesses certified Leizer and Zenia's wedding in the Vilna ghetto
BART FAMILY COLLECTION

assigned a bed in officers' class, Leizer made do in troop class.

They met up on the deck during the day to huddle under blankets as they crossed the Atlantic. They were still young—twenty-five and thirty-two years old—and beginning to feel it

Receipt for passage on
the Marine Perch
BART FAMILY COLLECTION

was safe to think they had a future, even if they didn't know what it held. Still, like other survivors, they were afloat in time, with nothing to hold them in place but the dark waters of a past in which they did not wish to anchor.

The golden path across the water began with the setting sun and ended in the white foam that hissed against the waterline of the ship. Leizer and Zenia sat in a gray wool cocoon, in the middle of an enormous ocean. Soon they would emerge and take on the changed shape of their life, but for now they just lay still, as the ocean whispered below them and the silent moon hovered on the horizon.

Epilogue

PERHAPS—UNTIL LIGHT

Remember: until our last breath—our first proclamation read. That
was many long days ago. Two years of bloody conflict. We shall continue until the last breath! And perhaps—until light.
—FROM THE BATTLE REGULATIONS OF THE FPO

Everybody smile," the waiter says, raising the camera and
poising his finger on the button.

The men turn to look at him. Their hands rest comfortably
on the table, their fingers curled around cigarettes and wine-
glasses. Two offer slight smiles to the camera while one, his
shoulders turned almost square, confronts the lens as if daring
the viewer to interpret his feelings. A woman at the far end,
leaning on her elbow, looks at a young couple on the other
side of the table with a smile that seems to mix puzzlement
with admiration.

It is that couple whose presence has brought the group together to celebrate. They are Leizer and Zenia Bart. That
morning they had stepped ashore in New York from the *Marine Perch*. Within hours they were seated here, in the Old Romania Restaurant, Zenia and Leizer together, with Uncle Aaron

Leizer and Zenia, with Uncle Aaron to their left and cousin Jeanette Greenberg across the table, at the Old Romanian Restaurant upon arrival in New York BART FAMILY COLLECTION

on her left. Perhaps he is understanding for the first time what Zenia meant in her postcard from Vilna, that she was "left one of the family." He will have to search her face for glimpses of everyone he remembers, for he will never see any of his other Vilna relatives again.

Zenia and Leizer push stiffly against the back of their chairs, their shoulders thrown back and their hands on their thighs, as if bracing themselves for whatever might come next. Perhaps they do not quite understand that it is over, that they have left war behind, left Europe behind, and that they are now in a place where what will begin to seem surreal is the

*Uncle Aaron Balcwinik, also
known as Aaron Fineberg*
BART FAMILY COLLECTION

ghetto and the forest, and
what will seem normal is
this crowded restaurant,
with its white tablecloths,
its crystal, and its starched
napkins.

Zenia looks at the cam-
era, with a focused, pre-
pared expression. Wearing
a jaunty hat over her coiffed
hair, and a crisp, white-
collared blouse under a plain, dark suit, she looks the picture of
propriety. A smile plays on her lips, but her eyes are tired. Perhaps in time she will look her age, but today the camera has
recorded someone who might be taken for older.

Leizer is a study in frozen angularity. His fingers are
splayed on his thighs, and his legs are braced forward under
the table, as if to save the extra half second that might be required for him to spring to his feet. The muscles of his jaw
have retracted his chin toward his ears.

Has he heard the call to smile for the camera? Perhaps, but
he is not ready to respond to it. In later years, as he learns to
speak the language of his new land, as he holds his babies in
his arms, as he builds a career and buys a home, he will come
to smile at a raised camera, but for now he stares, not amus-
edly at the commotion around him, but at nothing.

Nothing? Or possibly everything. Is he picturing the ghetto gate, or the forest? Is he picturing bodies thrown from derailed and crumpling trains, or running from burning homes in Koniuchi? Or is his mind a blank, overwhelmed with the events of a day that concluded his journey out of Europe with an extravaganza of plenty—a crowded restaurant, wine, and the promise of more food than his stomach can bear? Or is he simply a shy man, tongue-tied by the buzz of English being spoken at the tables around him, amazed at how different this table of Jews is from any other he has known? Whatever is on his mind, it is clear that he is not there.

He will go to a hotel that night and sleep beside Zenia in a bed with sheets that give off the smell of no past, that receive the weight of a body still not yet completely reconnected with a mind that keeps wandering, keeps seeing what it wishes to avoid.

She will put her arms around him. She will smell clean, like flowers. Tomorrow they will pack their meager belongings and go with Aaron to his home in "America Springfeld." It will be Zenia's turn to stare at faces that remind her of what she has lost. It will be the first chance they have to discover that, despite everything, there still is a family they can call their own. It will take years for that to feel like a victory.

But victories will come. Leizer will work four years as a shipping clerk for Uncle Aaron while he and Zenia go to night school to learn English.[1] After a year, Leizer's English will be good enough to start a career as a sales representative. Eighteen months after arriving in the United States, they will have their first child and buy their first house. Perhaps in that moment they will experience, for the first time, what it means to have survived.

Still, the scars will never leave. Leizer will live the remainder of his life with serious damage to his lung capacity caused by the months in the forest and his participation in many all-night missions during one of the coldest winters on record. It will take excellent medical care, and Zenia's love and constant support and companionship, to enable him to live beyond the five to ten years predicted by his doctors. Zenia will be plagued for years by headaches and nervous conditions.[2] Eventually she will develop Alzheimer's disease, and before her death she will suffer severe anxiety and hallucinations about being forced into a concentration camp. An MRI will reveal evidence of the brain trauma she experienced at the hands of a Nazi soldier in the ghetto, an injury which may well have contributed to her memory loss and dementia.

In 1966, Leizer, age fifty-one, and Zenia, age forty-four, will buy the home they will live in for the rest of their lives. Zenia will devote her life to being a homemaker, wife, and mother. They will join various Jewish social organizations, contributing tirelessly to charitable causes and building a large circle of friends. Leizer will die first, at age eighty-one, leaving Zenia behind for six more years before she too will take her last breath, shortly before her own eighty-first birthday.

But for now, in the restaurant, they can do nothing but sit, blown back by the moment, and by the experiences of the past. The cameraman finishes his count of three, and the flash explodes.

MEMBERS OF THE FAMILY
WHO DIED IN THE HOLOCAUST

This list includes members of the immediate Lewinson-Bart family among the six million Jews who perished in the Holocaust. In addition, there are countless other relatives known to Zenia and Leizer whose names have been lost to us.

Vilna, Lithuania

Bluma Rosaler-Balcwinik

Rikla (Rose) Balcwinik-Lewinson-Botwinik

Gershon (Hillel) Botwinik

Michael (Misha) Lewinson

Elizabeth (Lizzie) Balcwinik-Skolnicki

Avraham Skolnicki

Shashka Skolnicki

Nachum Skolnicki

Sonia Balcwinik-Bulkin

Avraham Bulkin

Sima Bulkin

Hrubieshov, Poland

Israel David Bart

Ida Bayla Gal-Bart

Michael Bart

Munia (Mindy) Bart

NOTES

Note: Zenia Bart wrote a number of letters now in Michael Bart's possession; unless otherwise indicated, any reference to or quotation from a letter is attributable to her.

Preface

1. Laurel and I are listed as coauthors on the book, although our contributions were distinctly different. She did all the writing for the text. I shared information with her about my family, told to me either by my parents, other Holocaust survivors, or relatives. I provided her with numerous books, articles, documents, letters, and other material I had collected during my years of research. I was also responsible for reviewing the text to ensure, to the best of my ability, that it was accurate.

2. Sakowicz, *Ponary Diary,* vi.

One: Before and After

1. Yad Vashem Central Database of Testimony given by Fania Bulkin-Wolozni-Srebernik, June 1956, states that Gershon (Hillel) Botwinik, married to Rikla (Rose), was a wood merchant.

Notes

2. A 1989 letter states, "My parents had a store"; the *1929 Annuaire De la Pologne* and *1929 Vilna Business Directory* list the Lewinsons' stationery (office supply) business at 7 Sadowa Street.

3. A 1989 letter states, "I was going to a private school, my brother Michael was very nice, [and we were a] close family."

4. A 1989 letter states, "Our grandma lived on 29 Zawalna Street"; the *1929 Annuaire De la Pologne* and *1929 Vilna Business Directory* list the Balcwiniks' hay and grain business. Fania Bulkin-Wolozni-Srebernik's letter dated February 2004 to Michael Bart states, "Your mother [Zenia] and family lived with Grandma Bluma at 29 Zawalna Street."

5. February 2, 1985, letter states, "Lizzie was the oldest, she had three sons: Shashka, Avraham, and Nachum, born in Vilna. [Next oldest daughter] Sonia, [married to] Avraham Bulkin, born in Vilna a girl Sima, [and] Fania"; Yad Vashem Central Database of Testimony given by Fania Bulkin-Wolozni-Srebernik, June 1956, states, "Lizzie was married to Wolf Skolnicki; Nachum Skolnicki, born in 1920, was married to Bluma and had one child, Tzila; Avraham Skolnicki was married."

6. A 1950s letter states, "Our family (one brother, mother, father, and myself) were comfortably well off."

7. Rickie Leiter's genealogy of the Balcwinik family tree done with the help of Bluma Balcwinik's son Aaron Fineberg and her granddaughter Zenia Bart in 1985 states, "Bluma ran [a] grain business. Shrewd business woman, sold grain to Russian army for their horses."

8. A 1989 letter states, "Before the war we could go or do what we wanted, of course the Jews weren't the chosen people, but everyone made a living. Vilna had a large Jewish population, lots of schools, seminars."

9. Maks Etingin has provided a great deal of information through numerous conversations with Michael and in his family's videotaped interview in 2001. Maks Etingin's videotape states, "My family celebrated the Jewish holidays and went to the synagogue a couple of times per year. My parents weren't that religious, but my grandfather was"; Zenia Bart told her son Michael that Maks Etingin's mother was good friends with her mother, Rose Lewinson. And Rose Lewinson married Maks Etingin's great-uncle Hillel Botwinik.

10. Zenia Bart's friend Louis Niebulski from Lida, now living in San Diego, told Michael in 2005 that Zenia attended the Epstein-Szpeizer Gymnasium. A graduate of the Epstein-Szpeizer Gymnasium videotaped in 2005 recalled living at 10 Zawalna, now 8 Zawalna. It took him twenty-five minutes to walk to school. He went to school every morning at 9:00 A.M., except on Shabbos. The school was private, and was the most expensive school in Vilna—costing six hundred zlotys per month. In comparison, Rachel Margoles, who worked in the ghetto library, told Michael in Vilnius in 2005 that she paid only two hundred zlotys per month to attend the Tarbut Gymnasium.

11. The Etingin family lived on Zeligowsky Street, according to a statement written by Sonia Etingin dated November 1971.

12. Zenia Bart told Michael, "I should have been killed many times. The first time was the day of the bombing in Vilna when I was taking something over to a relative's house. Later I found out that the building had been flattened"; Maks Etingin's videotape states, "Our house was bombed out the first day. We were in a park across the street from the house. And our neighbor's son was killed, on the same stairs. I remember when I came to the apartment; it was completely demolished—completely demolished. Everything we had was completely in shambles. We ended up not having anything."

13. Arad, *Ghetto in Flames,* 27.

14. Kowalski, *Secret Press,* 30–31; Arad, *Ghetto in Flames,* 10–12, 35–38.

15. Dawidowicz, *From That Place and Time,* 164–185; Gilbert, *The Holocaust,* 53–56, 60; Levine, *Fugitives of the Forest,* 191–192.

16. Arad, *Ghetto in Flames,* 25–26.

17. Kostanian, *Jewish Life in Lithuania,* 68; Shneidman, *Jerusalem of Lithuania,* 11.

18. Shneidman, *Jerusalem of Lithuania,* 11.

19. Kostanian, *Jewish Life in Lithuania,* 68–70; Shneidman, *Jerusalem of Lithuania,* 30.

20. Maks Etingin's videotape states, "Poland was divided by the powers, by Hitler and Stalin, into two parts: the part which was occupied by the Germans, and where we were living was occupied by the Soviets. The

life changed completely because it was a different type of regime. My father's [car dealership] business was taken away. And he had a job that he went to for eight hours . . . people who were pretty well off and had anything to do with the government started to be deported into Russia—deep into the Soviet Union. And at the time there was fear at home that we will be deported."

21. Levin, *Fighting Back,* 23; Shneidman, *Jerusalem of Lithuania,* 19. Note that statistics in regard to the Jewish population of Vilna before and during the Nazi occupation vary from source to source.

22. Mike Zaks, a member of the New Life Club of San Diego videotaped in 2007, states, "Leizer Bart I met in 1938 [in Czestochowa, Poland] sometime in the spring, when I was thirteen [years old] in April. Then I joined the youth organization of Shomer Hatzair and we went this time to visit a *hakhsharah,* which is a farm. . . . All the youngsters, and later on the young teenagers and so on, they went to work on a farm. The farms trained them farming and growing of fruits on the trees, and with animals, so that if they go to Palestine they will not be greenhorns, they will learn what they should know about farming. And that was most of the youngsters who went to the kibbutzim because the young Jewish people in Poland had no future because of anti-Semitism." Michael asked him if he recalled any hooliganism at the *hakhsharah.* Mike replied, "I didn't read about it, I experienced it. The day after [I went to the *hakhsharah*] the Polish hooligans attacked the *hakhsharah* of several hundred Jewish children. They beat them up, they cut them up. And we as youngsters, we ran to the Jewish hospital, there was a large Jewish hospital. About a mile and a half from *hakhsharah,* two miles. And we ran to see what was going on because we heard that the *hakhsharah* was attacked by hooligans. And they did quite a lot of damage to the Jewish children. They cut them up terrible." Michael asked, "These were local Poles?" Mike replied, "Yes." Mike also mentioned that at that time Leizer had been there for several years studying agronomy, in order to go to Palestine. Leizer was one of the leaders at the *hakhsharah* when Mike Zaks met him.

23. Cohen, *Avengers,* 17; Arad, *Ghetto in Flames,* 19.

24. Leizer Bart told Michael that he worried about his parents, sister, and brother, but he always thought that if the Germans invaded, his family

could cross the Bug River into Russia. He said that his sister was too young, but he begged his brother to leave Hrubieshov with him, and he refused because he wanted to stay with his parents.

25. Sugihara, *Visas for Life,* 29; Shneidman, *Jerusalem of Lithuania,* 24. Leizer Bart told Michael that he had gotten a visa from a Japanese woman in Kovno, but he had run out of time to use it.

Two: The City That Went Forth a Thousand

1. Guzenberg, *List of Ghetto Prisoners,* vol. 1, 52: census in the Vilna ghetto taken by the Lithuanians in 1942 and transcribed by the Vilna Gaon Jewish State Museum. Sources vary widely about population figures, but this is a widely accepted approximation.

2. Maks Etingin told Michael Bart in 2004 that he remembered his great-uncle Hillel Botwinik's farm called the Boulders.

3. A 1985 letter states, "Rose and Lizzie lived in Springfield [Mass.] for a couple of years, and returned back to Vilna, so then Aaron came, but he was smart to stay [in the United States]"; Rickie Leiter's genealogy of the Balcwinik family done in 1985 states, "Lizzie Balcwinik returned to Vilna after hearing about the 'easy life [in Vilna]' from her sister Rose."

4. Shneidman, *Jerusalem of Lithuania*, 56.

5. Maks Etingin's videotape states, "It took a couple of days for the Germans to roll into Vilna. As soon as they came, right away we felt a great deal of trouble for us."

6. Arad, *Ghetto in Flames,* 46; Levin, *Fighting Back,* 95.

7. Arad, *Ghetto in Flames,* 43.

8. Ibid., 44–46.

9. Shneidman, *Jerusalem of Lithuania*, 56.

10. Arad, *Ghetto in Flames,* 65–67; Shneidman, *Jerusalem of Lithuania,* 55–56; Maks Etingin's videotape states, "Together with the German army, the special troops came—the Gestapo, and the SS—and they were lining through the Jewish neighborhoods and starting to administer new anti-Jewish laws . . . we ended up a couple of blocks away from our house. My parents' friends took us in—an engineer, and his wife a doctor. . . . [After we moved,] every couple of days the Germans were coming in and looking for documents, looking for valuables, and making things difficult for the

Jewish population. And the local population—the Poles and the Lithuanians—weren't much better because somehow they felt they were getting even with the Jews and they were very much happy that they can cause the Jewish population all kinds of troubles. And their life became very difficult."

11. Shneidman, *Jerusalem of Lithuania,* 58.

12. A 1950s letter states that "for our daily bread we formed lines—waiting for hours."

13. Kruk, *Last Days,* 60. Kruk's diary states, "An order was posted that Jews are not allowed to appear on many streets, for example, Wielka, Niemiecka, Trocka, Zawalna, Mickiewicz, etc. Jews who live on those streets must go to the closest corner and walk from there through the side streets."

14. A 1989 letter states, "As my high school graduation was near, war broke off all normal life. All our hopes and plans were destroyed."

15. Maks Etingin's videotape states, "The consequences at that time if you were helping the Jews, you became as guilty, or as hounded as the Jews. People used to get shot just for helping the Jews. There were not many people that were helping, but certainly the people who were helping were prosecuted."

16. Arad, *Ghetto in Flames,* 67–68.

17. Kostanian, *Jewish Life in Lithuania,* 188–189.

18. Arad, *Ghetto in Flames,* 69.

19. Sakowicz, *Ponary Diary,* 12. Sakowicz, a local Pole, witnessed the extermination site at Ponary. He lived in a cottage overlooking the site. Sakowicz's diary states, "By the second day, July 12, a Saturday, we already knew what was going on, because at 3 P.M. a large group of Jews was taken to the forest, about 300, mainly intelligentsia with suitcases, beautifully dressed, known for their good economic situation, etc. An hour later the volleys began. Ten people were shot at a time. They took off their overcoats, caps, and shoes (but not their trousers!). Executions continue on the following days: July 13, 14, 15, 16, 17, 18, and 19, a Saturday. The Lithuanian Riflemen's Association does the shooting"; 1950s letter states, "One day the Germans took Jewish men to do one day's work, supposedly. That was the last time I saw my father"; Zenia's reply to a letter dated April 25, 1965, states, "My father . . . was taken away July 13, 1941, and

liquidated at Ponary—that is outside of Vilna"; Maks Etingin's videotape states, "For the first time in my life, I started to know what fear is . . . when you are a teenager, you don't know what fear is, but I started to experience fear. I started to see the menacing German soldiers beating up Jews on the street, I started to hear about Lithuanian militia taking Jews, supposedly, to work groups and they did not return home. Those people who were picked up on the street did not return home. Somehow there was a belief that they were taken to camps. Actually, later on we found out they were not taken to camps, but taken outside of Vilna, to a place that is called Ponary, and they were shot to death."

Three: The Stones Burst into Tears

1. Arad, *Ghetto in Flames,* 77.
2. Isaiah 1:8.
3. Arad, *Ghetto in Flames,* 58–59; Kruk, *Last Days,* 52. Kruk's diary states that "on July 4, 1941 an automobile arrived on Zydowska Street, in front of the Synagogue yard, and two Germans emerged with rifles on their shoulders. . . . [T]hey announced 'we order you to set up a Jewish representative body today and present it to us tomorrow.' "
4. Arad, *Ghetto in Flames,* 95–97; Lazar, *Destruction and Resistance,* 19.
5. Kruk, *Last Days,* 72.
6. Arad, *Ghetto in Flames,* 77.
7. Ibid., 74
8. Ibid., 72.
9. Ibid., 102.
10. Ibid., 108.
11. A 1950s letter states, "At five minutes notice we were all ordered to leave the homes we had known for generations and all of our possessions. Our destination was the concentration camp." Ghettos were, in fact, properly called concentration camps.

Four: Days with No Answer

1. Guzenberg, *List of Prisoners,* vol. 1, 101, records the Lewinson and Etingin families as residing at 5-3 Karmelitu, the Lithuanian name for Bosaczkowa Street.

2. Maks Etingin's videotape states, "All the Jews were rounded off and put into a designated ghetto place. It just so happened that our family moved to the area which became ghetto before the ghetto was established. So in one way we were lucky that we did not have to move when the whole Jewish population of Vilna moved to ghetto."

3. Maks Etingin's videotape states, "I remember standing in the window when the Jews of Vilna were evacuated from the places they lived into the ghetto. I remember the streams of people moving to the ghetto being beaten by the Lithuanian policemen, and by the German SS. It was really a horrifying picture—the elderly, with children's wagons, with small children on them, with very few possessions. A mass of people, just moving towards the ghetto—it was a picture that I will never forget. It somehow very much stands out in my mind."

4. Arad, *Ghetto in Flames*, 204.

5. Fania Bulkin-Wolozni-Srebernik's letter to Michael Bart dated 2004 states, "Zenia's Grandmother Bluma lived with her mother [Rose], and Zenia, they all lived in one room [in the ghetto]"; Maks Etingin's videotape states, "There were twenty to twenty-five people in the one small room, and there were four rooms, so there were about one hundred people in the apartment. . . . Four or five people slept in one bed, and more slept around the bed. There was only one bathroom, one kitchen, one stove, so you really had to share everything. You share everything under those conditions, people get very irritated. They are getting angry at each other, they are getting at each other's throats. There were many fights. There were incomplete families because some of the families were already decimated—their father was taken away, their brother was taken away. In the beginning they believed that those people were alive, then they started to realize that those people were done with already. So there was a lot of nervousness and a lot of tension"; 1950s letter states that "our family and five other families were thrown into one room."

6. Arad, *Ghetto in Flames*, 121.

7. Kruk, *Last Days*, 470.

8. Ibid., 104.

9. Guzenberg, *List of Prisoners*, vol. 1, 71–80. Many of the Jewish ghetto administration and the ghetto police were housed at 3 Arkliu Street; Arad, *Ghetto in Flames*, 128. Konska Street was known in Lithuanian as Arkliu.

10. Maks Etingin told Michael Bart, "We hung sheets from the ceiling, dividing the room into sections for each family, in order to have some privacy."

11. February 2, 1985, letter states, "Lizzie was in the ghetto, she had three sons"; Fania Bulkin-Wolozni-Srebernik's letter dated 2004 states, "Lizzie and her husband [Wolf Skolnicki] lived in the ghetto."

12. Guzenberg, *List of Prisoners,* vol. 1, 101, shows Maks Etingin's father Abram's profession as a mechanic. According to Michael Bart's conversation with Maks, his father worked at the same location as Zenia, and he remembered the name of their workplace as the "Lost Gathering Point"; Fania Bulkin-Wolozni-Srebernik's letter to Michael Bart postmarked August 2001 states, "Your mother worked at the rail station in Vilna, and she worked very, very hard—Cleaning, sweeping, etc"; Zenia Bart told Michael that she cooked and did laundry for the Germans.

13. Guzenburg, *List of Prisoners,* vol. 1, 101, shows Michael Lewinson's profession as a bricklayer.

14. Arad, *Ghetto in Flames,* 112–113; Shneidman, *Jerusalem of Lithuania,* 59; Maks Etingin's videotape states, "In Vilna there were, from the beginning, two ghettos. One was liquidated almost instantly. And the second one [the large ghetto] remained there. There were *Aktions,* the Germans used to call, or the inhabitants of the ghetto used to call *Aktions.* They used to take out groups of people. While we still believed they were sent to labor someplace outside Vilna, they were basically being killed."

15. Shneidman, *Jerusalem of Lithuania,* 59.

16. Maks Etingin's videotape states that the owner of the apartment, the engineer, "built a trap in his attic where you could hide. So during *Aktions* we used to hide in that attic, which had a false entry, which was masked and was not seen from the outside. It looked like it was the end of the attic, but you could crawl in there and close the trapdoor and be hidden. . . . It had a three-foot height and you used to stay in there under

a thin roof. It was a tin roof, and the sun would beat on the roof, and the temperature [inside the *maline*] must have been 150 degrees. . . . It felt like you were frying in there. At one point [during an *Aktion*] I said to my father, 'I want to get out. Let them shoot me, rather than stay here. Staying here is impossible.' And somehow my father prevailed on me to stay in there, under that hot tin roof. At that time [when we were in the attic] my mother and brother were in the apartment because they were only looking for men, not women and children."

17. A 1989 letter states, "My grandma had always for Saturday dinner everyone come over, and she served cholent—you cook this all night"; Zenia's prewar memories of her grandmother were often shared with Michael.

18. Arad, *Ghetto in Flames,* 123, 285.

19. Ibid., 125; Harmatz, *From the Wings,* 76. Joseph Harmatz told Michael Bart that he was classmates with Gens's daughter Ada before the war and had great respect for her father.

20. A 1950s letter states, "There were no sanitary facilities what so ever."

21. Kruk, *Last Days,* 154–155; Shneidman, *Jerusalem of Lithuania,* 61.

22. Maks Etingin's videotape states: "There was some kind of technical school. I remember for a couple of weeks or months I was going to that school—it was teaching some kind of technical skills." Also: "Most able-bodied men were going to work every day. They were working in different sections of town. They were not allowed to go on the sidewalk. They were walking on the street, with yellow patches, and with a leader of the group. Very often they were stopped by the Germans or by the Lithuanians. They were going to work in the morning and coming back in the evening into the ghetto. And the trick was to be able to bring something into the ghetto—some food for the family, or for yourself."

23. A 1950s letter states, "My good fortune of being able to do heavy work and laundry for the Germans entitled me to a daily plate of soup." In an interview, Maks Etingin stated that when they lived in the ghetto everyone was depressed, but Zenia's upbeat personality made everyone around her feel better. She was always concerned about everyone else's well-being.

24. Arad, *Ghetto in Flames,* 126; Motl Gurwitz, videotaped in 2005, states, "I knew all the policemen. Levas was from Betar. Meir Levas was on the

political right. Salek Dessler was the chairman of the Betar Union at the university, and he betrayed Jacob Gens." Motl Gurwitz mentioned that he was also a member of Betar.

25. Arad, *Ghetto in Flames*, 305–306.
26. Kruk, *Last Days*, 163.
27. Arad, *Ghetto in Flames*, 340.
28. Ibid., 147; 1950s letter states, "Each day more people were removed from our group. The only thing uncertain about our fate was who would be removed next. People prayed for death to end their suffering"; Maks Etingin's videotape states, "Every couple months the Lithuanians, under the order of the Germans, called for an *Aktion*. That means that they used to reduce the number of the people in the ghetto—five hundred to one thousand people at a time. . . . As time went on, the ghetto became smaller and smaller population wise because people were taken out."
29. Maks Etingin's videotape states, "I worked in a brick factory four miles outside the ghetto. The food situation was very bad. . . . The amounts were limited and very often we were hungry together. We were hungry and deprived of vitamins . . . we used to smuggle some food into the ghetto—a piece of bread or a piece of ham. People working outside weren't allowed to bring contraband inside. Jewish police at the gate cleared people of any food. Very often, the Germans were watching, and would beat up returning Jews. If they found a small piece of bread, they would beat you until you were bleeding—it was very unpleasant. . . . I never got caught with food. As you came closer to the ghetto—and if there were Germans on guard that day—people, rather than going to the ghetto, sort of circled away trying to get to the ghetto later. You used to get messages that Germans are by the tower and you used to shed all illegal stuff that you had with you on the street. We had to devise ways of bells and whistles that we used to get warnings when to get rid of the illegal contraband that we had on us."
30. Motl Gurwitz, videotaped in 2005, states, "The leader of the gate police, Meir Levas, was a terrible person. Levas was a hound."
31. Kruk, *Last Days*, 255.
32. Arad, *Ghetto in Flames*, 229; Cohen, *Avengers*, 39–40.

33. Joseph Harmatz stated during a phone conversation with Michael Bart, "Your dad was a good guy. He was working at the ghetto gate and allowed food and weapons to be smuggled into the ghetto"; Motl Gurwitz, videotaped in 2005, states, "In the forest, after the ghetto was liquidated, the policemen who were wicked in the ghetto were put on trial in the forest by the Jewish partisans and killed"; Stanley Wulc stated during a phone conversation with Michael Bart, "You know your father was a good ghetto policeman, otherwise he would have been shot in the woods." During Michael's visit with Maks Etingin in 2004, Maks stated, "It was always favorable when I saw your dad stationed at the ghetto gate."

Five: A Different Rhythm

1. Guzenberg, *List of Prisoners*, vol. 1, 140, shows Fania Bulkin resided at 10-8 Szpitalna, also known as Ligonines; Fania's letter to Michael Bart dated June 17, 2001, states, "Though, I didn't live with Zenia in the same house [in the ghetto], but we lived nearby in the same area, and visited often."

2. Scene and dialogue re-created from Zenia Bart's and Fania Bulkin-Wolozni-Srebernik's recollections; Fania's letter to Michael Bart dated June 17, 2001, states, "I knew your parents well. I met your father when I was in the ghetto, he was there too, and he was a friend of mine. He came to Vilna from Poland, he was a Hashomer Hatzair, he came to my place in Vilna, in the ghetto, and your mother came too"; Fania's letter to Michael Bart dated July 16, 2001, states, "I saw your father in the ghetto, he came to my house, when he was in the Hashomer Hatzair group. Your mother was Betar."

3. Zenia Bart told Michael that "I had never kissed a boy before because I thought if I kissed a boy that I would get pregnant." Zenia was known by Maks Etingin and all of her friends to have a very outgoing and flirtatious personality.

4. Fania Bulkin-Wolozni-Srebernik's letter to Michael Bart dated June 17, 2001, states, "Your father was a policeman in the ghetto. He was kind and good to everyone."

5. Cohen, *Avengers*, 39.

6. Arad, *Ghetto in Flames*, 145.

7. Ibid., 181.

8. Shneidman, *Jerusalem of Lithuania,* 64, 69.

9. Leizer would not have known that other groups such as Betar were also secretly holding discussions with their members in the same time period.

10. Scene re-created from stories told by Leizer and Zenia Bart. Zenia Bart told Michael that in order to curry favor with her mother, Leizer wanted to do something nice for her family. The favor he performed was greatly appreciated.

11. Shneidman, *Jerusalem of Lithuania,* 60.

12. Maks Etingin's videotape states, "I remember that there was an incident in the ghetto. . . . A group of people were taken there [to Ponary] during an *Aktion.* The Germans, or the Lithuanians, probably the Lithuanians shot them. But they did not kill one girl when she fell into the trench. She was wounded but she was not killed. She was able to get out from there at night. Dig herself out, and come wounded, bleeding into the ghetto, and she was telling the people what really happened. The people just did not believe her. The people were saying that she went out of her mind or something. . . . The people in the ghetto did not believe that they are being exterminated. It was just the last year [of the ghetto period] it became obvious to most of the people in the ghetto that we are being killed. Life is so strong that people did not want to believe that something like that would happen."

13. Cohen, *Avengers,* 39.

14. Scene and dialogue re-created from Arad, *Ghetto in Flames,* 226–228, and Shneidman, *Three Tragic Heroes,* 50.

15. Cohen, *Avengers,* 48.

16. Quotations from manifesto of Abba Kovner. Scene re-created from several sources, including Shneidman, *Three Tragic Heroes,* 48–49; Arad, *Ghetto in Flames,* 231–232; Cohen, *Avengers,* 50–51; Lazar, *Destruction and Resistance,* 61.

Six: We Dreamers Must Turn Soldiers

1. Harmatz, *From the Wings,* 76; Shneidman, *Jerusalem of Lithuania,* 62, 67–68; Arad, *Ghetto in Flames,* 257–258, 268, 306; Michael Bart had many conversations with underground members, including Joseph Harmatz, who described the duties of an underground gate guard.

Notes

2. Memoirs of ghetto inhabitants show that few knew who the underground agents were.

3. Shneidman, *Three Tragic Heroes,* 51; Arad, *Ghetto in Flames,* 261; Lazar, *Destruction and Resistance,* 40; Cohen, *Avengers,* 53.

4. Kowalski, *Secret Press,* 108; Lazar, *Destruction and Resistance,* 39.

5. Arad, *Ghetto in Flames,* 258; Cohen, *Avengers,* 54–55.

6. Arad, *Ghetto in Flames,* 306; Harmatz, *From the Wings,* 77–78. During a phone conversion in 2005, Joseph Harmatz told Michael Bart that he was one of the leaders in charge of smuggling arms for the FPO into the ghetto. Joseph said that he had a location within the ghetto slightly higher than the gate where he could monitor who was approaching the gate. Underground members had a way of signaling each other when returning into the ghetto through the gate with smuggled items, in order to alert each other of pending trouble; Fania Bulkin-Wolozni-Srebernik's letter to Michael Bart dated June 11, 2004, states, "Your father was in the FPO."

7. Joseph Harmatz told Michael Bart that Leizer's nickname was "no bullshit" because he was quiet and kept to himself. Leizer Bart told Michael growing up, "You never get in trouble keeping your mouth shut."

8. Maks Etingin, for example, states in his videotape that he didn't know about the resistance in the ghetto.

9. Arad, *Ghetto in Flames,* 308–309; Shneidman, *Jerusalem of Lithuania,* 61.

10. Arad, *Ghetto in Flames,* 294.

11. Ibid., 302.

12. Kruk, *Last Days,* 176.

13. Kostanian-Danzig, *Spiritual Resistance,* 105.

14. Ibid., 42–43.

15. Arad, *Ghetto in Flames,* 317.

16. Kostanian-Danzig, *Spiritual Resistance,* 43–47.

17. Arad, *Ghetto in Flames,* 318.

18. Maks Etingin's videotape states, "The Germans created a scene that made us believe we could survive. They allowed us to build a basketball court. Being hungry, I don't know how we could play basketball, but we played basketball."

19. Kruk, *Last Days,* 342.

20. Kostanian-Danzig, *Spiritual Resistance,* 87.

21. Ibid., 87–89; Arad, *Ghetto in Flames,* 321.

22. Chasia Spanerflig, videotaped in 2004, states that she sang in the choir. She remembers singing songs in the ghetto written by ghetto poets and composers, such as Hirsh Glik's "Never Say."

23. Kowalski, *Secret Press,* 140–142; Cohen, *Avengers,* 57–58.

24. Maks Etingin told Michael Bart in 2004 that he found it curious that the cook working for Anton Schmidt would walk Zenia back to the ghetto in order to ensure her safety; Zenia Bart told Michael that Sergeant "Fedel" Schmidt looked out for her, and referred to her as a "good girl."

25. Cohen, *Avengers,* 57.

26. Arad, *Ghetto in Flames,* 197.

27. Ibid., 225, 228.

28. Ibid., 197.

29. Ibid., 282–283.

30. Ibid., 283.

31. Ibid., 304–305; Kruk, *Last Days,* 323, 440.

32. Lazar, *Destruction and Resistance,* 61–62.

33. Dworzecki, *Histoire du Ghetto de Vilna,* 390–392. He states that "Yechiel Scheinbaum's group, divided into fifths, consisted mainly of weapons lessons, which took place three times a week at Strashun Street 2 and Hospital Street 5."

34. Arad, *Ghetto in Flames,* 264–265, 266; Kaplinsky, in *Pinkas Hrubieshov,* xiii, notes the experiences of Israel Weiss and Shlomo Brand, who were both from Leizer Bart's hometown; Dworzecki, *Histoire du Ghetto de Vilna,* 390. Dr. Leon Bernstein states, "What Ilya's group represented at the end was a fusion of different groups which finally combined into one strong group under the moral influence and under the energetic leadership of Yechiel."

35. Shneidman, *Three Tragic Heroes,* 50; Arad, *Ghetto in Flames,* 266; Dworzecki, *Histoire du Ghetto de Vilna,* 390. Dr. Leon Bernstein states, "Although the FPO stirred up the ghetto more, in their results both [groups] were completely equal in the ghetto, both were unable to produce a mass uprising, as there was in the Warsaw, or Bialystock ghettos."

36. Dworzecki, *Histoire du Ghetto de Vilna*, 391–392. Dworzecki states, "Dessler was capable of removing, with bestial brutality, people who knew too much about him or were just inconvenient for him."
37. Arad, *Ghetto in Flames*, 342–344, 350.
38. Scene and dialogue re-created from Zenia Bart's and Fania Bulkin-Wolozni-Srebrenik's recollections.
39. Arad, *Ghetto in Flames*, 304.

Seven: Graves Are Growing Here
1. Lazar, *Destruction and Resistance*, 53.
2. Ibid., 55.
3. Ibid., 56.
4. Ibid., 57.

Eight: A Fire Inside
1. Arad, *Ghetto in Flames*, 383.
2. Ibid., 383.
3. Lazar, *Destruction and Resistance*, 69.
4. Chasia Spanerflig, Borka Friedman's wife, videotaped in 2004, states, "The first person to leave the ghetto for the forest was Borka Friedman. . . . After the Warsaw ghetto uprising, he created a separate group to smuggle armament, and to leave the ghetto to the forest. He wanted to create a brigade of partisans to revenge the enemy, to explode trains. Staying in the ghetto was impossible. No one was in the forests in April 1943. Friedman got help from some partisans in Byelorussia. Then Gens gave a warning that anyone leaving the ghetto to the partisans, their families will be destroyed. Myself, his parents, his niece, his brother, and our two-and-a-half-year-old son were all taken to the prison on Lydos Street. At twelve midnight the Gestapo was coming to take the people from the prison. We were all waiting. But at 11:30 P.M. we were stolen from the prison. Our family went and hid at Strashun 1 in a *maline* for three weeks."
5. Dialogue re-created from Arad, *Ghetto in Flames*, 384.
6. Shames, "Memoirs of a Machine-Gunner," 400.
7. Arad, *Ghetto in Flames*, 386–387; Lazar, *Destruction and Resistance*, 63–64.

8. Fishman, *Embers Plucked from the Fire*, 7–10.

9. Shneidman, *Three Tragic Heroes*, 57.

10. Kowalski, *Secret Press*, 260.

11. Leizer and Zenia Bart told Michael that his grandmother and great-grandmother were very skeptical about Leizer, for a number of reasons, including his involvement with Ha-Shomer ha-Tzair. They also did not know his family, since he was not from Vilna, he didn't "look Jewish," and he was from a poor family. Bluma especially wanted proof that he was really Jewish. Growing up, Michael heard Leizer and Zenia joke about how her mother and grandmother gave him such a hard time. Zenia Bart's friend Louis Niebulski from Lida, now living in San Diego, told Michael in 2005, "The difference between the Betar and the Ha-Shomer ha-Tzair is like fire and water."

12. Scene and dialogue re-created from Zenia Bart's and Fania Bulkin-Wolozni-Srebernik's recollections. Zenia Bart told her son Michael, "Your father had a difficult time getting out the words—asking me to marry him"; Fania Bulkin-Wolozni-Srebernik's letter to Michael dated June 17, 2001, states, "Leizer told her he loved her. Your father was a nice gentleman."

13. Kowalski, *Secret Press*, 253. According to Kowalski there were four rabbis left after the Yellow Schein Aktion: Gutman, Mendel Zalmanowicz, Pilovski, and Yitzhak Kroniks.

Nine: Love as Fierce as Death

1. Scene and dialogue re-created from recollections of Zenia and Leizer Bart.

2. Scene and dialogue re-created from recollections of Zenia Bart and from the traditional Jewish wedding ceremony.

3. Leizer Bart told Michael that he had found a makeshift metal ring in the ghetto.

4. February 2, 1985, letter states, "Got married 1943, May 23"; Fania Bulkin-Wolozni-Srebernik's letter to Michael Bart dated June 2001 states, "The love was so strong that they married in the ghetto"; a friend of Zenia and Leizer's, June Schwartz, from the San Diego New Life Club, once said to Michael, "If you only remember one thing about your parents, remember that they were a love story—a love story."

5. Shneidman, *Three Tragic Heroes,* 53.
6. Zenia Bart told Michael that Rose divided her remaining jewelry and coins between Zenia and her brother. Rose also gave Zenia some of the silverware engraved with her initials, *RL.*
7. Dworzecki, *Histoire du Ghetto de Vilna,* 390–391. Dworzecki states, "Nathan Ring's group consisted of Mitia Lippenholz, Nisan Roitbart, Meir Lichtenson, Leizer Bart, Israel Weiss, Shlomo Brand, Yanek Faust, Benjamin Jacobson, the Lalke brothers, Hirsh Warshavchik and Israel Ben Asher"; Kaplinsky, in *Pinkas Hrubieshov,* xiii, notes Israel Wiess and Shlomo Brand were from Leizer Bart's hometown.
8. Dworzecki, *Histoire du Ghetto de Vilna,* 391. Dworzecki states, "In the ghetto Nathan Ring at first was service-director and then deputy for the ghetto police commissar in the third district, and later ghetto police commissar of the first district. Nathan's position in the ghetto police was very useful for various affairs of the combat group, such as carrying in weapons and such. Nathan's group was well armed. Nathan himself, and even more his bold friend Mitia Lipenholz, often went to the city and brought weapons. Nathan would keep the weapons in his own desk drawer in the ghetto police station. He was sure that in case of major searches for weapons, such a taboo place as a police headquarters would not be searched."
9. Joseph Harmatz told Michael during a phone conversation in 2005 that the members of the Yechiel group were older and more mature than the members of the FPO, and for that reason Yechiel members were more cautious and less compulsive in their actions.
10. Joseph Harmatz told Michael Bart in 2005 that he was one of the FPO fighters who jumped the soldiers.
11. Shneidman, *Three Tragic Heroes,* 61; Arad, *Ghetto in Flames,* 389.
12. Shneidman, *Three Tragic Heroes,* 61.
13. Dialogue re-created from several memoirs.
14. Arad, *Ghetto in Flames,* 390.
15. Shneidman, *Three Tragic Heroes,* 55; Arad, *Ghetto in Flames,* 389.
16. There were no eyewitness accounts of Wittenberg's death, and several versions have been put forward. Those who saw his body said it showed signs of torture, but it is unclear whether the abuse was inflicted before

or after his death. The suicide and Gens's role in it is one of the most commonly accepted versions of what occurred.

Ten: Into the Free Forests

1. Arad, *Ghetto in Flames,* 393–395.
2. Kovner, *Missive to Ha-Shomer ha-Tzair Partisans,* ix. Kovner states, "We saw ourselves in the FPO as a *shomer* collective, members of the Hashomer Hatzair movement."
3. Arad, *Ghetto in Flames,* 239.
4. Quotations from Kovner's September 1 declaration, in *Missive to Ha-Shomer ha-Tzair,* xi–xii, xix. Kovner states: "The major aim of the FPO was to organize, and to serve as the vanguard of the armed resistance movement of the Jewish masses of the ghetto in the face of destruction. . . . The FPO attempted to provide a socionational answer to the Jewish masses who lacked all hope in the ghetto, who were doomed to die: to organize a united fighting force, that would strike at the enemy and fight them and in the eventuality of liquidation, would arouse the ghetto to combat and defense. The way of the FPO demanded of each fighter an ultimate willingness to sacrifice, the supreme effort of heroism in all thoughts and feelings, of the entire soul to look forward to battle no matter what the outcome. For the vanguard of the FPO, the meaning of such battle meant—death!"
5. Shneidman, *Jerusalem of Lithuania,* 104–105; Shames, "Memoirs of a Machine-Gunner," 401–403. There are many versions of this event, depending upon the observer's position on Strashun Street. Morton (Motl) Shames recounted his experiences commanding the middle position at 6 Strashun Street. He states that there was an exchange of fire, and that some of the fighters expressed impatience and asked for orders to shoot. He refused, because he felt there was nothing to gain. Their position was too far out of range to shoot the two soldiers he had in his line of sight, and he was afraid to provoke the Germans into destroying the entire ghetto.
6. Motl Gurwitz, videotaped in 2005, retold the story of the shoot-out, stating, "Ilya Scheinbaum was killed next to me. When the Germans and Estonians entered into the ghetto, the FPO gathered together. We occupied the position at the beginning of the street on the second floor. We

were ready to fight. We had rifles, explosives, and explosives with liquid fuel. Another group armed with a machine gun took the position on 6 Strashun, where the library, public bath, and prison courtyard used to be. The Estonians found out that we were armed. We saw through the window that the Estonians were retreating. When Yechiel saw them leaving, he leaned out the window and was killed by a bullet through his throat, and fell down. A sniper from below shot him. Then we got the order to retreat to 6 Strashun—there was no fire [from his position]. The ghetto was surrounded by Estonians. Our group leaped out the window."

7. Maks Etingin's videotape states, "We knew the ghetto was coming to an end. The leaders of the ghetto were either trying to escape, or they were taken out and shot, or disposed of. The police of the ghetto sort of dispersed."

8. Lazar, *Destruction and Resistance,* 103.

9. A 1950s letter states, "My mother turned gray overnight. I tried to carry on for her sake."

10. Fania Bulkin-Wolozni-Srebernik's letter to Michael Bart dated February 2004 states, "Your [Great-]Grandma Bluma lived in the ghetto, and remained after I left for the partisan forest."

11. Guzenberg, *HKP Jewish Labor Camp,* 140, #259. Documents of the HKP Jewish labor camp in the Lithuanian Central State Archives show Michael Lewinson's name and signature on a January–February 1944 list of prisoners' names; he is #259. Rose's name is absent, but eyewitnesses place her there with Michael. The work camp was established sometime in late August or mid-September 1943. Several hundred skilled workers and their families were moved there from the ghetto. They were mostly mechanics, tinsmiths, turners, glaziers, and others who worked in the vehicle repair shop.

12. Scene and dialogue re-created from recollections of Zenia Bart. The three pieces of this silverware she and Leizer took to the Rudnicki forest remained with them and are still in Michael Bart's possession today.

13. Los Angeles relatives Arthur and Leona Lewinson heard the story from their cousin Zenia Bart during the 1950s; they told Michael that this story was "one we will never forget." In a videotaped interview of Arthur and Leona Lewinson in 2007 Leona told us, "Evidently, she was being

segregated to the concentration camp, and she ran up saying, 'I can work, I can work.' And he flung her, and she hit her head." Leona said, "When she went to ask the guard, he pushed her, she hit her head, and they took her for dead, because most of them were dead, they shot them. Yes, at the camp she was at they shot them all. But they took her for dead, and she lived because a Nazi knocked her down. Had he not done that she would have died with the rest of them. . . . I even remember where we were sitting when she was telling us the story. We were sitting in my dining room, at the dining room table. And she made me come over and feel the bump that was still on her head—she still had the bump." Scene and dialogue re-created from Leona and Arthur's account.

14. A 1950s letter states, "I tried to escape [the German soldier] but was caught and imprisoned. They pushed me against an iron gate—injuring my head. I was unconscious for some time and still do not know how I finally escaped. . . . I still have the head bump received when I was thrown against the iron prison. I got in touch with the underground, there met my husband. . . . After two years that camp [the ghetto] was [being] liquidated, and the remaining prisoners were moved to another camp [HKP]." Zenia told Michael this story as well.

15. Arad, *Ghetto in Flames,* 424; Lazar, *Destruction and Resistance,* 133; Kowalski, *Secret Press,* 394; Dworzecki, *Histoire du Ghetto de Vilna,* 478–479. Dworzecki states that the last group of Yechiel's combat organization left for the forest after Jacob Gens was shot. The group of fourteen included Leon Bernstein, Pesia Scheinbaum, Mitia Lipenholz, Leizer and Zenia Bart, Israel Weiss, Shlomo and Masha Brand, Nisan Rortbart, Janek and Rita Faust, Zenia Berkowitz, Hugo Griner, and Masha Schneider; Fania Jocheles-Brancovski told Michael Bart that his parents left through the side gate by bribing a Lithuanian policeman; Fania Bulkin-Wolozni-Srebernik's letter to Michael Bart dated December 2003 states, "Your parents came out of the ghetto, driven out by the Germans."

16. Maks Etingin's videotape explains why most ghetto inhabitants didn't try to escape from the ghetto. He states, "There was no place where to escape because you were surrounded by an unfriendly population. Who

if they caught you, well, they didn't have to catch—they just had to point you out. So there was really no place to escape. And the war was going on probably one hundred miles away, more to the west. The only thing that you could hope for is that eventually, somehow the Germans would lose the war. But for a long time it looked as though they are prevailing."

17. Fania Bulkin-Wolozni-Srebernik's letter to Michael Bart dated December 2003 states, "They walked all night in the forest, and it was very difficult to survive."

18. Recollection of Zenia Bart.

19. Leizer Bart told Zenia's cousin Sidney Baldwin this story: "When Zenia and I were on the outskirts of the forest I heard what I thought were German soldiers. I immediately pushed Zenia off into a ravine, then I jumped on the top of her to shield her from the pending bullets. Then I felt a rifle in my back. Fortunately the men were not German soldiers, but rather Russian partisans." Scene and dialogue re-created from Baldwin's account.

20. Fania Bulkin-Wolozni-Srebernik told Michael that she escaped the ghetto on September 13 with Meyer Wolozni; Fania Jocheles escaped the ghetto on September 21 through the side gate with Doba Debeltov. Others, such as Maks Etingin and his family, escaped the ghetto as well. Maks Etingin's videotape states, "We tried the last day in the hardest way to possibly get out of the main gate of the ghetto. We stood there for hours and we couldn't get out. We were so discouraged, so disappointed, and so tired that we went back to our place. We all went to sleep knowing that tomorrow will be the end of the ghetto. About two or three o'clock at night my mother, who certainly wasn't a leader, woke everybody up. And said, 'Let's try again.' She dressed us all up in the best clothes that we had—we still had holiday clothes. And we went down. The house where we were living was bordering on the outside of the ghetto, and the tower leading to the outside was nailed shut during the ghetto time. When we went down the nails were already pulled out. There was a policeman standing there watching haphazardly. A group of people sort of shoved him aside, and pulled the door leading to the outside open. Somehow the four of us—my mother, father, brother and myself—were outside of the ghetto. . . ."

Eleven: Vanished Like Smoke

1. Shneidman, *Three Tragic Heroes,* 130–131.

2. In *Missive to Ha-Shomer ha-Tzair,* xxii, Kovner states: "That same week, thousands of Jews were removed from the ghetto and we had to send the major part of the [FPO] organization, with most of its weapons, to Markov! Only at the very last moment, when we, the last group, were about to leave the ghetto, the order was given to us, and so we are here, and not in Naroch. Most of the people and weapons left for there. The tragedy experienced by our people is known to all of you. An unpredictable, tragic woe of anti-Semitic persecutions, of disarming and stealing weapons which were obtained with our blood, that was the reception prepared for people who came to the forest."

In "The Via Dolorosa of a Jewish Partisan," Keren-Paz states: "At dawn on that day [July 24], the first FPO unit, under the command of Joseph Glazman, headed for the Narocz forest. Because of treacherous misdirection, the unit found its path blocked by the German dragnet. . . . On Yom Kippur, 5704 [1944], all the fighters, Joseph, and his men fell before the German Amalekites, except one girl who survived the ambush and lived to tell the story."

Chasia Spanerflig, videotaped in 2004, states that when Glazman left for the Narocz forest in August, no one knew what had happened to her husband (Borka Friedman). They collected a second group to go to the forest, and there they found out from some Poles how Borka Friedman's group perished.

3. Dworzecki, *Histoire du Ghetto de Vilna,* 479. Dworzecki states, "On the day of the ghetto liquidation about sixty people of the FPO divided in groups and left the ghetto through the sewer pipes."

4. Cohen, *Avengers,* 100.

5. Shames, "Memoirs of a Machine-Gunner," 403.

6. Ibid.

7. Cohen, *Avengers,* 101; Dworzecki, *Histoire du Ghetto de Vilna,* 479. Dworzecki states, "On the way to the gathering place on Suboch Street, a German patrol stopped FPO members Jacob Kaplan and Abrasha Chvoinick, and the battalion contact Assia Bick. The three opened fire. Their bullets killed Max Gross, the interrogator for partisan affairs of

the Vilna Gestapo. The three were caught alive and brought to Rossa Square, where Kittel set up three gallows for them."

8. Fania Bulkin-Wolozni-Srebernik's letter to Michael Bart dated June 2001 states, "Your great-grandmother [Bluma] was buried in Ponary," but this was a presumption on her part, or meant to express simply that she had not survived. Her February 2, 1985, letter states, "Lizzie, she had three sons—Shashka, Avraham, and Nachum. They were all killed. Sonia & Avraham Bulkin, [and] Sima. They were all killed in Vilna"; Yad Vashem Central Database of Testimony given by Fania Bulkin-Wolozni-Srebernik, June 1956, states, "Lizzie Skolnicki died in Ponary. Nachum Skolnicki died in Ponary at the age of 18. Avraham Skolnicki died in Ponary."

9. Cohen, *Avengers*, 100.

10. Motl Gurwitz, videotaped in 2005, stated, "Zelda Treger was as tough as a man—she was blond and worked as a messenger with Vitka"; Fania Jocheles-Brancovski, videotaped in 2004, states that "the girls were messengers, such as Zelda Treger."

11. Cohen, *Avengers*, 64.

12. Levine, *Fugitives of the Forest*, 173. In *Missive to Ha-Shomer ha-Tzair Partisans*, xxii, Kovner states: "When we came here our first task was to establish a Jewish fighting unit. Immediately, with the first steps, we became aware not only of how great were the difficulties, but also, because of the human composition, the plight of having few weapons and the anti-Semitic atmosphere, that it was almost impossible to transform the hundreds of Jews around us into a Jewish fighting unit."

13. In Vilnius, Fania Jocheles-Brancovski told Michael Bart that Zenia cooked together with Pesia Scheinbaum; Motl Gurwitz also remembered Pesia as the camp cook.

14. Fania Jocheles-Brancovski, videotaped in 2004, states that while in the Rudnicki forest, before they built the bunkers, they made tents. There were five bunkers and one bathhouse in the Avengers' camp. She shared a bunker with Michael's parents. Zenia and Leizer slept on the left side of the bunker, and she slept across from them on the right side. Their bunker in the camp was situated next to Abba Kovner's bunker, where Vitka Kempner and Ruszka Korczak lived. Chiena Borowska, Zenia's cousin,

also lived in the same camp. In 2005, Michael Bart and his wife went with Fania Jocheles-Brancovski and Motl Gurwitz to the partisan camp. Fania recalled the thirty partisans who lived in their bunker: Leon Bernstein, Pesia Scheinbaum, Mitia Lipenholz, Masha and Shlomo Brand, and others. Inside they used spruce branches because they were very soft to sleep on. They began building the bunkers at the end of August, as it was just starting to get cold.

15. Cohen, *Avengers*, 113.
16. A few non-Jews were part of the Vilna detachments. Fania Jocheles-Brancovski recalled a Dutch man with the nickname Tolstoy, because his large girth reminded them of the Russian writer.
17. Kowalski, *Secret Press*, 405–407. Kowalski lists the names of partisans who were in the Rudnicki forest. Leizer and Zenia Bart's names are included on his list. Leizer Bart always kept Kowalski's book in a safe place—apparently it was very dear to him.

Twelve: Summon That Elusive Happiness

1. Levin, *Fighting Back*, 191.
2. Kramer, *Resistance: Untold Stories*, Vitka Kovner Interview.
3. In Vilnius in 2005, Motl Gurwitz told Michael Bart, "I did not know Leizer Bart in the ghetto since members of the underground knew only two or three other people within the organization; I met him in the forest—Leizer Bart was a good partisan, for sure!" Gurwitz remembered that he went on many missions with Leizer to blow up trains. Two groups would go out on a mission at the same time. One group would place explosives along the weak points of the railroad track, then attach something like a cord. Someone would smoke and light the explosive with the cigarette. The other group would cut telephone poles; Joseph Harmatz told Michael Bart in a telephone conversation, "Your dad was quiet and serious. I liked your dad because he was dependable when going out on missions—some weren't as levelheaded in uncertain situations"; Fania Bulkin-Wolozni-Srebernik's letter to Michael Bart dated June 17, 2001, states, "We were all partisans in the forest. Your father was a wonderful partisan."
4. Kowalski, *Secret Press*, 346.
5. Cohen, *Avengers*, 136–137.

6. Scene and dialogue re-created from recollections of Zenia Bart.

7. Zenia Bart told Michael that one of the many times she was almost killed was when she had found a bullet caught inside a comb located in the bag that she carried on her side.

8. Lazar, *Destruction and Resistance*, 193; Rachel Schwartz, a member of the New Life Club, and Zenia and Leizer Bart's close friend in San Diego, told Michael and his wife that Zenia had told her that she couriered needed items back and forth between the partisan camps.

9. Fania Jocheles-Brancovski, videotaped in 2004, states that she and her husband went together on two missions. One was at Christmas time, when five of them went to explode a bridge and paper plant. She said, "I was the only girl [on that mission]."

10. Fania Jocheles-Brancovski, videotaped in 2004, states that she got some kind of sickness from lack of vitamins.

11. A 1950s letter states, "We fought the Nazis anyway we could. Going without food for days at a time, existing under horrible conditions. The only thought that kept me going was the knowledge that in another camp my mother still lived."

12. Joseph Harmatz told Michael in a phone conversation that food missions were much more dangerous than blowing up trains. The fighters were more likely to be shot during food missions.

13. Kaplinsky, *Pinkas Hrubieshov*, xiii. Israel Weiss states, "Our supply lines were steadily improving, although it was not easy to induce the farmers to hand out food and other supplies merely against our receipt, promising payment after victory was achieved."

14. Scene and dialogue re-created from recollections of Leizer Bart. Leizer Bart told Michael at a young age that the hole in his side was from a bullet wound that he sustained while in the forest.

15. Fania Jocheles-Brancovski told Laurel Corona about the gramophone and the records they had in the forest; Dworzecki, *Historie du Ghetto de Vilna*, 390. Dr. Bernstein states, "The FPO and the Yechiel Struggle Group moved themselves to the forest after the end of the ghetto. There they did not stand as separate units, and their comrades fought well for the common cause. In the forest they mingled so well, that the once heterogeneous elements ceased to exist."

Thirteen: Under the Lofty, Silent Heavens

1. As Michael Bart, his wife, Laurel Corona, and Fania Jocheles-Brancovski were walking through the Ponary forest in 2004, Fania picked some of her favorite flowers, forget-me-nots, which she remembered from the camp. She remembered there being no flowers in the ghetto.
2. Ran, *Jerusalem of Lithuania,* vol. 2, 469.
3. Ibid., 468; Fania Jocheles-Brancovski, videotaped in 2004, remembered Dogim saying this.
4. Ran, *Jerusalem of Lithuania,* vol. 2, 468; Kowalski, *Secret Press,* 298–301; Harmatz, *From the Wings,* 93–95; Fania Jocheles-Brancovski, videotaped in 2004, states in great detail Motl Ziedel's and Isaac Dogim's experiences at Ponary: "The group was divided into brigades. There was one brigade responsible for the firewood—three to six meters long. The second brigade was digging out corpses—they had long hooks. They would put a layer of firewood and a layer of corpses. Afterwards, there was a person responsible for taking out the golden teeth—the doctor. Then they would make a fireplace, it was very high. The fireplace had a special elevator—as the corpses burned, they watched to see if the bones were still hard. The fire would burn for one week. Afterwards they would check again for any remaining hard bones. If there were some they used a hammer to break them up. They had a net to find gold and stones. Then they were supposed to mix the ashes with the earth. . . ."
5. Ran, *Jerusalem of Lithuania,* vol. 2, 468.
6. Fania Jocheles-Brancovski, videotaped in 2004, states, "They wanted to escape from their tasks. It was Dogim who was very creative and made a plan to escape. They started to dig a tunnel. . . . On April 15, they escaped . . . there was a terrible smell inside their skin—a smell of corpses. There was only thirteen who survived [the escape], some say twelve. Some hid in the wetlands. There was a pile of manure. The strong smell of manure hid the smell of the corpses. So they buried themselves in the manure. The Germans advertised a reward for whoever captured them. But the partisans saw that and were trying to meet them. . . . Zeidel was in my camp, and also with Leizer and Zenia."
7. They were ultimately dispersed to separate groups. Motl Zeidel stayed with Leizer and Zenia in their bunker in the Avengers' camp.

8. *Shomrim* is the plural of *shomer,* or guardsman.
9. Kovner, *Missive to Ha-Shomer ha-Tzair,* xxxiv.
10. Weiss, "Disaster and Heroism," viii.
11. Cohen, *Avengers,* 144–145; Kowalski, *Secret Press,* 333–334; Lazar, *Destruction and Resistance,* 174–175.
12. Motl Gurwitz told Michael Bart in 2005 that "only the main line fighters participated in the fight for Vilna, not the cooks etc. [camp support]."
13. Bak, *Painted in Words,* 8.
14. This general scene is based on eyewitness accounts, including Zenia Bart's. The narration of their actions and words upon discovering the bodies is true to what little Zenia said about this painful event, but the dialogue and specific actions are imagined. A 1950s letter states, "In 1944 my mother and brother were two of the living five hundred Jews interned [at HKP]. Before the Nazis left the city they were all destroyed. What a scene of horror greeted the Partisans on their arrival in the city the next day. That shock was the start of my continuous depression." 1965 statement states, "My mother Rose Lewinson . . . was in a camp HKP in Vilna and liquidated Sept 1944. My brother Misha [Michael] Lewinson, born Dec 1925 in Vilna, lived with my mother in camp HKP till Sept 1944 and was killed in Sept in 1944." Zenia Bart also told Michael that she found her mother and brother dead at HKP.

Fourteen: A World Was Here
1. When asked what the Avengers did to celebrate the liberation of Vilna, Fania Jocheles-Brancovski said flatly, "Nothing"; Rickie Leiter's genealogy of the Balcwinik family, done with the help of Bluma Balcwinik's son Aaron Fineberg and her granddaughter Zenia Bart in 1985, states, "Sonia Bulkin died 1944 in Holocaust, daughter Sima died 1944 Holocaust, Lizzie's three sons—all killed in the ghetto"; February 2, 1985, letter states, "Sonia & Avraham Bulkin, Sima they were killed in Vilna, just Fania is alive."
2. Scene and dialogue re-created from recollections of Zenia Bart: 1945 letter from Rome states, "In the last month, when they liquidated the concentration camp (HKP) that was five days before the liberation of Vilna by

the Red Army, there were a few comrades of my brother who succeeded in escaping and urged my brother to join them in escape. My brother refused, and his last words were, 'I'm not going to leave my mother. I'll die with her.' And that is how he died with her. When together with the Russian Partisans we entered liberated Vilna, the bodies of my loved ones were still lying sprawled out in the courtyard of the Concentration Camp. Not a day goes by that I can forget that awful sight. A wound has remained in my heart that will never heal."

3. A 1989 letter states, "They had a place *Ponary,* they killed a lot of Jews, before we left Vilna we attended memorial services."

4. When asked what life was like in the camp, Fania Jocheles-Brancovski told Laurel Corona, "We were happy."

5. Scene and dialogue re-created from the surviving postcard and Zenia's recollection of events.

6. Weiss, "Disaster and Heroism," xiii. Israel Weiss states, "In February 1945, I returned to Hrubieshov, only to find it occupied by gentiles. Just a few residents remained alive."

7. Scene and dialogue re-created from Leizer and Zenia Bart's recollection of events. A 1950s letter states, "Not one member of my husband's family escaped"; another 1950s letter states, "In 1947, I was again sent to a sanitarium where I was told that my nerves were weak and only I could help myself which I tried to do because my husband had no one"; a 1945 letter from Rome states, "The German bandits also killed my husband's entire family. He also, has been left entirely alone like I have been. The only survivor he has is that of an uncle in America, whose address is unknown to him"; Sol Margoles retold the story to Michael and his wife, one week before he died, stating that Leizer had been haunted by the fact that his younger sister, who was a very pretty girl, was taken to a field by locals, raped, and then killed.

8. Leizer Bart told Michael that he went to his family's home in Hrubieshov and found Gentiles occupying the house. Leizer, pointing a pistol at a man at his front door, told him they had forty-eight hours to leave. As he was walking away, he was recognized by a Catholic priest who had grown up nearby. The priest warned him that he should leave town now

because it wasn't safe. The priest said, "These people have no intention of giving back your house, there will just be another dead Jew." On another occasion, Zenia Bart told Michael that they went to Leizer's hometown, and he ran into a neighbor. The neighbor informed him that Jews were hauled off in two different roundups, but that his sister was taken earlier by some local townspeople.

9. Leizer Bart told Michael that he traveled from country to country on top of trains, including Romania, Austria, and Italy; February 2, 1985, letter states, "Fania moved to Israel from Romania 11/27/1945."

10. "Jew?" Harmatz, *From the Wings,* 112.

11. Scene and dialogue re-created from Zenia Bart's recollection of events.

12. A 1950s letter states, "We had no one and belonged no where, so we traveled from one country to another, trying to forget the horrors we had lived through. I was undernourished and anemic and had continuous headaches. In 1946 the doctor recommended a stay at the sanitarium where for a few weeks I was given treatment for nervousness. It was impossible for me to control my eyes and all of the doctors gave me the same diagnoses—nerves. The constant nightmares and crying spells made me want to avoid people—especially those I had known before the war."

13. Scene and dialogue re-created from Leizer and Zenia Bart's recollection of events.

14. A 1950s letter states, "At war's end in 1945 we arrived in Italy where my husband found temporary employment and help for us with the Joint Distribution Committee."

15. Scene and dialogue re-created from Leizer and Zenia Bart's recollection of events.

16. Aaron Fineberg's letter to his niece Zenia Bart dated January 2, 1946, states, "Everyone has been receiving your letters and we are all anxious to know how you are doing and Leizer are. Zenia if there is anything you need in the way of food—*you must tell us,* for we have no other way of knowing. My nephew Sidney has sent several packages to you for me, so you should receive them soon. And we will send you more in the future . . . *Please tell us if you need anything in food.* Also, we want you to know how many meals you eat each day, and what sort of living place you have. *Don't be ashamed to ask for what you need!!!* Love from your

Uncle Aaron"; 1946 letter states, "As soon as we received the letter from Aunt Bessie, we went directly to the American Consul in Naples. No one is allowed in the consulate, but after great hardship, after showing the English letter, and the picture, we were allowed entrance. We were told we couldn't be registered until we show our affidavits. Now it depends on our Uncle, how soon they can send us papers . . . the only hope we have is that we will be able to come to you . . . I was so happy looking at you [your picture] that tears of joy came to my eyes, and to know there is some left of my family. It all seems like a horrible dream that I've been left all alone from my entire family. Today is Hanakah, my brother's birthday. I look back into the past when all our family would get together, and be happy and merry, in celebrating his birthday. Today, he is lying in his grave, so innocent and young."

Epilogue: Perhaps—Until Light

1. A 1985 letter states, "We lived three years in Rome (Italy), until we got papers to come to the U.S.A. We arrived in Jan 1948 in New York. Janette, and Uncle Aaron came to meet us. Almost one year we lived with Aaron and Sid [his wife]. We became citizens in 1953. Leizer worked four years in Aaron's shop—shipping clerk. I worked in Carter Shop, sewing. What education we had we got in Europe, but in the U.S.A. we were going to night school."

2. A 1950s letter states, "On a lucky day in 1948 we arrived in the U.S.A. I thought all of the horrible past would be forgotten. After a while the week long headaches—numb lips and sore and choking feelings of my throat started again. I have great difficulty in doing my housework as being unable to relax and feeling nervous and tense. I feel nauseous very often. My legs itch and I find the nights are a time of dread nightmares."

BIBLIOGRAPHY

Arad, Yitzhak. *Ghetto in Flames: The Struggle and Destruction of the Jews in Vilna in the Holocaust.* Jerusalem: Yad Vashem, 1980.

Bak, Samuel. *Painted in Words: A Memoir.* Bloomington: Indiana University Press, 2001.

Cohen, Israel. *History of the Jews in Vilna.* Philadelphia: Jewish Publication Society of America, 1943.

Cohen, Rich. *The Avengers: A Jewish War Story.* New York: Alfred A. Knopf, 2000.

Dawidowicz, Lucy S. *From That Place and Time: A Memoir, 1938–1947.* New York: W.W. Norton and Company, 1989.

Donin, Hayim Halevy. *To Be a Jew.* New York: Basic Books, 1980.

———. *To Pray as a Jew.* New York: Basic Books, 1972.

Dworzecki (Dvorzetsky), Mark. *Yeruschalayim D'Lita in Kamf un Umkum: Histoire du Ghetto de Vilna.* Paris: The Jewish Popular Union in France, 1948.

Ehrenburg, Ilya, and Visily Grossman. *The Complete Black Book of Russian Jewry.* 1946. David Patterson, trans., ed. Edison, New Jersey: Transaction Publishers, 2002.

Etingin, Maks. *A Life of Miracles.* DVD. New York: Private Collection Video, 2001.

Fishman, David E. *Embers Plucked from the Fire: The Rescue of Jewish Cultural Treasures in Vilna.* New York: YIVO Institute of Jewish Research, 1996.

Gilbert, Martin. *The Holocaust: A History of the Jews of Europe During the Second World War.* New York: Henry Holt and Company, 1986.

Godel, Zvi. *Forest of Valor.* VHS. Israel Educational Television, 1989.

Good, Michael. *The Search for Major Plagge: The Nazi Who Saved Jews.* New York: Fordham University Press, 2005.

Gutman, Israel, ed. *Encyclopedia of the Holocaust.* 4 vols. New York: Macmillan Publishing Company, 1990.

Guzenberg, Irina. *The HKP Jewish Labor Camp, 1943–1944.* Vilnius: The Vilna Gaon Jewish State Museum, 2002.

———. *Vilnius Ghetto: The List of Prisoners.* 2 vols. Vilnius: The Vilna Gaon Jewish State Museum, 1996–1998.

Harmatz, Joseph. *From the Wings: A Long Journey, 1940–1960.* Sussex, England: The Book Guild, 1998.

Harran, Marilyn. *The Holocaust Chronicle: A History in Words and Pictures.* Lincolnwood, IL: Publications International, 2000.

Keren-Paz, Avraham. "The Via Dolorosa of a Jewish Partisan." *Anthology on Armed Jewish Resistance, 1939–1945.* Isaac Kowalski, ed. New York: Jewish Combatants Publishers House, 1985.

Kostanian-Danzig, Rachel. *Spiritual Resistance in the Vilna Ghetto.* Vilnius: The Vilna Gaon Jewish State Museum, 2002.

Kostanian, Rachel. *Jewish Life in Lithuania.* Vilnius: The Vilna Gaon Jewish State Museum, 2001.

———. *Vilna Ghetto Posters: Jewish Spiritual Resistance.* Vilnius: The Vilna Gaon Jewish State Museum, 2001.

Kovner, Abba. *My Little Sister.* Shirley Kaufman, trans. Oberlin, Ohio: Oberlin College Press, 1986.

Bibliography

———. *A Missive to Ha-Shomer ha-Tzair Partisans.* 1944. Israel: Morshet Publishing House, 2002.

———. *Scrolls of Testimony.* Philadelphia: The Jewish Publication Society, 2001.

Kowalski, Isaac. *A Secret Press in Nazi Europe: The Story of a Jewish United Partisan Organization.* New York: Central Guide Publishers, 1969.

Kramer, Seth. *Resistance: Untold Stories of Jewish Partisans.* VHS. PBS Home Video, 2002.

Kruk, Herman. *The Last Days of the Jerusalem of Lithuania.* New Haven: Yale University Press, 2002.

Lazar, Chaim. *Destruction and Resistance: A History of the Partisan Movement in Vilna.* New York: Shengold Publishers, 1985.

Levin, Dov. *Fighting Back: Lithuanian Jewry's Armed Resistance to the Nazis, 1941–1945.* New York: Holmes and Meier Publishers, 1985.

Levin, Nora. *The Holocaust: The Destruction of European Jewry, 1933–1945.* New York: Thomas Y. Crowell Company, 1968.

Levine, Allan. *Fugitives of the Forest: The Heroic Story of Jewish Resistance and Survival During the Second World War.* Toronto: Stoddart, 1998.

Ran, Leyzer. *Jerusalem of Lithuania.* 3 vols. New York: The Laureate Press, 1974.

Rudashevski, Yitskhok. *The Diary of the Vilna Ghetto.* Ghetto Fighters' House, Israel: Hakibbutz Hameuchad Publishing House, 1973.

Sakowicz, Kazimierz. *Ponary Diary, 1941–1943.* Yitzhak Arad, ed. New Haven: Yale University Press, 2005.

Shames, Morton. "Memoirs of a Machine-Gunner." *Anthology on Armed Jewish Resistance, 1939–1945.* Isaac Kowalski, ed. New York: Jewish Combatants Publishers House, 1985.

Shneidman, N. N. *Jerusalem of Lithuania: The Rise and Fall of Jewish Vilnius.* New York: Mosaic Press, 1998.

———. *The Three Tragic Heroes of the Vilnius Ghetto: Wittenberg, Sheinbaum, Gens.* New York: Mosaic Press, 2002.

Bibliography

Sugihara, Yukiko, and Anne Hashiko Akabor. *Visas for Life*. San Francisco: Edu-Comm, 1995.

United States Holocaust Memorial Museum. *Historical Atlas of the Holocaust*. New York: Macmillan Publishing USA, 1996.

Waletzky, Josh. *Partisans of Vilna: The Untold Story of Jewish Resistance During WWII*. VHS. A Ciesla Foundation Production. The National Center for Jewish Film, Brandeis University, 1986.

Weiss, Israel. "Disaster and Heroism." *Pinkas Hrubieshov: Memorial to a Jewish Community in Poland*. Baruch Kaplinsky, ed. Tel Aviv: The Israel Press, 1962.

ACKNOWLEDGMENTS

Heartfelt thanks to the following for sharing their memories with Michael:

Maks and Rochelle Etingin. Maks, along with his parents and brother, lived with Zenia and her grandmother, mother, and brother in the same Vilna ghetto room for twenty-one months.

Fania Bulkin-Wolozni-Srebernik, Zenia's cousin who introduced Zenia to Leizer in the Vilna ghetto, a partisan fighter in the Rudnicki forest, now living in Israel.

Fania Jocheles-Brancovski, ghetto underground member, partisan fighter who shared the same underground bunker as Zenia and Leizer in the Rudnicki forest, now living in Vilnius, Lithuania.

Joseph Harmatz, ghetto underground leader, ghetto policeman, partisan fighter in the Rudnicki forest, and former director general of World ORT, now living in Israel.

Motl Gurwitz, ghetto underground member, partisan fighter in the Rudnicki forest who went on numerous train sabotage missions with Leizer, now living in Israel.

Morton (Motl) Shames, ghetto underground member and weapons

instructor, machine-gun commander and partisan fighter in the Rudnicki forest, now living in New Jersey.

Sol Margoles, husband of Bea, Zenia's cousin in Springfield, Massachusetts, who was a great confidant and friend to Leizer and Zenia upon their arrival in the United States, and to his daughter, Rickie Leiter, for her moral support to Michael in telling his parents' story.

The Lewinson family in Los Angeles. Zenia's cousins: Rachel, Saul, Anne, Arthur, and Michael. Rachel and Saul were born in Vilna.

Members of the New Life Club.

Thanks to Yearl Schwartz for introducing Michael to the Freedom Fighters of Nekamah, and to the dozens of other Holocaust survivors, relatives, and friends too numerous to mention, for their endless help and support to Michael in his ten years of research.

Thanks to Regina Kopilevich, our guide in Vilna, for making Leizer's and Zenia's experiences more real to us. And to the following organizations for their research help to Michael: United States Holocaust Memorial Museum, Simon Wiesenthal Center Museum of Tolerance, Yad Vashem, Ghetto Fighters' Museum, American Friends of the Ghetto Fighters' Museum, YIVO Institute for Jewish Research, the Vilna Gaon Jewish State Museum, and the American Joint Distribution Committee.

With love and endless appreciation to Pamela Shekinah Perkins, who cajoled and challenged Laurel; to her son, Ivan Corona, who energized her by his confidence; and to James Fee, who cheered her on.

To our agent, Barbara Braun, and our editor, Daniela Rapp, who saw the importance of this story, and helped us share it.